macromedia®

FLASH™ MX

CREATING DYNAMIC APPLICATIONS

INTEGRATED TECHNOLOGIES

Macromedia Flash™

Java™

ColdFusion®

.NET

Tim K. Chung Sean Clark Eric E. Dolecki Juan Ignacio Gelos

Michael Grundvig Jobe Makar Max Oshman Dr. William B. Sanders Scott Smith

Macromedia Flash MX: Creating Dynamic Applications

Tim K. Chung, Sean Clark, Eric E. Dolecki, Juan Ignacio Gelos, Michael Grundvig, Jobe Makar, Max Oshman, Dr. William B. Sanders, Scott Smith

Macromedia Press
1249 Eighth Street
Berkeley, CA 94710
510/524-2178
510/524-2221 (fax)

Published by Macromedia Press, in association with Peachpit Press, a division of Pearson Education.

Find us on the World Wide Web at:
www.peachpit.com
www.macromedia.com

To report errors, please send a note to errata@peachpit.com

Macromedia Press Editor: Angela C. Kozlowski
Development Editor: Maryann Steinhart
Production Coordinator: Connie Jeung-Mills
Page Layout: Owen Wolfson
Indexer: Ron Strauss
Interior Designer: Mimi Heft
Cover Designer: Kurt Wolken, Wolken Communica

ISBN 0-321-11548-1

9 8 7 6 5 4 3 2 1

Printed and bound in the United States of America

Bios

Tim K. Chung is a Programmer/Analyst and has been coding Flash and ActionScript since Flash 2. His site `www.cruddog.com` was featured in the Flash 3 Bible. During his freelance days he developed Flash-based games like Puyo Puyo Flash and The Legends of Tao-Woo. He has worked with design agencies developing games for client sites such as 7-Up. Tim retains a BSc. in Computer Science from the University of Calgary and is currently living in London, U.K., building Flash MX-based Web applications.

Sean Clark was born in Canada in Saskatoon, Saskatchewan. I lived there for three years, than we moved over to Kimberley, in BC. After about five of years living there, we got our first computer. It's amazing how expensive they were back then; for around $3500 Canadian, we got a mid range computer (if only I could spend that now!). Two years later, we moved to Kamloops, the place I am currently living in. It is here that I first started programming, on good 'ol Microsoft QBasic. I started off with simple stuff: the PRINT statement, and the always powerful IF statement. I played around with that a little, and made a few games. These were very simple games… quite linear story games. Kind of like "You are in a dark room, should you a) turn on the light, b) run away…" etc. Later on we got another computer, a cheap bargain one. The best part was that we got the connected to the Internet. It was here I learned about Web design. After viewing a whole bunch of gaming Web sites, I decided to make my own. Armed with Microsoft Paint, and Corel WordPerfect, I made my first Web site.

I soon got tired of these limiting programs. I started searching for better ones, and discovered Flash 4. I really enjoyed playing around with it, and making simple animations. After Flash 5 came out, I rediscovered my passion for programming. I started to master ActionScript, delving into the world of object oriented programming. I never turned back. Now that I'm 17 and have Flash MX in my arsenal, new doors are opening. As my skills grow, I someday hope to become a famous programmer, right up there with the big guys.

Eric E. Dolecki is currently Senior Interactive Designer and Interactive Technology Manager at Boston-based Directech eMerge. Clients include notable high-technology clients such as Teradata, WorldCom, and Connected. His Flash work appears on the Macromedia/Centennial Media Advanced Flash 5 ActionScripting Training CD-ROM, and past issues of Computer Arts UK magazine.

Eric was a co-author of the advanced Flash book *Macromedia Flash Super Samurai*, and also Flash MX Audio Magic. In addition to published works, he has won numerous international Flash awards. He is a regular contributor to several open source Flash sites, and he maintains his personal site: `www.ericd.net`, which showcases experiments, manages his personal clients' work, and serves as a conduit between himself and those seeking to learn more about Flash. His mobile Pocket PC Flash application "FlashForward 2K2 NYC Event Guide" was chosen as a Macromedia Site of the Day for June 22, 2002.

Eric actively maintains a personal client list.

Juan Ignacio Gelos is founder and chief executive officer of RSA Internet (www.rsainternet.com), an Internet development and services provider company located in Buenos Aires, Argentina. He's been in the Internet industry since 1997.

Michael Grundvig is a co-founder of Electrotank Inc. (www.electrotank.com). He has co-authored and contributed to several books on Flash, presented at an international Flash conference, and moderates on several prominent Flash community Web sites. He is currently employed at Hallmark Cards Inc. in the IT Solutions Center Of Excellence focusing primarily on Java and application architecture development.

Jobe Makar is co-founder of Electrotank Inc. (www.electrotank.com), a game development company located in Raleigh, North Carolina. He has been building applications with Macromedia Flash since version 3. With a strong education in physics Jobe also uses ActionScript to program realistic interactions in games which have won several international awards for his work in Flash game creation and have been recognized in over a dozen publications.

Max Oshman is the lead backend programmer at pLot Multimedia Developers (www.plotdev.com) and president of Webworks, Ltd., a Web development firm. He specializes in data-driven Flash sites and is fluent in server-side scripting languages such as ColdFusion, PHP, and ASP. Clients for whom he has worked include Motown Records, Universal Studios and Sean John Clothing. During his spare time, Max helps moderate the ColdFusion and Flash forums at one of the leading resource sites, Flashcfm.com. In addition to authoring numerous articles, this is his second book addressing advanced techniques in Flash programming.

Dr. William B. Sanders is a Professor of Interactive Information Technology at the University of Hartford. He has written three previous books on Flash, his latest being *Server-Side Flash*, co-authored with Mark Winstanley. All together he has written some 40 computer-related books covering a range of topics from programming to eBusiness. Currently, he is interested in developing rich interactive interfaces for the Internet that combine both Web usability and natural social interaction. He maintains an interactive Web site at www.sandlight.com that is in constant need of updating.

Scott Smith has a Bachelor of Science in Computer Information Systems from William Jewell College. I am a Sun Certified Programmer for the Java 2 Platform, and a Sun Certified Web Component Developer for J2EE Platform. Currently employed at Hallmark Cards Inc. in the IT Solutions Center Of Excellence focusing primarily on Java and application architecture development.

Acks

Tim would like to thank Mike Grundvig for the opportunity to help out, Rem Cmiral for the excellent hosting at entropik.com, Diwa Fernandez for the fun interview and jaw-dropping Flash anime artwork, Louie Penaflor for the Mac info and game breaks, and the lovely Janet Lau for being so patient, supportive, and understanding.

—Tim Chung

There are many people I need to acknowledge here; the main one being the always wonderful Flash community. Without Web sites like Flashkit, Were-Here, and Ultrashock, I would never have learned as much ActionScript as I know now. There is no one person who has helped me the most; however, I would like to thank Brandon Hall for all of his contributions to the Flash community, and also Mike Grundvig for giving me the chance to help author this book. Thank you to you all.

—Sean Clark

Deanna, thank you for all your support and patience. I hope that you know how much it means to me. It can't be easy when I have so many deadlines to tackle that pull me away for hours on end. I love you.

For my family: thank you for your patience as well. My deadlines and workloads haven't made things easy for me to stay in touch with you as much as I would like, and I have missed a lot of things during all of this.

To Mike Grundvig: you have been a great friend and inspiration to me, and I really appreciate your ability to often field my lame questions. You'll make a fine developer out of me yet. I owe you a few steak dinners!

I would also like to thank: Max Oshman, Bill Sanders, Jobe Makar, Mike Chambers, Greg Burch, Phillip Torrone of Flashenabled, Ian Chia, Bill Perry, Chris Pelsor, Bob Clagett at VelocityWorks, Miko at Ultrashock, BJ Mace, Anthony at Ant Mobile Software, Craig Swann, Braden Hall, Eric Jordan, and of course all the wonderful people at Peachpit Press.

—Eric Doleki

To Carlos Bernardo Gonzalez Pecotche (Raumsol), my Master, creator of the Logosophy (www.logosophy.org), for teaching me the art of conscious thinking and showing me the path towards a new inner life.

—Juan Ignacio Gelos

I first need to thank Jamie, my wonderful wife for putting up with me while I worked on this book. I would also like to thank Angela Kozlowski and the wonderful people at Peachpit who helped me so much with this book. You are all absolute miracle workers with the patience of saints! I also need to thank all the other authors and developers who made this book possible: Jobe Makar, Tim Chung, Sean Clark, Juan Gelos, Scott Smith, Robert Firebaugh,

Max Oshman, and many others. You know who you are! Without all of your help and support, none of this would have been possible, thank you! Finally, I would like to thank Eric Doleki for pitching in so much at the end when it was needed the most. Thanks so much man!

—Michael Grundvig

I would like to thank my loving wife Kelly for giving me the support needed to create the work seen in this book. Next I would like to thank Mike for creating the sophistocated socket server that made my chapter possible. Eric, thank you so much for the amazing screenshots and figures. Thank you Robert for creating the killer graphics used in my chapter, your work is always great! A big thank you goes out to everyone at Peachpit who has had a hand in making this book what it is. As always, thanks to my entire family their constant support. And of course, thank you Free. You will always be my fluffiest supporter.

—Jobe Makar

I would like to dedicate this book to my grandfather Aaron Oshman, who passed away this year. He was a great man who taught me much about the importance of integrity and intellect in life. I must also give thanks to my parents for giving me the encouragement and oppurtunity to reach this point in my life. To my brother, Charlie, for giving me some competition on XBOX, and to my sister, Sophie, for always bringing me Starbucks for those late night writing sessions.. Thanks to my friends Bellisimo, Rodeo, Twersk, Jeffersonian and Scottchua for putting up with me. To my new partner, Yves, and the rest of the crew at pLot Development (`www.plotdev.com`). Many thanks to `nexpoint.net` for being the best host on the Net. And of course, I would like to thank everyone at Peachpit Press and Macromedia Press for having faith in me for a second time. Finally, thanks to Moses for taking my people out of Egypt.

—Max Oshman

In the Beta group for Tincan I received help from Sudhir Kuman, aYo Binitie, Eric Dolecki, Brian Lesser, Phillip Kerman, Beau Ambur, Melvyn Song Kian Guan, Den Ivanov, Robert Walch and others who either provided information or helped test my application. From Macromedia, massive assistance was provided by Manish Anand, Giacomo Guillizzoni, Colin Cherot, Asa Whillock Barbara Herbert, Pritham Shetty, Sarah Allen, Jim Whitfield, Bryan Payne, Jeremy Allaire, Damian Burns, Elliot Winard, Srinivas Manapragada, Edward Chan, and Henriette Cohn. Demian P. Sellfors at Media Temple provided Beta hosting that allowed development in a real-world environment.

—Bill Sanders

I would like to thank Mike Grundvig for coming up with the idea of doing the book and providing me the opportunity to lend a hand. I would also like to thank my beautiful wife Cassandra for her patience, tolerance, and support while I spent countless hours over the keyboard coding for the book. Lastly I would like to thank some of my code-junkie friends: Ike Eggers and Russ Hampleman for continually raising the coding high-bar and always being there to help out and give advice whenever it is needed.

—Scott Smith

Table of Contents

5: Multiplayer Game 118

6: Instant Messenger 148

Introduction

This book is not like other Flash MX books. In fact, it isn't like many computer programming books in general. When we first started talking about this book, we decided that we wanted to make something different. We wanted to create a book that would not cover the principles so much as the implementation. There are many Flash MX books available to cover how to perform some technical concept in ActionScript. We want this book to help you develop applications from scratch.

It seems that the best way to teach someone how to develop an application is to walk through existing applications. To this end, we've created a book full of applications. Each chapter contains a fully functional application built in Flash MX. We've tried to keep these applications complex to make them more than just simple samples. All of the applications follow similar methods for communicating with the server but each is implemented in its own way.

We realize that developers use many languages in their projects. We also recognize the fact that no single language dominates the world of application development. Because of this, we used many languages to develop the server-side portions of the applications. All of the smaller applications support ColdFusion, ASP.NET, and Java. The larger applications are created in Java and ASP.NET. This means that if you use only ASP.NET for projects, you can just use the ASP.NET source code from the CD-ROM for all of the applications in this book.

We've made the code as reusable as possible on both the client and the server. By defining some common formats for data into and out of the client, we are able to reuse many pieces across applications. As you go through the book, you'll see the same components used in different places. We've called these out by placing them in external .AS files.

We wanted to illustrate how pieces of an application can be decoupled from each other. We created an object in ActionScript that hides how data is sent to or received from the server. By changing a single property of this object, the Flash client can be used with a different server-side language.

This book is about Flash MX and not ASP.NET, Java, ColdFusion, or any other server-side language, so we do not cover how the server-side portions of these applications are created. Because of this, it's important that you have a good understanding of the correct language before really digging into the code. To make this as easy as possible, we've included readme files on the CD-ROM to walk you through installing the server-side code into an application server.

We had a lot of fun and learned a great deal while writing this book, and it is our hope that you will do the same as you build your own Flash MX applications!

1: Dynamic Polling System

by Max Oshman

Often times you may find yourself wondering what people think about your Web site and what you can do to bring in more traffic. There are many possible solutions; however, only one solution is both simple and not annoying for your visitors to partake in: a polling system.

Everyone has an opinion, and everyone loves to share what's on his mind. What better way to let your users say what they feel than by taking a poll?

In this chapter we take an in-depth look into a dynamic polling system coded in ColdFusion, ASP.NET, and Java. Of course, Flash is used as the front end, and many of MX's new capabilities are put on display.

It is recommended that you have intermediate to advanced knowledge of Flash, ColdFusion, and XML before continuing or you will have trouble understanding many of the concepts and techniques used in this application. If you meet the prerequisite, let's go!

What Is It?

A polling system is an excellent way of obtaining information from visitors. Users are often very intimidated by surveys because they can take time to fill out, and in our fast-paced world of cable connections and TV dinners, almost nobody wants to spend his scarce free time filling out a survey. A polling system asks one question at a time and gives possible answers. A poll is a great way to get answers to the questions you need answered quickly, such as "What would you like to see next on the site?" or "Do you like the new layout?" The questions and answers are easily updatable and the results are effortlessly obtainable. All in all, a poll is an easy and efficient way of obtaining information from your site's visitors.

How Is It Going To Work?

We all need a little structure in our lives (that's why we love XML so much), therefore, before starting any project, it's imperative that you understand what you are making and how you are going to make it. Many people like to graph and draw up flow charts, but what you do is solely up to you as long as you have a guide to follow. For this particular application, the poll consists of an admin done in HTML that has the ability to change the question and possible answers. Each question can have an unlimited number of answers. A user can only vote once for each question. There can only be one active question in the system at a given time, with an unlimited number of answers. The following lists describe how Flash will communicate with the server.

Client-to-Server Execution Order

1. Flash calls the server and asks for the currently active polls results and data.
2. Flash calls the server and asks if this user has already voted on the currently active poll.
3. Flash posts back the data if the user hasn't already voted. If he has, only the results are displayed.

Client-to-Server Interaction Points

1. Flash gets the poll question and the list of answers.
   a. Sends in a "GetPollData" transaction request.
   b. Server responds with the poll question and answer as well as the vote tallies.
2. Flash asks the server if the user has already voted on this poll.
   a. Send in a "HasVoted" transaction request.
   b. Server responds with either a true or false based on the user having voted.
3. Flash sends in the user's vote.
   a. Sends in a "VoteOnPoll" transaction request that contains PollIDs associated with AnswerIDs.
   b. Server responds with a success message or error.

XML is used to transfer data between the server-side language and Flash, and vice versa. An Access database is used to store all of the data (questions, answers, results, and so forth).

The Database

The database is the backbone of this application. It's used to store the questions, answers, and results of the poll. Since this is a small project, we'll use Microsoft Access as the database. If you intend to create applications that need the database to hold very large amounts of data, I recommend using Oracle (currently in version 9i). Let's look at the database's key points in order to gain a better understanding of how the poll works.

Open Poll-97.mdb from the CD-ROM. **Figure 1.1** shows the completed database.

You'll see two tables: Answers and Polls. Each table plays a different role; together, they make the poll function properly.

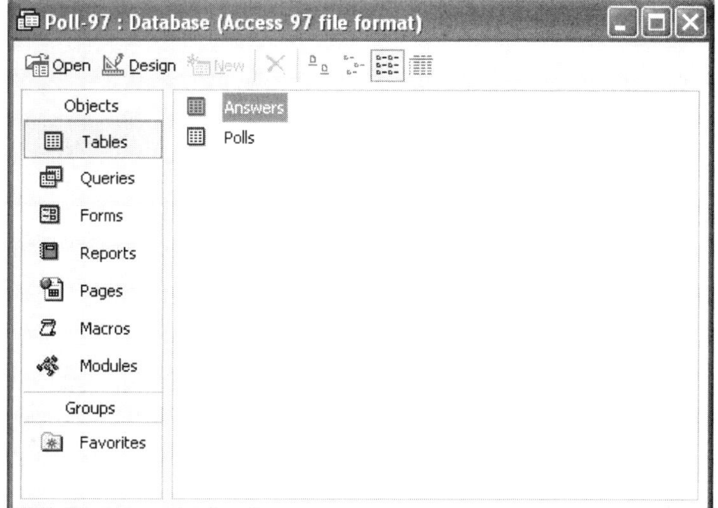

Figure 1.1 *The database that powers the poll has two tables.*

Answers

The Answers table stores the answers to the polls (answers are given to the questions in the admin). The number of votes given to each answer is also stored in this table.

Polls

The Polls table stores every question, the date it was created, whether it is the active question, and the total number of votes the question has received. The question is designated from the admin, just like the answers are.

The XML Document

As I stated before, the data is passed between the server-side scripts, to and from Flash, using XML. Parts of this XML document show up in different codes in order to organize the information that is either sent to the database, or extracted from the database. As we discuss the ColdFusion, Java, and ASP.NET code, you'll recognize much of the XML used because you'll already be familiar with it.

Open Poll.xml from the CD-ROM.

The following is the XML document that is used for all three variations of the poll (ColdFusion, ASP.NET, and Java):

```
<Blah>

<!– The request to get the poll question and answers –>
<Request>
    <TransactionType>GetPollData</TransactionType>
    <Data />
</Request>

<!– The response to GetPollData –>
<Response>
    <Status>Success</Status>
    <Data>
        <Poll ID="" TotalVotes="">
            <Question ID="">
                <Text></Text>
                <Answers>
                    <Answer ID="" Votes="">
                        <Text></Text>
                    </Answer>
                    <Answer ID="" Votes="">
                        <Text></Text>
                    </Answer>
                </Answers>
            </Question>
        </Poll>
    </Data>
</Response>
```

```
<!— The request to vote —>
<Request>
    <TransactionType>VoteOnPoll</TransactionType>
    <Data>
        <Vote PollID="" QuestionID="" AnswerID="" />
    </Data>
</Request>

<!— The response to vote —>
<Response>
    <Status>Success</Status>
    <Data>
        <Message>Your vote was recorded</Message>
    </Data>
</Response>

<!— The request to see if you have voted already on the
currently active poll —>
<Request>
    <TransactionType>HasVoted</TransactionType>
    <Data></Data>
</Request>

<!— The response to HasVoted —>
<Response>
    <Status>Success</Status>
    <Data>
        <VotedAlready>True | False</VotedAlready>
    </Data>
</Response>

<!— The response in case of an error —>
<Response>
    <Status>Error</Status>
    <Data>
        <Message>An error has occurred!</Message>
    </Data>
</Response>

</Blah>
```

The Admin

The admin is used to update the poll's questions and answers. You could very easily go into Flash and change the question and answers manually, but that process would be extremely tedious. Using the admin, you can change the entire poll in minutes. Additionally, when you have much larger applications that need their data updated quickly, the techniques behind the admin will help you greatly.

Open admin.cfm from the CD-ROM. **Figure 1.2** shows the finished admin.

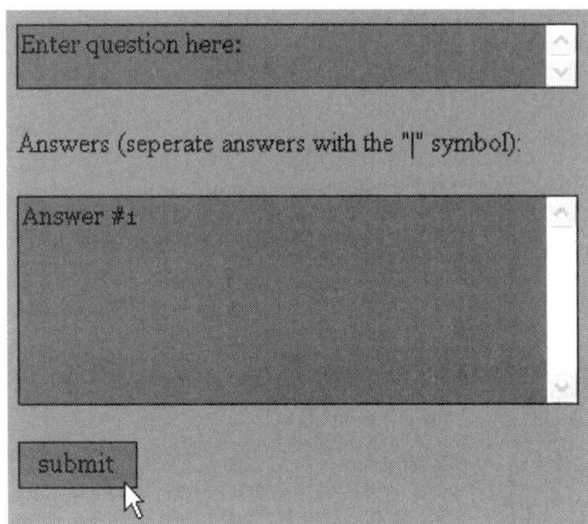

Figure 1.2 *The admin updates the poll's data.*

The following is the code behind the poll's admin:

```
<html>
<head>
<Title>Poll Admin</title>

<!-- Define the look of the form using CSS-->
<style type="text/css">

TEXTAREA, INPUT {
    font-family: Georgia, "MS Serif", "New York", serif;
    padding: 1px;
    font-size: 10px;
    color: #000000;
    background-color: #666666;
    border: solid 1px #000000;
}
```

```
</style>
</head>

<body bgcolor="#999999">

<cfparam name="action" default="none">

<cfswitch expression="#action#">
    <cfcase value="none">

        <form name="info" method="post">
    <p>
    <textarea name="question" cols="50" class="texta1"
    → wrap="VIRTUAL">Enter question here:</textarea>
    <p> Answers (seperate answers with the "|" symbol):
    <p>
        <textarea name="answers" cols="50" class="texta1"
        → wrap="VIRTUAL" rows="7">Answer #1</textarea>
    <p>
        <input type="submit" value="submit">
        <input type="hidden" name="action" value="insert">
        </form>


    </cfcase>

    <cfcase value="insert">

        <!-- Insert the question and date into the Poll
        → table -->
        <cfquery name="InsertQuestion" datasource="POLL"
        → dbtype="odbc">
            insert into Polls
            (pollquestion, createdate)
            values ('#form.question#', #CreateODBCDate(Now())#)
        </cfquery>

        <!-- Get the largest PollID and assign it the name
        → of HighID -->
        <cfquery name="GetNewID" datasource="POLL"
        → dbtype="ODBC">
```

continues on next page

```
            Select Max(PollID) as HighID from Polls
        </cfquery>

        <!-- Deactivate all the poll questions -->
        <cfquery name="deactivate" datasource="poll">
            UPDATE Polls
            set active = 0
        </cfquery>

        <!-- Reactivate the poll whos PollID equals HighID
        → (reactivates the last entered poll) -->
        <cfquery name="active" datasource="poll">
            UPDATE Polls
            set active = 1
            where PollID=#GetNewID.HighID#
        </cfquery>

        <!-- Loop through the answers and insert them into
        → the database 1 by 1-->
        <cfloop list="#form.answers#" index="list_index"
        → delimiters="|">

        <cfquery name="InsertAnswer" datasource="POLL"
        → dbtype="odbc">
            insert into Answers
             (pollID, answer)
            values (#GetNewID.HighID#, '#list_index#')
        </cfquery>

        </cfloop>

        <!- Tell the user that the poll has been updated
        → successfully ->
        <cfoutput>
            <br>The poll has been updated
        </cfoutput>

    </cfcase>
</cfswitch>

</body>
</html>
```

All of the HTML should look familiar to you, except for possibly the code between the <style> tags. This is code for Cascading Style Sheets (CSS). CSS enables you to control the layout of your HTML documents with simple, reusable code. To find out more about CSS, go to www.w3.org/Style/CSS/.

The ColdFusion behind the admin is fairly simple as well. The first things to be inserted into the database are the question and the date of its creation. Subsequently, the largest PollID is extracted from the database and saved as HighID. Then, all the polls are made inactive, just so the last created poll can be made the only active poll (if more than one poll was active, the entire application would be shot because the ColdFusion and Flash code that are discussed later would not work). Finally, we loop through all the answers in the answers text field, break them up one by one (using the | as the delimiter) and insert the answers one by one into the database. This is how the poll's questions and answers can be updated. Be cognizant of the fact that all the vote tallies go back to 0 when you update. Therefore, make sure when creating a new poll that all the possible answers are included because you won't be able to change the answers for a specific question unless you reset the entire poll.

The Poll: ColdFusion Version

Now that we have the XML document, database, and administrative system set up, there is only one task left to handle before we dig into the Flash code: the ColdFusion code that connects Flash to the database. The main language for this chapter is ColdFusion. It is an obvious choice because of its easy syntax and database connectivity. Java or ASP.NET is not a necessity for this particular project because speed isn't a concern due to the minimal amount of information being sent to and from the server. In the following sections we take a look at and dissect the four ColdFusion scripts used in the polling system.

Where Do You Begin?

Some developers like to do the Flash end before the backend (whether it's ColdFusion, Java, ASP.NET, PHP, or whatever), but the general practice is to do the backend before the Flash. It is up to you as a developer to formulate your own routines to make your programming process easier, speedier, and more efficient.

Controller.cfm

The Controller.cfm file is used to define a few global variables, dynamically build the include, determine the transaction type, and catch any errors. It's almost impossible to say that any one script is more important than the next because the absence of any script causes your application to be faulty, but, as its name indicates, controller.cfm is the most important (for lack of a better word) file because it controls the entire application. Let's look at the code so you can get a better understanding of what I'm trying to convey:

Open controller.cfm from the CD-ROM.

```
<cfsetting enablecfoutputonly="Yes" showdebugoutput="No"
→ catchexceptionsbypattern="No">
<!-- Set global values for the datasource name and database
→ type -->
<cfset DATASOURCE_NAME = "Poll">
<cfset DATABASE_TYPE = "ODBC">

<!-- Create a default doc variable if it wasnt passed -->
<cfparam name="URL.doc" type="string" default="">

<!-- If the doc variable is empty, throw an error -->
<cfif URL.doc is "">
    <cfoutput>
        <Response>
            <Status>Error</Status>
            <Data>
                <Message>No XML data sent</Message>
            </Data>
        </Response>
    </cfoutput>

    <!-- Stop the page from executing further -->
    <cfabort>
</cfif>

<!-- Wrap everything a try block -->
<cftry>

    <!-- Parse the XML document -->
    <CF_XMLParser xml = URL.doc output="xmlDoc">
```

```
        <!-- Find the transaction type -->
        <cfset transaction =
        → xmlDoc.Request.TransactionType.INNER_TEXT>

        <!-- Include the transaction dynamically -->
        <cfinclude template = "#transaction#Transaction.cfm">

        <!-- Handle database errors -->
        <cfcatch type="Database">
            <cfoutput>
                <Response>
                    <Status>Error</Status>
                    <Data>
                        <Message>Error accessing database</Message>
                    </Data>
                </Response>
            </cfoutput>
        </cfcatch>

        <!-- Handle any other errors -->
        <cfcatch type="Any">
            <cfoutput>
                <Response>
                    <Status>Error</Status>
                    <Data>
                        <Message>Error handling transaction</
                        → Message>
                    </Data>
                </Response>
            </cfoutput>
        </cfcatch>

    </cftry>

    <!-- Turn off enablecfoutputonly -->
    <cfsetting enablecfoutputonly="No" showdebugoutput="No"
    → catchexceptionsbypattern="No">
```

The code is heavily commented so you should be able to understand what it does, but let's review it anyway. Unfortunately for programmers, ColdFusion often outputs extra whitespace. Thankfully, however, there are ways to eliminate the extra whitespace, such as using the `<cfsetting>` tag and setting the ENABLECFOUTPUTONLY attribute to Yes. Once that is taken care of, it is time to set two global variables: DATASOURCE_NAME and DATABASE_TYPE. These variables are used in all ColdFusion scripts to determine the data source name (DSN) and the type of database. If a doc variable isn't passed, it is created. (If the doc variable is empty, it means that there was no request for a transaction to be made, and an error message is sent and the script stops executing.) If the doc variable isn't empty, a transaction request was made, the XML document is parsed, and the transaction type is determined (there are three types of transactions: GetPollData, VoteOnPoll, and HasVoted). Once the transaction is determined, the appropriate file is loaded into the controller.cfm file using <cfinclude>. Database errors are checked for, as are all other errors. Finally, enablecfoutputonly is disabled. As you can now easily see, controller.cfm is extremely important to this application because it defines the DSN and database type, determines the transaction type, loads the appropriate file based on the transaction type, and checks for errors.

GetPollDataTransaction.cfm

The GetPollDataTransaction.cfm file is used to extract all the information (question, answers, total votes, and so on) from the database and put it into XML form to be handled by Flash. Let's take a look:

Open GetPollDataTransaction.cfm from the CD-ROM.

```
<!-- Execute the query to get the poll data -->
<cfquery name="GetPoll" datasource="#DATASOURCE_NAME#"
→ dbtype="#DATABASE_TYPE#">
    Select PollID, PollQuestion, TotalVotes
    From Polls
    Where Active = 1
</cfquery>

<!-- If no polls were found, set the poll ID to -1 -->
<cfif GetPoll.RecordCount is 0>
    <cfset pollID = -1>
<cfelse>
    <cfset pollID = GetPoll.pollID>
</cfif>

<!-- Get all answers for the poll -->
```

```
<cfquery name="GetAnswers" datasource="#DATASOURCE_NAME#"
→ dbtype="#DATABASE_TYPE#">
    Select AnswerID, Answer, Votes
    From Answers
    Where PollID = #pollID#
</cfquery>

<!-- Build the XML document to return -->
<cfoutput>
    <Response>
        <Status>Success</Status>
        <Data>
            <Poll ID="#GetPoll.PollID#" TotalVotes=
            → "#GetPoll.TotalVotes#">
                <Question>
                    <Text>#GetPoll.PollQuestion#</Text>
                    <Answers>
                        <cfloop query="GetAnswers">
                            <Answer ID="#AnswerID#" Votes=
                            → "#Votes#">
                                <Text>#Answer#</Text>
                            </Answer>
                        </cfloop>
                    </Answers>
                </Question>
            </Poll>
        </Data>
    </Response>
</cfoutput>
```

To start off, the poll's id, question, and total votes where active equals 1 (as I stated before, if active equals 1, it is the last entered poll. All other polls have active set to 0) is extracted from the database. If no poll was found, pollID is set to -1, but if a poll was found, pollID is set to the pollID retrieved from the GetPoll query. Then, the answerID, answers, and votes are extracted from the database. Finally, the XML document is built to be returned into Flash.

VoteOnPollTransaction.cfm

Once the question, answers, and votes are retrieved, it is time to give the user the option to vote. VoteOnPollTransaction.cfm sends the user's vote to the database and dumps a cookie on the user's machine saying that a vote was made. Let's go over VoteOnPollTransaction.cfm:

Open VoteOnPollTransaction.cfm from the CD-ROM.

```
<!-- Get the answerID -->
<cfset answerID = xmlDoc.Request.Data.Vote.AnswerID>

<!-- Execute the query to update the poll -->
<cfquery name="UpdatePollVotes"
datasource="#DATASOURCE_NAME#" dbtype="#DATABASE_TYPE#">
    update Polls, Answers
        set Polls.TotalVotes = (Polls.TotalVotes + 1),
        Answers.Votes = (Answers.Votes + 1)
    where Polls.Active = Yes and
        Polls.PollID = Answers.PollID and
        Answers.AnswerID = #AnswerID#;
</cfquery>


<!-- Dump the cookie on the users machine -->
<cfcookie name="hasVoted" value="#pollID#" expires="NEVER">

<cfoutput>
    <Response>
        <Status>Success</Status>
        <Data>
            <Message>Voted properly</Message>
        </Data>
    </Response>
</cfoutput>
```

First, the answerID is retrieved from the XML document. Then, the total votes for the active poll is incremented by 1. The total votes for the specified answer is also incremented by 1. A cookie named hasVoted, with a value of pollID and no expiration date is then dumped on the user's machine. Finally, an XML document is built to tell the user that everything was successful and that the vote was recorded properly.

HasVotedTransaction.cfm

You know that there is going to be someone who has so much time on his hands that he's going to sit in front of his computer, vote 100 times, and screw up your poll with faulty results. For that reason, in the VoteOnPollTransaction file, we dump a cookie on the user's machine after he votes the first time. With the HasVotedTransaction.cfm file, we check to see if the cookie exists on the user's machine. Let's have a look at the file:

Open HasVotedTransaction.cfm from the CD-ROM.

```
<!-- Execute the query to get the pollID -->
<cfquery name="GetPollID" datasource="#DATASOURCE_NAME#"
→ dbtype="#DATABASE_TYPE#">
    Select PollID
    From Polls
    Where Active = 1
</cfquery>

<!-- Get a convenient reference to the pollID -->
<cfset pollID = GetPollID.PollID>

<!-- Get the cookie value and set it to a default if
→ necessary -->
<cfparam name="cookie.hasVoted" default="-1">

<!-- Return the response -->
<cfoutput>
    <Response>
        <Status>Success</Status>
        <Data>
            <!-- If the cookie has a value that is NOT the
            → same as the pollID, they havent voted -->
            <cfif pollID IS cookie.hasVoted>
                <VotedAlready>True</VotedAlready>
            <cfelse>
                <VotedAlready>False</VotedAlready>
            </cfif>
        </Data>
    </Response>
</cfoutput>
```

The code first obtains the PollID of the active poll. A convenient name is assigned to the pollID. The cookie value is retrieved, and, if necessary, a default value of -1 is assigned to it. An XML document is then built, and if the cookie has a value of PollID, `<VotedAlready>` is set to true; if the user does not have a cookie with the same value as PollID, `<VotedAlready>` is set to false. Notice how ColdFusion checks whether the cookie has a value of PollID, not just whether the cookie exists. By doing this, the user is allowed to vote on other questions, just not on the same question more than once from the same computer.

Why Not JavaScript?

A lot of people like to use JavaScript for their cookies, so I have included files on the CD-ROM named cookie_test.fla, cook_test.html, and cookie.js, which shows you how to set cookies using JavaScript and Flash. If you compare setting cookies in JavaScript to setting cookies in ColdFusion, you see that the latter is much easier to use than the former.

The Flash Front End

Now that the backend is completed, it is time to start programming the Flash front end. It consists of one scene with multiple parts.

Why Only One Scene?

While it may seem logical to make multiple scenes for such an application, working with one scene makes it easier for you to locate loaded variables. You could load the data in multiple times, but that slows down your application drastically, not to mention annoys your anxious users.

Open poll.fla from the CD-ROM. There are three parts to this application. The first part loads the data (**Figure 1.3**); the second part displays the answers (**Figure 1.4**); and the final part displays the poll's results (**Figure 1.5**). These three sections make up the polling system.

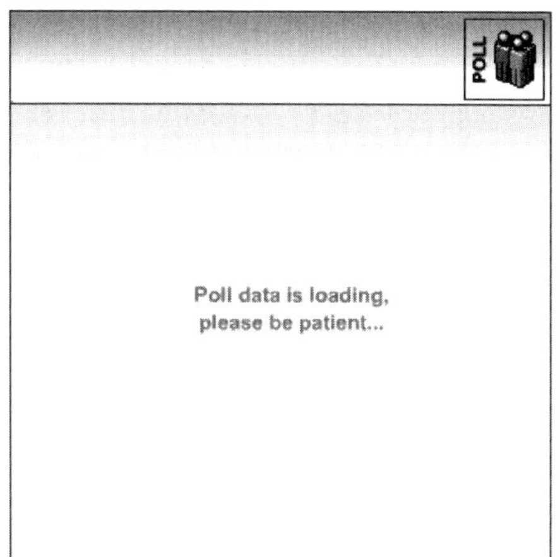

Figure 1.3 *The completed poll loading in the data.*

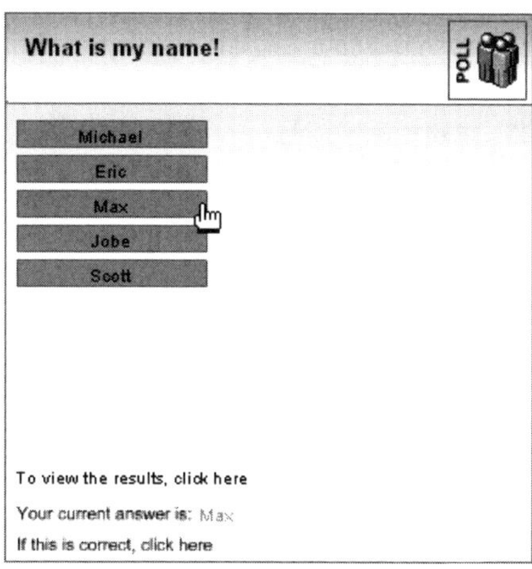

Figure 1.4 *The completed poll displaying the answers and enabling the user to vote.*

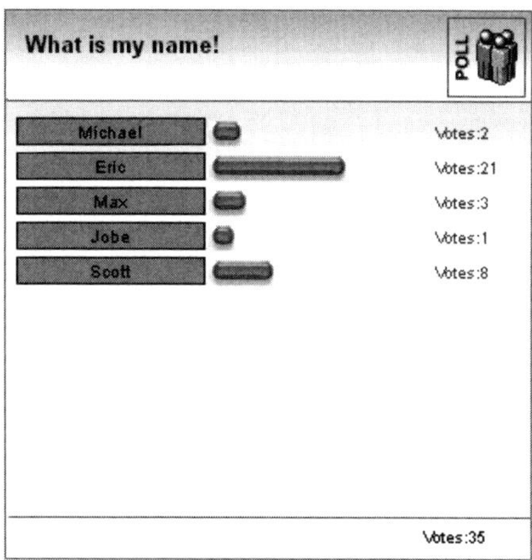

Figure 1.5 *The completed poll displaying the poll's results.*

Before starting to program the front end, I set up the movie's properties. The movie's size is set to 320X325, the background color is set to #FF6600, and the publishing setting is left at its default of Flash 6. Once this is done, I add a layer named actions and, on frame one, I create a bunch of custom functions in order to handle the different types of data transactions. The following are the actions for the first frame of the actions layer:

```
#include "ServerData.as"
#include "CommonTransactionFunctions.as"
// stop the movie
stop();
// do this once:
sd = new ServerData();
sd.setMethod(sd.SEND_AND_LOAD);
sd.setLanguage(sd.COLD_FUSION);
sd.setURL("http://www.yourserver.com/Controller.cfm");
// set the document to send to the server
sd.setDocOut(buildGetPollDataTransaction());
// set the document you want to contain the response
sd.setDocIn(new XML());
// set the call back for when its done
sd.onLoad = parseGetPollData;
function parseGetPollData() {
    xmlDoc = this.getDocIn();
    worked = wasSuccessful(xmlDoc);
    if (worked) {
        var mainNodes = xmlDoc.firstChild.childNodes;
        var dataNode = mainNodes[1];
        var pollNode = dataNode.firstChild;
        var pollNodeAttributes = pollNode.attributes;
        pollID = pollNodeAttributes["ID"];
        pollTotalVotes = pollNodeAttributes["TotalVotes"];
        var questionNode = pollNode.firstChild;
        var questionNodeChildren = questionNode.childNodes;
        pollQuestion = questionNodeChildren[0].firstChild.
        ⇢ nodeValue;
        var pollAnswers = questionNodeChildren[1].childNodes;
        answers = new Array();
        for (i=0; i<pollAnswers.length; i++) {
            var tempAnswer = pollAnswers[i];
            var tempAttributes = tempAnswer.attributes;
            var tempAnswerValue = tempAnswer.firstChild;
```

```
            answers["ID_"+i] = tempAttributes["ID"];
            answers["Votes_"+i] = tempAttributes["Votes"];
            answers["Answer_"+i] = tempAnswerValue.firstChild.
            → nodeValue;
        }
        totalAnswers = pollAnswers.length;
    }
    // Kick off the next step
    determineVoteStatus();
}
// execute it
sd.execute();
function determineVoteStatus() {
    // set the document to send to the server
    sd.setDocOut(buildHasVotedTransaction());
    // set the document you want to contain the response
    sd.setDocIn(new XML());
    // set the call back for when its done
    sd.onLoad = parseHasVoted;
    // execute it
    sd.execute();
}
function parseHasVoted() {
    xmlDoc = this.getDocIn();
    trace(xmlDoc);
    if (wasSuccessful(xmlDoc)) {
        var xmlDoc = new XML(pollVotedXML);
        var mainNodes = xmlDoc.firstChild.childNodes;
        var dataNode = mainNodes[1];
        var votedAlreadyNode = dataNode.firstChild;
        votedAlready = votedAlreadyNode.firstChild.nodeValue;
        if (votedAlready) {
            gotoAndStop("results");
        } else {
            gotoAndStop("Vote");
        }
    }
}
// buildGetPollDataTransaction function
// This function creates a 'get poll data'
// transaction
```

continues on next page

```
function buildGetPollDataTransaction() {
    // Build a basic 'get poll data' transaction
    getPollDataRequest = buildBaseRequest("GetPollData");
    // Return the xml object
    return getPollDataRequest;
}
// end buildGetPollDataTransaction function
// buildHasVotedTransaction function
// This function builds a 'has voted' transaction
function buildHasVotedTransaction() {
    // Build a basic 'has voted' transaction
    hasVotedRequest = buildBaseRequest("HasVoted");
    // Return the xml object
    return hasVotedRequest;
}
// end buildHasVotedTransaction function
// buildVoteOnPollTransaction function
// This function builds a 'vote on poll' transaction
function buildVoteOnPollTransaction(pollID, answerID) {
    // Build a basic 'vote on poll' transaction
    voteRequest = buildBaseRequest("VoteOnPoll");
    // Get the data node
    dataNode = findDataNode(voteRequest);
    // Create the vote node
    voteNode = tempDoc.createElement("Vote");
    // Get the vote node attributes
    voteAttributes = voteNode.attributes;
    // Set the attribute values
    voteAttributes.PollID = pollID;
    voteAttributes.AnswerID = answerID;
    // Append the vote node to the data node
    dataNode.appendChild(voteNode);
    // Return the transaction request
    return voteRequest;
}
// end buildVoteOnPollTransaction function
```

Before you start gasping for air, let me reassure you, it isn't as complicated as it looks. These functions are the key to the rest of the poll, so do not read hastily through the explanations. Each type of transaction, as set forth in the interaction points, has its own function. Before any functions are made, the ServerData.as and CommonTransactionFunctions.as files are loaded into Flash. Then the movie is stopped; it is sent to another frame once it is determined whether the user has already voted on the current poll. The type of method, language, and URL of the controller file are all set. The XML document to be sent to the server and the document that contains its response are both set. The `onLoad` event for sd (the new server data) is set to `parseGetPollData`, so when sd is executed, the `parseGetPollData` function is performed. The first function, `parseGetPollData`, is then created. If the XML document loads into Flash successfully, the `pollID` is set to the current poll's ID, `pollTotalVotes` is set to the total amount of votes on the current poll, and `pollQuestion` is set to the poll's current question. In addition, an array named answer is created to contain the poll's answers, the answers' IDs, and the total number of votes for each answer. The `totalAnswers` variable is set to the length of the `pollAnswers` variable (this is used later to determine how many times a movieclip will need to be duplicated). Finally, the `determineVoteStatus` function is called upon and sd is executed (when sd is executed, it means that a certain transaction is taking place. In this case, the `GetPollData` transaction is taking place). If you refer back to the development plot, you'll see that I am being consistent with the scheme that was drawn up.

The next function is `determineVoteStatus`. The XML document to be sent to the server and the document that contains its response are both set. Then, the `onLoad` event for sd is set to `parseHasVoted`, so when sd is executed the `parseHasVoted` function is performed. sd, with its new settings, is once again executed.

The third function, `parseHasVoted`, first checks to make sure that the document was sent back by the server. If it was successfully sent back to Flash, then the `VotedAlready` variable is set to either true or false, depending on whether the user has voted on the current poll. If the user has voted, then he is sent to the results frame in order to see the current results. If the user has not yet voted, he is sent to the vote frame in order to cast his vote. Once again, I am following the development plot. I just completed number 2 on both numbered lists.

The `buildGetPollDataTransaction` function simply builds a getPollData transaction and returns the XML document.

Next, the `buildHasVotedTransaction` function is created. It builds a `hasVoted` transaction and returns the XML document.

The sixth and final function is `buildVoteOnPollTransaction`. It takes two parameters: `pollID` and `answerID`. First, this function builds a `VoteOnPoll` transaction. Then, the data node from the VoteOnPollTransaction file is found. A node with a name of Vote is created and given two attributes, pollID and answerID. The Vote node is added onto the data node. Finally, the transaction request is returned. The third and final task set forth in the development plot is now complete.

Well, that was certainly a lot of code to digest! If you don't completely understand how the functions work, I strongly suggest going back and rereading the comments and explanations. The functions are the basis to the rest of the application; if you don't understand them, you won't understand the rest of the code.

Next, I create a second layer and name it loading. On the first and only keyframe, I add the text "Poll data is loading, please be patient." This means that before the user is sent to another frame, he is notified that the data is loading.

Subsequently, I add a layer, name it voteElements, and set a keyframe on the second frame. On the new keyframe I create a movieclip with a textbox named answer and an invisible button with the following actions:

```
on (release) {
    _root.answer = this.answer;
    _root.answerID = this.answerID;
}
```

This code sets the answer variable on the main timeline to the answer variable in the movieclip, and the answerID variable on the main timeline to the answer variable in the movieclip.

The movieclip is dragged onto the stage and given an instance name of Vote. I then add the text "Your current answer is:", and adjacent to it I create a textbox named answer to display the currently selected answer. Next, a button is made underneath the textbox with the following actions:

```
on (release) {
    sd.onLoad = buildVoteOnPollTransaction (pollID, answerID);
    sd.setDocOut(buildVoteOnPollTransaction (pollID,
    → answerID));
    sd.execute();
    gotoAndStop("results");
}
```

This sets the onLoad event to buildVoteOnPollTransaction, which is used to update the poll's results. Then, the XML document that is being sent to the server is set to buildVoteOnPollTransaction, because the function also creates an XML document with the user's currently selected answer. The function is executed and the XML document with the pollID and answerID is sent to the server to be handled by VoteOnPollTransaction. Finally, the user is sent to the results frame in order to see the poll's current standings.

Another button is then created with the following actions:

```
on (release) {
    gotoAndPlay("results");
}
```

Obviously, this button sends the user to the results frame without having to actually vote on the poll.

I then add a second keyframe on the actions layer and add the following action script:

```
loop_length = totalAnswers;
// handle the clip duplication
ystart = vote._y;
for (i=0; i<loop_length; i++) {
    duplicateMovieClip("vote", "vote"+i, i);
    setProperty("vote"+i, _y, ystart+20*i);
    set("vote"+i+".answer", answers["Answer_"+i]);
    set("vote"+i+".answerID", answers["ID_"+i]);
}
stop();
```

First, I set the variable loop_length to toalAnswers, which is a variable set back in frame 1 that contains the total number of answers returned from the database. Then, ystart is set to the y-value of the vote movieclip. Now it's time to duplicate the movieclip, one time for each answer. To do this, I set up a for loop, which begins with i equaling 1, and ends when i is greater than loop_length. Each time it loops, the movieclip vote is duplicated and named "vote"+i, which means that if there are 3 answers, there will be three movieclips: vote1, vote2, and vote3. The movieclip is given a y-position, which is 20 pixels greater than the movieclip before it. The answer variable in the movieclip is set to an element in the answers["Answer_"+i] portion of the answers array. The answerID variable is then set to an element in the answers["ID_"+i] portion of the answers array. Finally, the movie is instructed to stop.

Lastly on the second frame (**Figure 1.6**), I add a layer and name it question. A textbox is created with a variable name of pollQuestion. It is used to display the poll's question.

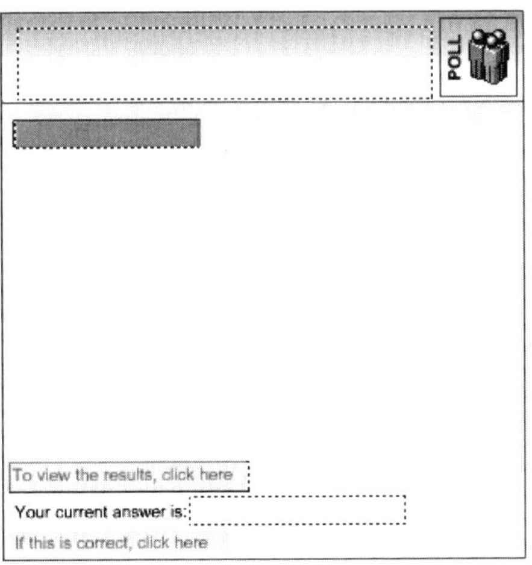

Figure 1.6 *The poll's second frame.*

Going back to the question layer, I insert a frame on the third frame. I then add another layer, name it resultElements, and add a keyframe on its third frame. On that keyframe I create a textbox and give it a variable name of `totalvotes`; the textbox will be used to display the total amount of votes on the poll. I then create a movieclip that displays the results of the poll. In this movieclip, I create two textboxes: answer (to display the poll's possible answers) and votes (to display the total number of votes given to the answer). The movie clip also consists of a graphic, which is scaled from 7.0 pixels wide to 115 pixels wide over the course of 100 frames. Each layer in the movieclip has a keyframe on frame 1 and on frame 100, so when the graphic is scaled (the graphic is used as a bar graph to graph the number of votes each answer receives), the textboxes do not disappear. I go back to the main timeline, drag an instance of the movieclip onto the stage, and give it an instance name of `result_mc`. Next, I add a keyframe on the third frame of the actions layer and add the following action script:

```
totalVotes = "Votes:"+pollTotalVotes;
loop_length = totalAnswers;
// handle the clip duplication
ystart = result_mc._y;
for (i=0; i<loop_length; i++) {
    duplicateMovieClip("result_mc", "result_mc"+i, i);
    setProperty("result_mc"+i, _y, ystart+20*i);
    set("result_mc"+i+".answer", answers["Answer_"+i]);
    set("result_mc"+i+".votes", "Votes:"+answers["Votes_"+i]);
    set("result_mc"+i+".percent", answers["Votes_"+i]/
    → pollTotalVotes*100);
}
stop();
```

The totalVotes variable is first set to display the word Votes: and then the total number of votes on the particular poll. Just like in keyframe 2, I set the variable loop_length to toalAnswers. Then, ystart is set to the y-value of the result_mc movieclip. Now it's time to duplicate the result_mc movieclip, once for each answer. A for loop is set up, which loops from i until it is greater than loop_length. Each time it loops, the movieclip result_mc is duplicated and named "result_mc"+i. The movieclip is given a y-position, which is 20 pixels greater than the movieclip before it. The answer variable in the movieclip is set to an element in the answers["Answer_"+i] portion of the array; the votes variable is then set to an element in the answers["votes_"+i] portion of the array; and the percent variable is then set to answers["Votes_"+i] divided by the total number of votes and multiplied by 100 (number over the total number multiplied by 100 gives you a percentage).

Finally, I go back to the result_mc and add the following code to the first keyframe:

```
stop();
percent = Math.round(percent);
gotoAndStop(percent);
```

This stops the movieclip from looping through its 100 frames, rounds off the percent variable, and sends the movieclip to the frame equal to the value of the percent variable. This sets up a bar graph, which is simply a way of displaying results. **Figure 1.7** shows the poll's third frame.

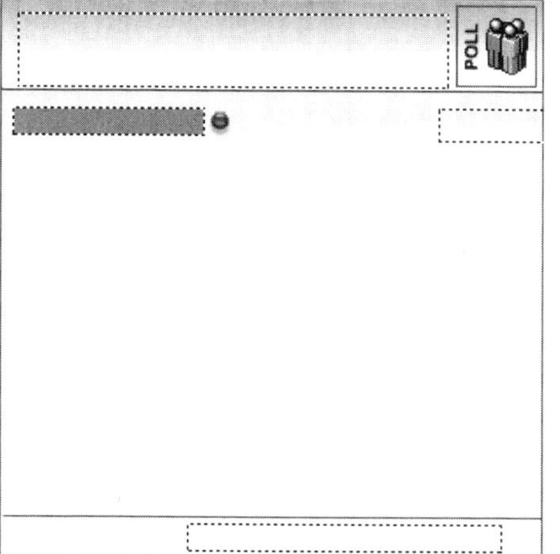

Figure 1.7 *The poll's third frame.*

These are all the key points behind the Flash front end to the poll. Other than what we just reviewed, the only other objects in the Flash movie are graphics and eye candy.

The Poll: Other Versions

It is extremely easy to make the polling system work with another server-side language, such as Java or ASP.NET. There are a number of reasons you might want to change the language that is used. For example, you might be more proficient in Java than ColdFusion, so you would be more comfortable using a Java version. Additionally, your server might support Java, but not ColdFusion. The next two sections talk about versions of the poll using server-side languages other than ColdFusion.

Java

To get the Java code found on the CD-ROM working, you only need to change two code lines. Look in frame 1 on the actions layer for the following code:

```
sd.setLanguage(sd.COLD_FUSION);
sd.setURL("http://www.yourserver.com/Controller.cfm");
```

And change it to this:

```
sd.setLanguage(sd.JAVA);
sd.setURL("http://www.yourserver.com/ TransactionController ");
```

ASP.NET

Just like the Java code, all you need to do to get the ASP.NET code found on the CD-ROM working is to change following code:

```
sd.setLanguage(sd.COLD_FUSION);
sd.setURL("http://www.yourserver.com/Controller.cfm");
```

To this:

```
sd.setLanguage(sd.ASPNET);
sd.setURL("http://www.yourserver.com/
→ TransactionController.asp");
```

Moving Onward

Wondering where to go from here? Well, there are modifications that you could make to the poll to further meet your needs. For example, if you have 20 possible answers to the poll's question, many of the answers won't be visible to the user. To solve the problem, either make the stage area much bigger, or add scrollbars. If your answers are not one-word answers, use MX's new `TextField._width` property to dynamically set the width of the answer text fields. You may also need to redesign the artwork because the answers might overlap it and cause your Flash movie to look ugly and unorganized. One last suggestion would be to change the way the results are displayed. Instead of using the bar graph, you could set up a pie chart using MX's new `MovieClip.CurveTO` function or by going to the Exchange (which can be found at http://www.macromedia.com/exchange/) and grabbing the pie chart component. I hope this gives you a little food for thought on how to customize this poll to your needs. Even if you have no further needs to be met by this application, the best way to learn is through experimentation, so modify the poll for learning purposes as well.

Conclusion

The poll was used as a gentle introduction into the world of advanced dynamic application development using Flash MX. The concepts and techniques used in this chapter are used on a more advanced level in the rest of the chapters in this book, so it's imperative that you understand them. In this chapter we reviewed how to integrate ColdFusion, XML, and Flash; ASP.NET and Flash; and Java and Flash. Additionally, you learned how to plot out the development of an application. At this point, I would like to point out that the plot was followed verbatim in the ColdFusion, ASP.NET, Java, and Flash scripts. Once the plot is laid out nicely, the codes are easier to write because you have a structure to follow. This is just an example of how a little time in the beginning can save a lot of time at the end. Remember, knowledge is power, so use the knowledge gained from this chapter in the more advanced chapters and applications to come!

2: Guest Book with a Whiteboard

by Max Oshman

A guest book is probably the most popular component on the Internet today, and it is also probably one of the most useful. It's a fact: people love to talk and love to express themselves; a guest book gives them ample opportunity to do so.

In this chapter, we dissect and discuss a guest book coded in ColdFusion, Java, and ASP.NET, utilizing Flash as a front end. Some of Flash MX's new capabilities, including components, are discussed in the course of the chapter. Without further adieu, let's get right into the application.

What Is It?

A guest book is a great way to let your users leave their comments, questions, and suggestions. It is a forum for users to meet new people, discuss hot topics, and debate on controversial issues. A guest book is a worthwhile addition to any site, no matter what the topic. One feature of our guest book is that, in addition to leaving his comments, the user also can select an image to be tagged on to his entry. This project is a lot of fun and is sure to be a big hit with your Web site visitors.

How Is It Going To Work?

It is now time to look at how the project is going to work. Users are able to create new messages and post them as well as browse the existing messages. One of the features of the guest book is a drawing application that lets users tag an image to their posts. The server does not use this data in any way; it just stores the XML doc in the database directly.

Client-to-Server Execution Order

1. Client asks the server for a list of all guest book entries by date.
2. Client posts an entry if the user wishes.

Client-to-Server Interaction Points

1. Get entries.
    a. Client asks the server for a list of all the entries with a "GetEntries" transaction request.
    b. Server responds with the XML data.
2. Post new entry.
    a. Client sends in an XML document with transaction "PostEntry" and all necessary data.
    b. Server writes this data to the database and returns success or failure.

The Database

Just like the poll application in Chapter 1, this project employs a database. Let's take a look at the database (**Figure 2.1**), which has only one table: Entries.

Open GuestBook-97.mdb from the CD-ROM.

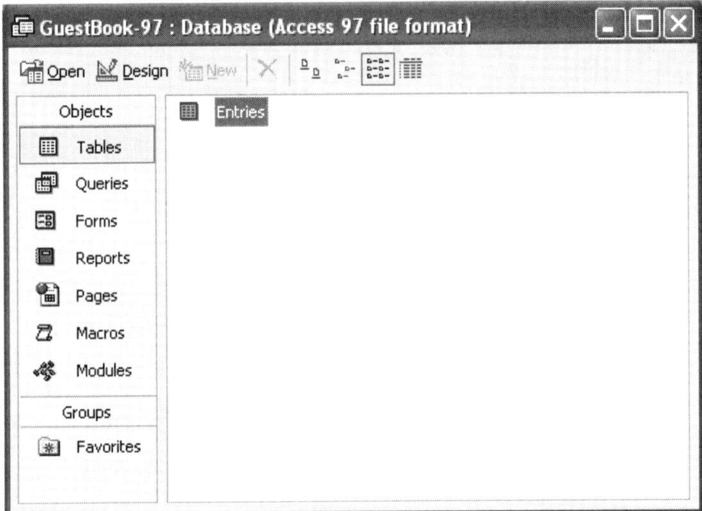

Figure 2.1 *The database that powers the guest book has one table.*

Entries

This is the database's only table. It contains all the information entered by the user: name, email address, subject, and message. Additionally, there is a column named Drawing, which contains information as to the user's selected image to be tagged with his entry. The date created and the user's IP address are also stored in the database.

The XML Document

Just like the poll application, the data is passed between the server-side scripts, both to and from Flash, using XML. Snippets of this XML document appear in the different ColdFusion, Java, and ASP.NET codes.

Open Guestbook.xml from the CD-ROM.

The following is the XML document that is used for all three variations (ColdFusion, ASP.NET, and Java) of the guest book:

```
<Blah>

<!– The request to get the guestbook entries –>
<Request>
    <TransactionType>GetEntries</TransactionType>
    <Data />
</Request>


<!– The response to GetEntries –>
<Response>
    <Status>Success</Status>
    <Data>
        <Entries>
            <Entry ID="" ShowEmail="True|False">
                <Name></Name>
                <Email></Email>
                <Subject></Subject>
                <Message></Message>
                <imagedata></imagedata>
            </Entry>
        </Entries>
    </Data>
</Response>


<!– The request to post an entry –>
<Request>
    <TransactionType>PostEntry</TransactionType>
    <Data>
        <Name></Name>
        <Email></Email>
        <Subject></Subject>
        <Body></Body>
        <ImageData></ImageData>
    </Data>
</Request>
```

continues on next page

```
<!— The response to PostEntry —>
<Response>
    <Status>Success</Status>
    <Data>
        <Message>Post entered</Message>
    </Data>
</Response>


<!— The response in case of an error —>
<Response>
    <Status>Error</Status>
    <Data>
    <Message>broke</Message>
    </Data>
</Response>


</Blah>
```

The Guest Book: ColdFusion Version

The database and XML documents are completed, so it is now time to work on the server-side code. The main language for this chapter is ColdFusion because of its easy database connectivity. Also, since it is not in real-time (such as a chat room or instant messenger would have to be), speed is not much of an issue. . In the following sections we take a look at and dissect the three ColdFusion scripts used in the guest book.

Controller.cfm

The controller.cfm file is the same as in the previous chapter. It defines a couple global variables, builds the include, determines the transaction type, and catches errors. Let's briefly look over it again:

Open controller.cfm from the CD-ROM.

```
<cfsetting enablecfoutputonly="Yes" showdebugoutput="No"
→ catchexceptionsbypattern="No">

<!-- Set global values for the datasource name and database
→ type -->
<cfset DATASOURCE_NAME = "Poll">
<cfset DATABASE_TYPE = "ODBC">

<!-- Create a default doc variable if it wasn't passed -->
<cfparam name="URL.doc" type="string" default="">

<!-- If the doc variable is empty, throw an error -->
<cfif URL.doc is "">
    <cfoutput>
        <Response>
            <Status>Error</Status>
            <Data>
                <Message>No XML data sent</Message>
            </Data>
        </Response>
    </cfoutput>

    <!-- Stop the page from executing further -->
    <cfabort>
</cfif>

<!-- Wrap everything a try block -->
<cftry>

    <!-- Parse the XML document -->
    <CF_XMLParser xml = URL.doc output="xmlDoc">

    <!-- Find the transaction type -->
    <cfset transaction =
    → xmlDoc.Request.TransactionType.INNER_TEXT>

    <!-- Include the transaction dynamically -->
    <cfinclude template = "#transaction#Transaction.cfm">
```

continues on next page

```
        <!-- Handle database errors -->
        <cfcatch type="Database">
            <cfoutput>
                <Response>
                    <Status>Error</Status>
                    <Data>
                        <Message>Error accessing database</
                        → Message>
                    </Data>
                </Response>
            </cfoutput>
        </cfcatch>

        <!-- Handle any other errors -->
        <cfcatch type="Any">
            <cfoutput>
                <Response>
                    <Status>Error</Status>
                    <Data>
                        <Message>Error handling transaction</
                        → Message>
                    </Data>
                </Response>
        </cfoutput>
        </cfcatch>

    </cftry>

    <!-- Turn off enablecfoutputonly -->
    <cfsetting enablecfoutputonly="No" showdebugoutput="No"
    → catchexceptionsbypattern="No">
```

Since this code has been previously explained, we'll just go over it quickly. First, we strip extra whitespace and then we define two variables, one for the DSN and one for the type of database. We make sure an XML document was sent to the server. If it wasn't, an error message is displayed. If it was sent to the server, the transaction type is determined and the proper ColdFusion code is loaded. Finally, we check for other possible errors.

GetEntriesTransaction.cfm

The GetEntriesTransaction.cfm file is used to take most of the guest book's data (everything with the exception of the drawing, createdate, and ipaddress columns) and throw it into an XML document to be loaded into and handled by Flash. Let's look it over:

Open GetEntriesTransaction.cfm from the CD-ROM.

```
<!-- Execute the query to get the Guestbook data -->
<cfquery name="GetGuestbook" datasource="#DATASOURCE_NAME#"
→ dbtype="#DATABASE_TYPE#">
    Select EntryID, name, email, showemail, subject,
    → message, drawing
    From Entries
</cfquery>

<!-- If no entries were found, set the poll ID to -1 -->
<cfif GetGuestbook.RecordCount is 0>
    <cfset entryID = -1>
<cfelse>
    <cfset entryID = GetGuestbook.entryID>
</cfif>

<!-- Build the XML document to return -->
<cfoutput>
    <Response>
        <Status>Success</Status>
        <Data>
            <cfloop query="GetGuestbook">
                <Entries>
                    <Entry ID="#EntryID#" ShowEmail=
                    → "#ShowEmail#">
                        <Name>#name#</Name>
                        <Email>#email#</Email>
                        <Subject>#subject#</Subject>
                        <Message>#message#</Message>
                        <imagedata>#drawing#</imagedata>
                    </Entry>
                </Entries>
            </cfloop>
        </Data>
    </Response>
</cfoutput>
```

This code can't possibly get any easier. First, we take the specified data out of the database. Then, we check to see how many results the query returned. If it does not return any, we set the EntryID to -1; if it does return results, we set EntryID to the number of results returned from the query. Finally, we build the XML document to be sent back into Flash. It contains the EntryID, ShowEmail, name, email, subject, and message data.

PostEntryTransaction.cfm

This script sends all of the user's entered data (everything from his name to the image he drew) into the database. Let's take a look at the code and review it:

Open PostEntryTransaction.cfm from the CD-ROM.

```
<!-- Make a convenient reference -->
<cfset dataNode = xmlDoc.Request.Data>

<!-- Get the Name -->
<cfset name = dataNode.Name.INNER_TEXT>

<!-- Get the email -->
<cfset email = dataNode.Email.INNER_TEXT>

<!-- Get the showemail -->
<cfset showemail = dataNode.ShowEmail.INNER_TEXT>

<!-- Get the subject -->
<cfset subject = dataNode.Subject.INNER_TEXT>

<!-- Get the message -->
<cfset message = dataNode.Message.INNER_TEXT>

<!-- Get the imagedata -->
<cfset imagedata = dataNode.imagedata.INNER_TEXT>


<!-- Execute the query to update the poll -->
<cfquery name="PostMessage" datasource="#DATASOURCE_NAME#"
dbtype="#DATABASE_TYPE#">
        Insert into Entries
            (name, email, showemail, subject, message,
            → drawing, createdate, IPAddress)
```

```
            values
                ('#name#', '#email#', '#showemail#', '#subject#',
                → '#message#', '#imagedata#', #Now()#,
                → '#REMOTE_ADDR#')
        </cfquery>

    <!— The response to PostEntry —>
    <Response>
        <Status>Success</Status>
        <Data>
            <Message>Message Recorded</Message>
        </Data>
    </Response>


    <!— The response in case of an error —>
    <Response>
        <Status>Error</Status>
        <Data>
            <Message>There was an error, please try again</
            → Message>
        </Data>
```

First, we get the values of the values of the XML elements, and assign them to variables. Then we insert the data into the database. Finally, an XML document with either a Success or Error message is outputted.

The Flash Front End

Well, here we are, the moment we have all been waiting for! We have laid the foundation of the application with the database, taken the information out of and put information back into the database using ColdFusion, and it is now time to tie it all together and display the information using Flash as our front end.

Open Guestbook.fla from the CD-ROM. There are three parts to this application. The first part loads the entries (**Figure 2.2**); the second part displays the entries (**Figure 2.3**); and the final part posts the user's entries (**Figure 2.4**).

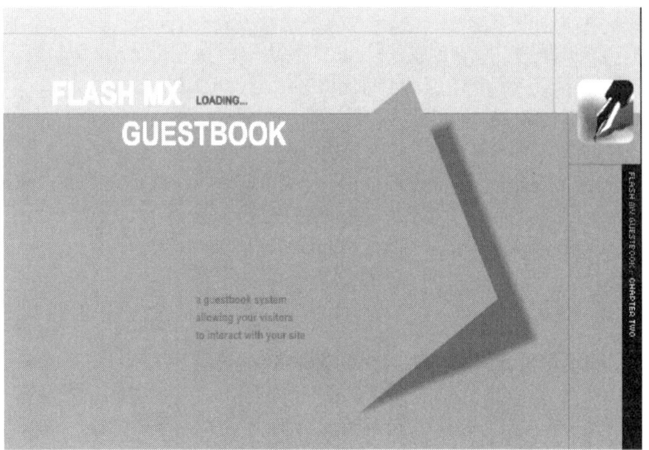

Figure 2.2 The guest book loading in the entries.

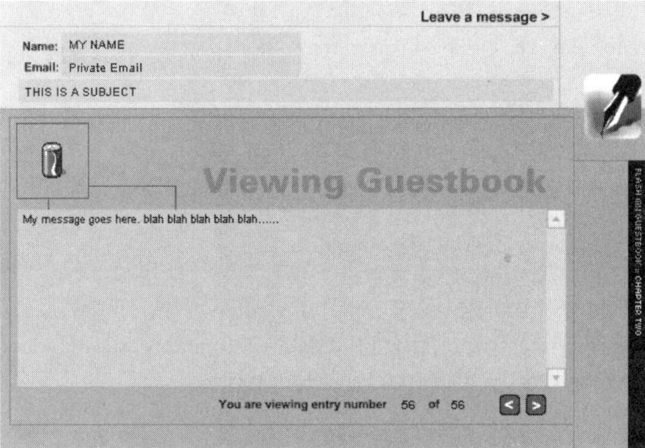

Figure 2.3 The guest book displaying the entries.

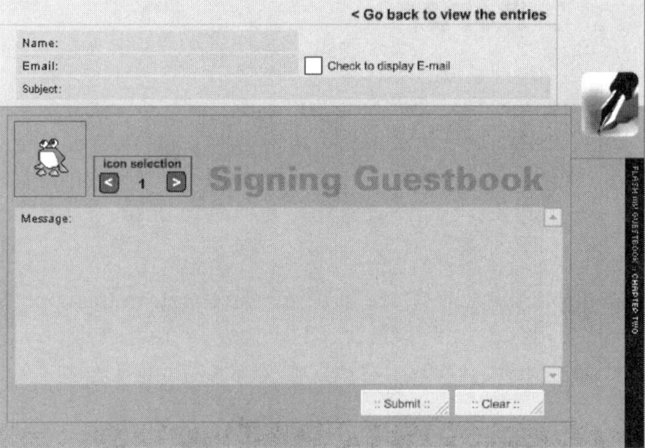

Figure 2.4 The frame that allows the user to post an entry.

First, I set up the movie. I leave the dimensions at their default, 550X400; change the background to gray (hex number #666666); and set the FPS to 120. Once the movie is set up, I name the pre-made layer actions, and add the following actions to it:

```
#include "ServerData.as"
#include "CommonTransactionFunctions.as"
// stop the movie
stop();
// do this once:
sd = new ServerData();
sd.setMethod(sd.SEND_AND_LOAD);
sd.setLanguage(sd.COLD_FUSION);
sd.setURL("http://www.yoururl/controller.cfm");
sd.setDocOut(buildGetEntriesTransaction());
// set the document you want to contain the response
sd.setDocIn(new XML());
// set the call back for when its done
sd.onLoad = parseGetEntries;
// gets the guestbook entries and organizes them properly
function parseGetEntries() {
    xmlDoc = this.getDocIn();
    worked = wasSuccessful(xmlDoc);
    if (worked) {
        var mainNodes = xmlDoc.firstChild.childNodes;
        var dataNode = mainNodes[1];
        var EntriesNode = dataNode.childNodes;
        var EntryNodeChildren = EntryNode.childNodes;
        // create the array which will contain all the data
        → for the guestbook
        entriesdata = new Array();
        for (i=0; i<EntriesNode.length; i++) {
            var tempEntry = EntriesNode[i];
            var tempAttributes =
            → tempEntry.firstChild.attributes;
            var tempEntryValue = tempEntry.firstChild;
            entriesdata["ID_"+i] = tempAttributes["ID"];
            entriesdata["ShowEmail_"+i] =
            → tempAttributes["ShowEmail"];
            entriesdata["Name_"+i] =
            → tempEntryValue.firstChild.firstChild;
```

continues on next page

```
            entriesdata["Email_"+i] =
            → tempEntryValue.firstChild.nextSibling.firstChild;
            entriesdata["Subject_"+i] =
            → tempEntryValue.firstChild.nextSibling.
            → nextSibling.firstChild;
            entriesdata["Message_"+i] =
            tempEntryValue.firstChild.nextSibling.nextSibling.
            → nextSibling.firstChild;
            entriesdata["imagedata_"+i] =
            tempEntryValue.firstChild.nextSibling.nextSibling.
            → nextSibling.nextSibling.firstChild;
        }
            // display the results
            total_entries = EntriesNode.length-1;
            i = i-1;
            _root.name = entriesdata["Name_"+i];
            _root.showemail = entriesdata["ShowEmail_"+i];
            _root.subject = entriesdata["Subject_"+i];
            _root.message = entriesdata["Message_"+i];
            root.images.gotoAndStop(parseFloat(entriesdata
            → ["imagedata_"+i]));
        // if the user requested not to show his email, set
        → email to private email
            if (_root.showemail == "0") {
                _root.email = "Private Email";
            } else {
                _root.email = entriesdata["Email_"+i];
            }
            gotoAndStop(2);
    }
}
sd.execute();
function buildGetEntriesTransaction() {
    GetEntriesRequest = buildBaseRequest("GetEntries");
    return GetEntriesRequest;
}
function postEntry() {
    // set the document to send to the server
    sd.setDocOut(buildPostEntryTransaction());
    // set the document you want to contain the response
    sd.setDocIn(new XML());
    // what to do once the data is loaded
```

```
    sd.onLoad = parseGetEntries;
    // execute it
    sd.execute();
}
function buildPostEntryTransaction() {
    postRequest = buildBaseRequest("PostEntry");
    // Get the data node
    dataNode = findDataNode(postRequest);
    // Create the nodes
    nameNode = postRequest.createElement("Name");
    showemailNode = postRequest.createElement("ShowEmail");
    emailNode = postRequest.createElement("Email");
    subjectNode = postRequest.createElement("Subject");
    messageNode = postRequest.createElement("Message");
    imagedataNode = postRequest.createElement("imagedata");
    // Give the values
    var nameValue = postRequest.createTextNode(name);
    var showemailValue =
    → postRequest.createTextNode(showemail);
    var emailValue = postRequest.createTextNode(email);
    var subjectValue = postRequest.createTextNode(subject);
    var messageValue = postRequest.createTextNode(message);
    var imagedataValue =
    → postRequest.createTextNode(imagedata);
    // Append the nodes to each other
    nameNode.appendChild(nameValue);
    showemailnode.appendChild(showEmailValue);
    emailnode.appendChild(emailValue);
    subjectnode.appendChild(subjectValue);
    messageNode.appendChild(messageValue);
    imagedataNode.appendChild(imagedataValue);
    // Append the nodes to each other
    dataNode.appendChild(nameNode);
    dataNode.appendChild(emailNode);
    dataNode.appendChild(showEmailNode);
    dataNode.appendChild(subjectNode);
    dataNode.appendChild(messageNode);
    dataNode.appendChild(imagedataNode);
    // Return the transaction request
    gotoAndPlay(1);
    return postRequest;
}
```

These are the functions that pretty much control the rest of the application. Before I start coding the functions however, there are some things that I need to take care of. I load in two .as files, ServerData.as and CommongTransactionFunctions.as. Then, I set some properties for the rest of the application, including the way I will work with the data (`SEND AND LOAD`), the language we'll use (`COLD FUSION`), and the URL where the controller.cfm file is located.

Now I can do the initial load of the data. To do so, I call upon the `buildGetEntriesTransaction` function to send a `GetEntries` transaction request to the server. Then I organize the loaded data using the `parseGetEntries` function. I must first make sure the data is loaded in successfully, and once I check to make sure it is, I target certain important nodes to make it possible for us to organize the data properly. I create an array named `entriesdata` that contains all the guest book's information (ID, ShowEmail, Name, Email, Subject, Message and imagedata), and set variables to the values of the retrieved and organized data. `Name`, `Email`, `ShowEmail`, `Subject`, `Message`, and `imagedata` are all set to the appropriate values. As you can see, they are only set to the first retrieved value because the guest book only displays one entry at a time. The values are set here so when the next frame is viewed, the variables already have values and there is no lag time. Then, I make sure `ShowEmail` is not set to 0, because if it is, this means that the user has selected to be anonymous and rather than his email address being displayed, "Private Message" appears instead. Finally, I go to the second frame so the guest book entries can be browsed.

The second function is `buildGetEntriesTransaction`, which builds the actual `GetEntries` transaction request to be sent to the server, to inform it that the data for the guest book is needed.

The third function, `postEntry`, says to send the data organized by the `buildPostEntryTransaction` function to the server. It also creates a new XML document for the information retrieved by the server to be sent back into Flash, and tells Flash what to do once the data is loaded. Once it is loaded, the `parseGetEntries` function is once again called upon for reorganizing the newly entered data.

The final function, `buildPostEntryTransaction`, builds the XML document to be sent back to the server. First, it makes the transaction type `PostEntry`. Then it finds the `dataNode` so the rest of the XML data can be appended to it and sent to ColdFusion to be inserted into the database. Once I find the `dataNode`, I create the `nameNode`, `showemailNode`, `emailNode`, `subjectNode`, `messageNode`, and `imagedataNode` elements. I create six TextNodes (`nameValue`, `showemailValue`, `emailValue`, `subjectValue`, `messageValue`, and imagedataValue) and append them to the elements. Then, I append all the elements to the dataNode. Finally, I go back to the first keyframe so the data can be reorganized (yes, I know we did other things to reorganize the data already, but this is completely necessary. If you remove one of the calls back to either the first keyframe or to the parseGetEntries function, the data isn't always reorganized).

With the functions created, I add another layer, name it loading, and on the first keyframe I add a little message to let the user know that the data is loading.

I create another layer and name it showmessage. I insert a keyframe on the second frame and add the objects to the stage that are needed to view the users' entries. I add four textboxes (name, email, subject, and message), open up the Components panel, and drag an instance of the ScrollBar component to the stage, snapping it onto the message textbox just in case a user has a lot to say and needs extra space to write. Then, I add Next and Previous buttons to enable users to browse through all of the entries. The Next button is given the following actions:

```
on (release) {
    // if the total entries doesn't equal i, then add 1 to it
    // and update the displayed data by showing the element in
    // the entriesdata array which is one above the previous
    // element.
    if (_root.total_entries != i) {
        i = i+1;
        _root.name = entriesdata["Name_"+i];
        _root.showemail = entriesdata["ShowEmail_"+i];
        _root.subject = entriesdata["Subject_"+i];
        _root.message = entriesdata["Message_"+i];
        _root.images.gotoAndStop(parseFloat(entriesdata
        → ["imagedata_"+i]));
        // if the user requested not to show his email, keep
        // his privacy
        if (_root.showemail == "0") {
            _root.email = "Private Email";
        } else {
            _root.email = entriesdata["Email_"+i];
        }
    } else {
        _root.i = _root.total_entries;
    }
}
```

To enable scrolling upward through the entries, I check to make sure that the total_entries value doesn't equal i. If it doesn't, then I add one to the value of i. The name, showemail, subject, message and imagedata sections of the entriesdata array are all increased by one. This then displays the one element above the currently displayed element, hence scrolling upward through the guest book's entries. Also, I must not forget about our user's privacy. I check to make sure that the user has not selected to remain anonymous. If he has, the email textbox displays "Private Email." If the user has not selected to keep his anonymity, his email address is displayed.

Next, I assign the following actions to the Previous button:

```
on (release) {
    // if i doesn't equal zero, then decrease i by one and
    // update the displayed data
    if (_root.i != 0) {
        i = i-1;
        _root.name = entriesdata["Name_"+i];
        _root.showemail = entriesdata["ShowEmail_"+i];
        _root.subject = entriesdata["Subject_"+i];
        _root.message = entriesdata["Message_"+i];
        _root.images.gotoAndStop(parseFloat(entriesdata
        → ["imagedata_"+i]));
        // keep the users privacy
        if (_root.showemail == "0") {
            _root.email = "Private Email";
        } else {
            _root.email = entriesdata["Email_"+i];
        }
    }
}
```

This does the same thing the Next button's actions did, except in reverse. First, I make sure i is not equal to 0. If it isn't, i is set to i-1. Then I update which element in the array is displayed in the textboxes. Finally, I check to make sure it is okay with the user to display his email address.

Then, a button is created that says "Leave a message," which takes the user to the third keyframe where he can post his own entry. The following actions are given to this button:

```
on (release) {
    name = "Name:"
    email = "Email:"
    showemail = "0"
    subject = "Subject:"
    message = "Message:"
    gotoAndStop(3);
}
```

Each variable is given a default value, and Flash is sent to the third keyframe.

A movieclip named images is created. Inside this movieclip are five keyframes, each an image options. If the person who posts the entry chooses an icon he wants to tag onto his guest book entry, it is displayed here. The movieclip is given an instance name of images.

I then create two more textboxes, give them variable names of `i` and `total entries`, and place them next to each other so the user can tell which entry he is looking at. For example, if the user is looking at the ninth entry of the 29 total entries, these textboxes say, "You are viewing entry number 9 of 29."

Finally, a second keyframe was added to the actions layer on its second frame. It was given a `stop ();` action so the movie stops and the user is able to view the entries. **Figure 2.5** shows the final result of the second frame.

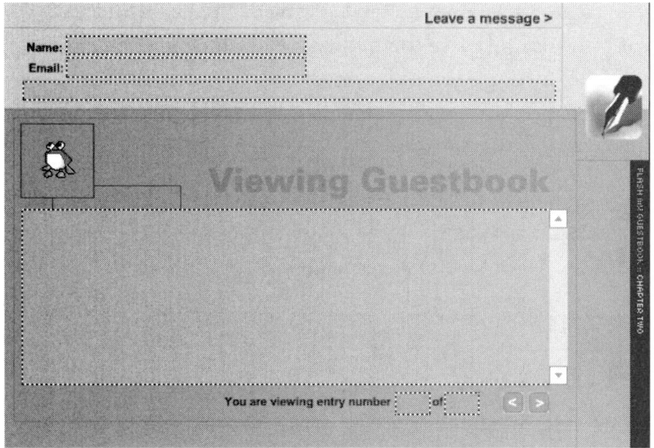

Figure 2.5 *The guest book's second frame.*

A third layer, named leavemessage, is added, and a keyframe is added on the third frame. On this keyframe, I add the same textboxes as in keyframe two of the showmessages layer, except this time I make them Input Text rather than Dynamic Text to let the user input his own data.

Then, I add a little user security to determine whether the user wants to remain anonymous. In order to do so, I create a movieclip, name it `check_box`, and give it two frames, one without a checked box and one with it. On the first frame, where the box is not checked, is a button with the following actions:

```
on (release) {
    _root.ShowEmail = 1;
    gotoAndStop(2);
}
```

This sets the variable `ShowEmail` to 1 (indicating to the server that it is okay to show the user's email address) and then sends Flash to the second frame.

On the second frame, where the box is checked, is a button with the following actions:

```
on (release) {
    _root.ShowEmail = 0;
    gotoAndStop(1);
}
```

This sets the `ShowEmail` variable to 0 (indicating that it is not okay for the user's email address to be shown) and then sends the user back to the first frame.

I then go back to the main timeline and drag an instance of the images movieclip onto the stage. I give it an instance name of images, and then add Next and Previous buttons and place them underneath the images movieclip. These are used to scroll through the different images that can be tagged onto the guest book entry. The Next button is given the following actions:

```
on (release) {
    if (images._currentframe != 5) {
        images.gotoAndStop(images._currentframe + 1);
        _root.imagedata = _root.imagedata + 1;
    }
}
```

This says that if the current frame of the images movieclip doesn't equal 5, go to the next frame and increment the `imagedata` variable by one (the current frame and the `imagedata` variable will be the same number because when the `imagedata` variable is loaded into Flash, the images movieclip is sent to the frame equal to the value of the `imagedata` variable).

The Previous button is assigned the following actions:

```
on (release) {
    if (images._currentframe != 1) {
        images.gotoAndStop(images._currentframe - 1);
        _root.imagedata = _root.imagedata - 1;
    }
}
```

This does the exact opposite of the Next button. If the current frame doesn't equal one, it sends the images movieclip to one frame less than its current position and decrements the `imagedata` variable by one.

A Submit button is then created and given the following actions:

```
on (release) {
    postEntry();
}
```

This calls upon the `postEntry` function, which takes the entered data and sends it to the server to be saved.

Another Clear button is created and given the following actions:

```
on (release) {
    name="Name:"
    email="Email:"
    subject="Subject:"
    message="Message:"
}
```

This sets the variables back to their defaults. That's all for frame 3. **Figure 2.6** shows the finished product.

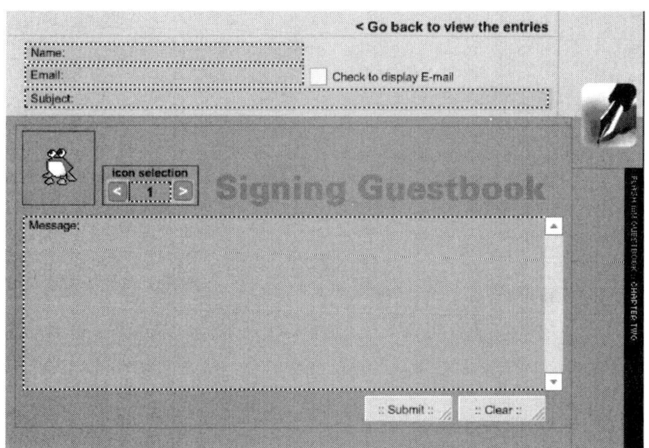

Figure 2.6 *The guest book's third frame.*

Believe it or not, that's it! Simple enough, right? If not, go back through the previous two chapters and read through the code explanations. Things really take off from this point and the next chapters are more difficult. Make sure you have a firm understanding of the code and the techniques behind the code before moving on.

The Guest Book: Other Versions

It is extremely easy to make the guest book work with another server-side language, such as Java or ASP.NET. There are a number of reasons you might want to change the language that is used in such an application, as discussed in Chapter 1. The next two sections talk about versions of the poll using server-side languages other than ColdFusion.

Java

To get the guest book to work with the Java code supplied with the CD-ROM, look in frame 1 for the following code:

```
sd.setLanguage(sd.COLD_FUSION);
sd.setURL("http://www.yourserver.com/Controller.cfm");
```

And change it to this:

```
sd.setLanguage(sd.JAVA);
sd.setURL("http://www.yourserver.com/TransactionController");
```

ASP.NET

To get the ASP.NET code working, change the following lines:

```
sd.setLanguage(sd.COLD_FUSION);
sd.setURL("http://www.yourserver.com/Controller.cfm");
```

To this:

```
sd.setLanguage(sd.ASPNET);
sd.setURL("http://www.yourserver.com/
TransactionController.asp ");
```

Where To Go From Here

There are not many modifications you could make to the guest book, but there are a few. For starters, since there could potentially be hundreds of entries, it might take a while for the data to load, so rather than a simple "data is loading message," add a preloader. You could do this by using the `getBytesTotal()` and `getBytesLoaded()` functions. Simply divide the BytesLoaded byBytesTotal and multiply by 100 and you get the percent of data loaded. Obviously you also could change the data that the user is asked to enter into the database. Just remember, you'd have to change the two major functions (`parseGetEntries` and `buildPostEntryTransaction`) to make them work with the new data. The most complex modification that I can think of would be to create a little application where the user can upload his own picture into your database and you would have Flash dynamically load the image when the user's entry is viewed. To load a picture dynamically into the images movieclip, use the following code:

```
images.loadMovie("http://www.yourdomain.com/someimage.jpg")
```

Other than that, it's up to you to be creative. Be imaginative; Flash has bounds not yet reached, so push the envelope.

Conclusion

The concepts in this chapter are extremely important. For example, the capability to display only certain information, which we used in this chapter, is the main concept behind projects such as an instant messenger. You also saw how to take a user's request (to show or not to show his email address, the icon selection, and so forth) and modify the look of another viewer's screen. The concepts and techniques discussed in each chapter of this book do not apply only to the example project, but can be applied to many, many applications. If you think you haven't grasped all the information discussed in the chapter, go back and skim the parts that still confuse you. When you're ready, let's move on to the next project: a message board.

3: Message Board System

by Eric E. Dolecki

In your online travels, chances are you've come across a message board of some kind. Message boards are complex data systems set up on certain Web sites that allow for online community interaction between the site visitors themselves.

Message boards can replace traditional help desks and customer support in many respects. They allow for the back-and-forth posting/replying to textual topics and threads.

Many are the nights when I run into a problem during the construction of a Flash project. When I need guidance quickly, I go to the Flash forums (message boards). They are well visited, and a lot of brilliant coders filter through the posts there supplying answers. After posting a specific problem, I can usually expect some sort of reply with corrected code in a day or so. That's a huge success for a community site. Before Flash MX was released, message boards were almost always HTML constructions. Now they can be deployed using Flash MX and a backend server-side system to great affect. This chapter shows you how.

Flash MX Message Board Features

The Flash MX message board presented in this chapter (**Figure 3.1**) has many of the features you expect from a traditional message board system:

- Topic entries (admin-defined—users cannot add topics)
- Any visitors can read posts, but must register and login first to be able to post themselves or reply to another post
- Threads based upon topic entries
- Replies to threads (messages)

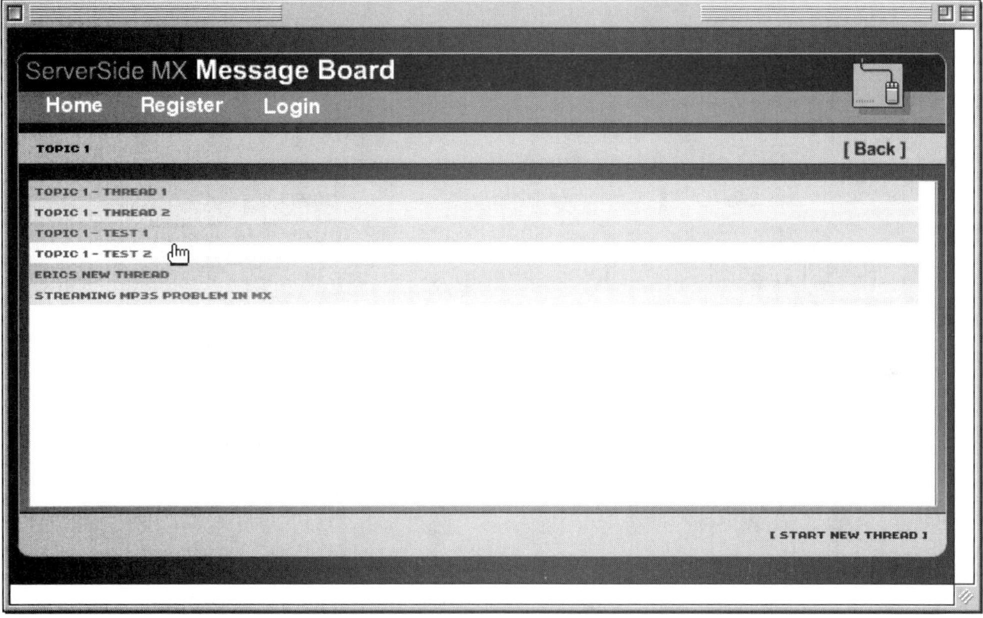

Figure 3.1 *Our Flash MX message board in action.*

A new Flash MX component, coupled with dynamic movie clip/text field creation, and new text formatting capabilities allow this system to go far beyond any previous Flash-based message board system. To administer this message board system, you can edit entries by hand (not advisable) or you can create your own admin panel (suggested).

Why Use Flash for a Message Board?

That's a fair question to ask. The overwhelming majority of message boards are HTML-based systems. They are usually composed of a series of individual ASP, JSP, or PHP pages that perform middleware operations between Flash and their respective databases. This still works well in most circumstances. However, developing a system like this from scratch may equate to a system of dozens of individual pages to perform individual operations.

The power of Flash MX as a GUI (graphical user interface) enables you to deploy your applications in a visually seamless fashion. There is no need to traverse multiple pages of a HTML-based system, and the experience is much less jarring to a visitor.

With the correct planning and development, conventional middleware pages (PHP, ASP, and so on) can be replaced with a single server application. The system could even work offline. This alone, however, wouldn't necessarily convince the casual developer to use Flash for such an application.

As Flash gains higher levels of usage, you'll find more sites and applications composed completely as SWF deployments. How elegant would it be to nestle your message board system directly within a greater application? Deploy a Flash-based Help Desk on an intranet—it could consist of a message board, email system, the ability to chat live with a customer service representative (audio), or even hold a video conference with someone from customer support who was specifically qualified to talk to your problem! All of this enclosed within one large Flash-based system, built of advanced components and allowing for the seamless integration of those components, all residing in a single browser window, accessible to you—and even customizable per the individual user's tastes. Deploy the system as an offline application, and now you're talking about a seriously elegant solution to solve particular needs.

If you are developing something like a Flash-based Web site for a company that sells computer hardware, for example, how nice would it be to have a tab on the side of the page that, when clicked, simply swings out a message board specific to a hardware part, so you could get available user feedback/ratings on a particular part you are considering for purchase? All without leaving the page you were already on? That's something you'll be seeing spring up in online applications. This is a movement you can embrace and further along by using MX in such ways.

That same message board system could communicate with another component, such as a live chat area, where an online admin would receive a message containing the topic of your recent message board post, and he could push a message window to you inviting you into a one-to-one personal chat to help resolve your technical problem. Within the span of a few minutes, you might be able to gain help from replies to your message board posting, or from an admin in a live chat session. That same admin could even push JPEG diagrams of a schematic to you now through Flash MX.

This idea is just the beginning in terms of possible uses of this type of integrated Flash-based solution. And with Flash, you don't need to worry so much about a client's browser or operating system (as you might with strictly HTML-based solutions) – you know that your front-end displays and functions with synergy, and that your backend solution processes information as needed.

All of this could be rather difficult to manage in a HTML-based system. You'd have to worry about client detection scripts, style sheet issues, possible JavaScript incompatibilities, tabling, and so forth. Not so with Flash.

How Our Message Board Works

One advantage of using Flash MX in development of a message board system is its ability to format data into a more presentable fashion than Flash 5 allowed. It also parses XML content like a demon. This system uses the ScrollPane component (a default Macromedia component that comes with Flash MX) and TextField formatting (via ActionScript) to present threaded information to viewers.

This message board uses .NET technology. It executes upon receipt of information and commands originating with the client, processes information, and returns information back to the client. It's a complicated system, but built in such a way that it can be used in a great many different applications, engaging and processing many different request types.

The following is a breakdown of the process this message board takes in terms of the backend communication that makes it work. It's quite technical in the details, and I present it so you get a better idea of how the backend is functioning. Afterward, we'll crack the `.FLA` open so you can see the guts of the front end itself.

The Backend Process

The first two chapters focused on using ColdFusion as the server-side language. While we have provided code in ASP.NET and Java, we haven't discussed how it was designed. One of the goals we set out with for this book was to teach how code could be reused across projects on both the client and the server. To this end, you'll see that many of the classes are used over and over again in all the projects. Because this is not a book on object-oriented application development, we only briefly cover the concepts involved.

The key piece of reusable code is called the `TransactionController`. This object in both Java and C# is used to field requests for work to be done. We have broken that work up into discrete transactions because that makes the most sense. In most of the projects, we have a transaction called `Login` or `CreateUser`. These are distinct pieces of work that need to be done in order. The Flash client sends a request to the server via XML over HTTP and the server responds once the transaction has completed.

In the following series of steps, we break down the basic process for you.

1. The client (Flash MX message board SWF) passes in an XML document that has been created in a standardized format over HTTP to the `TransactionController.aspx` page. This is the same basic XML format we use for all the projects in this book. Using a standardized format makes it much simpler to reuse code across projects. The code for this particular page is in the `TransactionController.cs` file. These files are included in the C-Sharp section on the CD-ROM.

2. The transaction controller passes the XML document and gets the transaction name as a string (such as `GetTopics`, `GetThreads`, `CreateUser`, and so forth). It takes that and the rest of the XML document and places it into a new `TransInfo` object.

3. The `TransactionController` instantiates a `TransactionService` object and passes in the `TransInfo` object.

4. The `TransactionService` gets the transaction name from the `TransInfo` object and dynamically instantiates a copy of the appropriate transaction class as an object of type `object`. It then casts this object to an `ITransaction` object. The `ITransaction` class is an interface that all transactions (`GetTopics`, `GetThreads`, `CreateUser`, and so on) implement.

5. The TransactionService calls the Execute method on the new transaction object. The transaction object takes the TransInfo object and uses the data within it to do its work. It then builds and returns a TransResult object to the TransactionService.

6. The TransactionService passes the TransResult object back to the TransactionController.

7. The TransactionController takes the XML out of the TransResult object and sends it back to the client (Flash MX message board).

Whew. That's a pretty in-depth explanation of the entire process, but you can see how powerful this system really is. It is set up to handle any kind of request, and it's self-moderating, meaning it can catch and handle any error it encounters along the way. **Figure 3.2** is a diagram of the system flow to try to make the whole process a little easier for you to understand.

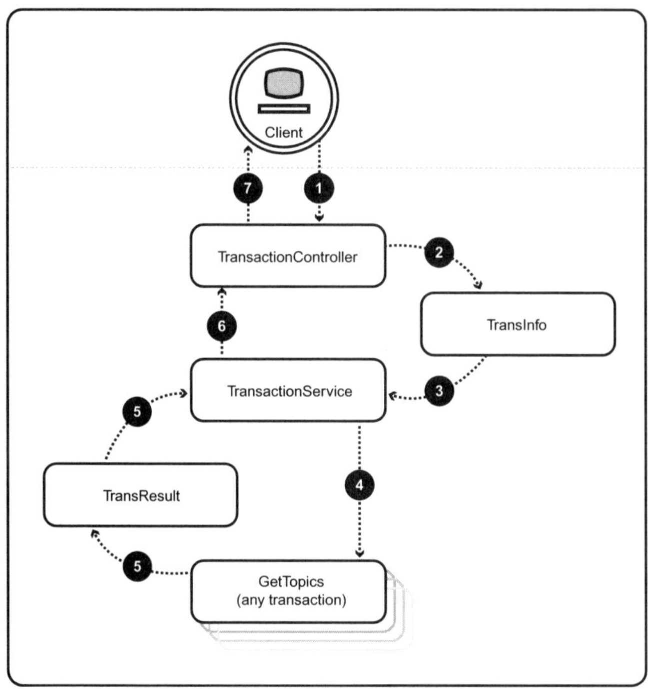

Figure 3.2 *Diagram of the backend process.*

If you are a C# developer, or are interested in the .cs files, feel free to open them with your favorite editor and examine the scripting. If you decide to modify any of the scripts, we have supplied a batch file (compileCSharp.bat in the chapter_3/C-Sharp folder on the CD-ROM) so that you can recompile your .dll file.

Remember, that the Flash `Transactions.cs` is the key to this whole system. It sits on the server ands is of a true OOP construction. It fields generic requests and works for all applications in this book. It is for .NET implementations only. You can expand its capabilities if you want. It will work the same with Access and SQL – the code is exactly the same for both. A helper file determines which to use and how.

Data Capture

The system writes to an Access database (.MDB). This database (**Figure 3.3**) contains all the information necessary (user information, topics, threads, and messages) for the fully-functioning message board. The Messages table maintains a circular association in the scheme of the database. A sample `.mdb` (`MessageBoard.mdb`) is included in the Chapter 3 folder on the accompanying CD-ROM; it contains data that was created during the testing of the message board.

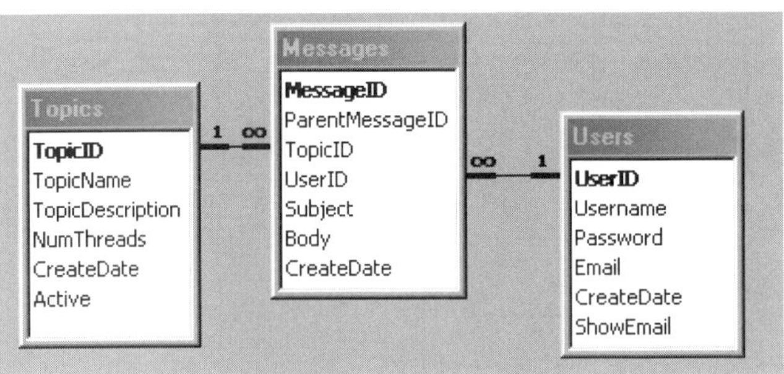

Figure 3.3 *The Access database tables and their relationships.*

The User Interface: The Application

Copy `MB.fla` from the Chapter 3 folder on the CD-ROM and open it from your desktop to see the general look of the message board on the Stage. Note that the `.fla` is set up with labels across the top, which denote functions of the message board and are used in order to process the many message board functions.

Load, Frame 1

Right now we are concerned with the Actions layer (**Figure 3.4**). On the first frame on the Actions layer (labeled Load), you find the following ActionScript (which is part of the loading process):

```
// Include the server data object
#include "ServerData.as"
// Include the common transaction functions
#include "CommonTransactionFunctions.as"
// Include the loading panel code
#include "LoadingPanel.as"
// Include the error panel code
#include "ErrorPanel.as"
// Include the error panel code
#include "MessagePanel.as"
// Global variables
    global.loadingPanelDepth = 100;
    global.errorPanelDepth = 101;
    global.messagePanelDepth = 102;
    global.clipDepth = 1000;
    global.topicsLoaded = false;
```

continues on next page

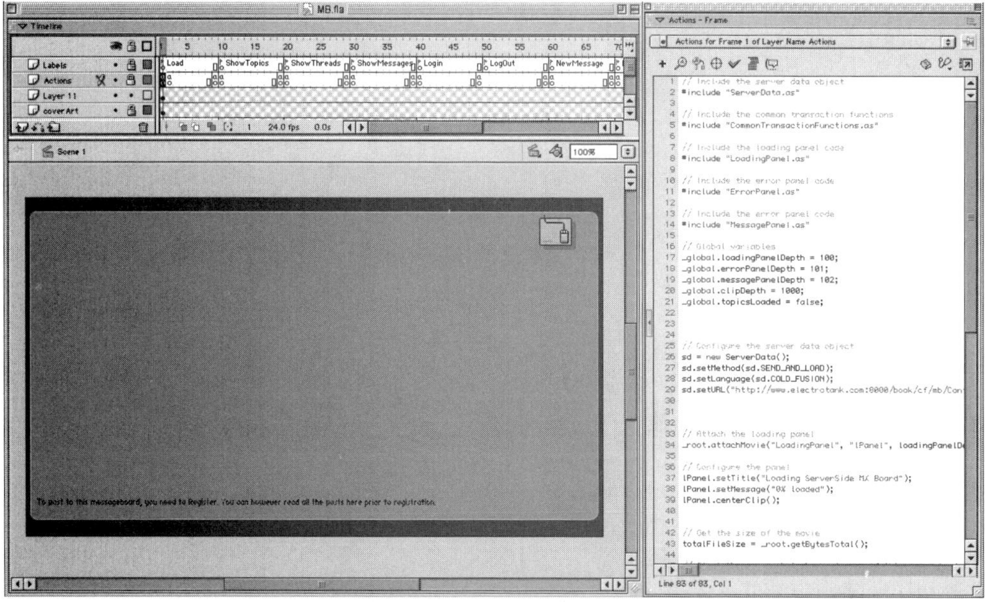

Figure 3.4 *The first frame in the Actions layer contains code for loading the SWF itself.*

```
// Configure the server data object
sd = new ServerData();
sd.setMethod(sd.SEND_AND_LOAD);
sd.setLanguage(sd.COLD_FUSION);
sd.setURL("http://www.electrotank.com:8000/book/cf/mb/
→ Controller.cfm");
// Attach the loading panel
    root.attachMovie("LoadingPanel", "lPanel",
    → loadingPanelDepth);
// Configure the panel
lPanel.setTitle("Loading ServerSide MX Board");
lPanel.setMessage("0% loaded");
lPanel.centerClip();
// Get the size of the movie
totalFileSize = _root.getBytesTotal();
// Start the event that checks to see if things are loaded
    root.onEnterFrame = function() {
    // See how much is loaded currently
    currentFileSize = _root.getBytesLoaded();
    // Handle if its done or not
    if(currentFileSize < totalFileSize) {
            // Get percentage
        percent = (currentFileSize / totalFileSize) * 100;
        percent = Math.round(percent);
        // Update the message
        lPanel.setMessage(percent + "% loaded");
    } else {
        // Kill the panel
        lPanel.unloadMovie();
        // Kill this event
        _root.onEnterFrame = null;
        // Start executing again
        _root.nextFrame();
    }
} // end onLoad event

// initiate click audio
click = new Sound();
click.attachSound("click");
click.setVolume(50);

// Stop the timeline from progressing
stop();
```

In this code you can see how the application takes shape. Several `include` files are declared that import the major application processing engine code upon SWF compiling and publishing. Feel free to go through this code on your own because there is simply too much of it to explain in the scope of this book. The code is heavily commented and that should go a long way in offering satisfactory explanations about it.

Global variables (new to Flash MX; variables that exist globally and can be called easily from anywhere) are defined, setting up the level position of interface elements, and the variable `topicsLoaded` is set to the Boolean of `false` (initially the topics are not loaded.) The server data model is defined next, including the server-side language and the location of the appropriate language HTTP page.

The loading panel (which gives graphical feedback on the SWF loading status) is configured for use. The lines below its configuration set and run the pre-loader information displayed in the loading panel (`lPanel`) and once the SWF has loaded, the panel is killed (no function association called upon `onEnterFrame`). If the SWF has preloaded, the movie progresses to the next frame, breaking it from the `onEnterFrame` loop of the preloader. The code also instantiates a sound object for rollover feedback that will be used in the topics display ScrollPane, which we'll look at shortly.

Load, Frame 2

On frame 2 of the Actions layer in the `.FLA`, you'll find the rest of the ActionScript that deals with loading the message board data itself:

```
// Include the properties manager class
#include "PropertiesManager.as"
pm = new PropertiesManager();
pm.load("MBProperties.xml");
pm.onLoad = propertiesLoaded;

// Attach the loading panel
    root.attachMovie("LoadingPanel", "lPanelProps",
    → loadingPanelDepth);

// Configure the panel
lPanelProps.setTitle("Loading Properties");
lPanelProps.setMessage("0% loaded");
lPanelProps.centerClip();
```

continues on next page

```
// Get the size of the properties file
totalPropsSize = pm.getBytesTotal();

// Start the event that checks to see if things are loaded
    root.onEnterFrame = function() {

    // See how much is loaded currently
    currentPropsSize = pm.getBytesLoaded();

    // Handle if its done or not
    if(currentPropsSize < totalPropsSize) {

        // Get percentage
        percent = (currentPropsSize / totalPropsSize) * 100;
        percent = Math.round(percent);

        // Update the message
        lPanelProps.setMessage(percent + "% loaded");

    } else {

        // Kill the panel
        lPanelProps.unloadMovie();

        // Kill this event
        _root.onEnterFrame = null;

        // Start executing again
        _root.nextFrame();
    }

} // end onEnterFrame event

function propertiesLoaded(success) {

    // Check to see if it worked
    if(success) {

        // get data
        _global._serverLanguage = this.getProperty
         → ("ServerLanguage");
        _global._controllerURL = this.getProperty
         → ("ControllerURL");
```

```
            // Move to the ShowTopics label
            gotoAndPlay("ShowTopics");

        } else {

            // Attach the error panel
            root.attachMovie("ErrorPanel", "propsErrorPanel",
            → errorPanelDepth);

            // Configure the panel
            propsErrorPanel.setMessage("Error Loading Properties");
            propsErrorPanel.centerClip();
        }
    }
    // Stop the move from progressing
    stop();
```

This code loads the code from the `PropertiesManager.as` files and dynamically instantiates the loading panel. Once the XML data has been loaded, the ActionScript checks to see if the data properly loaded and either is successful and kills the loading panel or declares that an error loading properties has occurred by displaying the error panel.

Here are the contents of the `MBProperties.xml` document:

```
<Properties>
    <Property>
        <Name>ServerLanguage</Name>
        <Value>ASPNET</Value>
    </Property>
    <Property>
        <Name>ControllerURL</Name>
        <Value>http://msgboard.flashbook.hostingdot.net/
        → TransactionController.aspx/</Value>
    </Property>
</Properties>
```

The server language is declared and the controller URL is defined for association with proper processing methods that occur later in the system.

Upon success, the application advances to the frame label ShowTopics. Because MBProperties XML data is now loaded, the application can proceed to the loading of topic data. All of the preceding code is processed very rapidly due to Flash MX's ability to quickly parse XML data. .NET is also pre-compiled, which allows for quicker processing of requested data.

Show Topics, Frame 10

On frame 10 on the main Timeline (**Figure 3.5**), you'll notice that now the message board has taken on the look of a more traditional message board system. Navigation to Home, Register, and Login is available at the top. Remember that viewers can read topics, threads, and responses, but to actively participate they need to first register and then login.

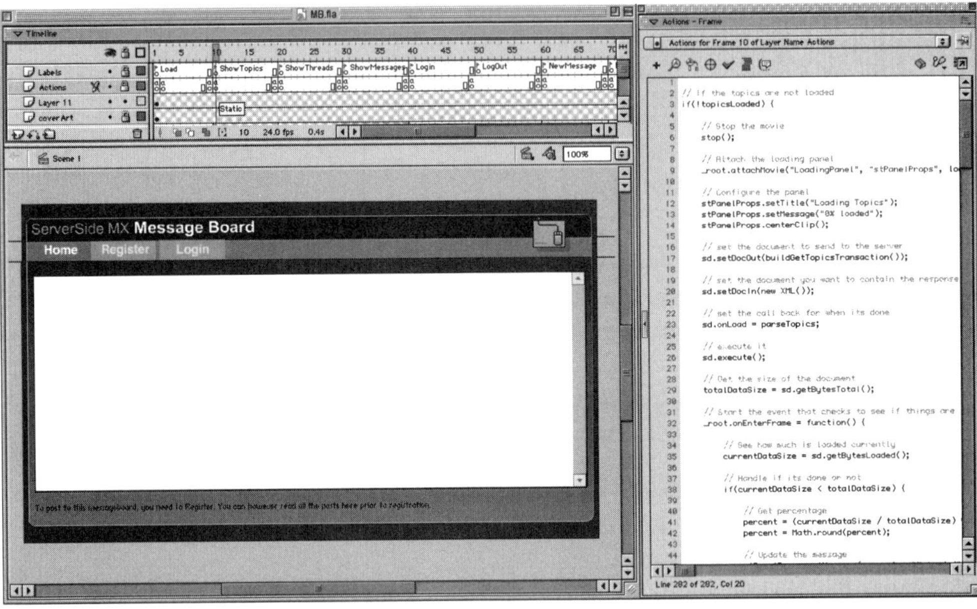

Figure 3.5 *Topics data loads in Frame 10.*

A ScrollPane with the MC instance name of `topicPane` resides on the stage (**Figure 3.6**). It has the following parameters:

- Horizontal Scroll = `false`
- Vertical Scroll = `auto` (`auto` means you will see a scroll bar if the content fills the area enough to warrant the use of a scroll bar. If this was set to `true`, you would always see a scroll bar, even when it didn't make sense to have one available.)
- Drag Content = `false` (the pane itself cannot be dragged)

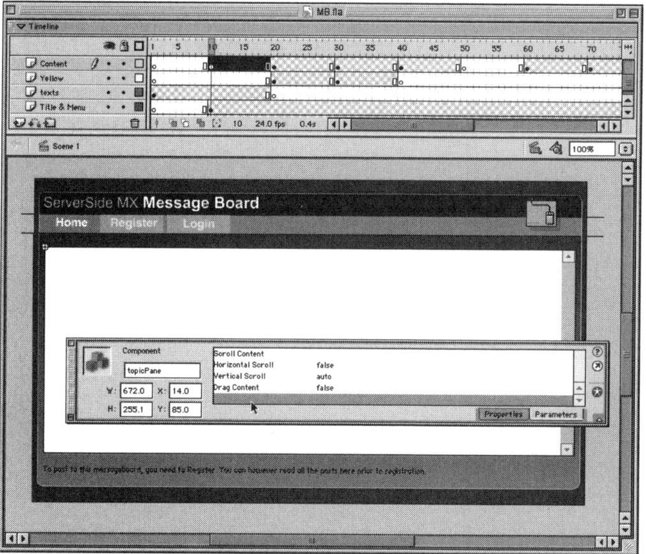

Figure 3.6 *The ScrollPane component will contain all the topics data in the system.*

The code following areas on the Timeline is very similar in most respects to the code in this section. This is where Flash MX's ability to deploy components, paired with text formatting, really shines.

Populating a ScrollPane with Many Items

The ScrollPane component can only scroll a single item, such as a loaded JPEG image or a movie clip. The message board system actually gets around the problem of loading multiple topic title objects into the ScrollPane for scrolling by actually dynamically creating a single movie clip into the ScrollPane and subsequently populating and associating nested movie clips that contain the textual topics title data.

Take note of the following code on frame 10 (there is a lot of magic that takes place here):

```
// If the topics are not loaded
if(!topicsLoaded) {
    // Stop the movie
    stop();

    // Attach the loading panel
    _root.attachMovie("LoadingPanel", "stPanelProps",
loadingPanelDepth);
```

continues on next page

```
// Configure the panel
stPanelProps.setTitle("Loading Topics");
stPanelProps.setMessage("0% loaded");
stPanelProps.centerClip();

// set the document to send to the server
sd.setDocOut(buildGetTopicsTransaction());

// set the document you want to contain the response
sd.setDocIn(new XML());

// set the call back for when its done
sd.onLoad = parseTopics;

// execute it
sd.execute();

// Get the size of the document
totalDataSize = sd.getBytesTotal();

// Start the event that checks to see if things are loaded
_root.onEnterFrame = function() {

    // See how much is loaded currently
    currentDataSize = sd.getBytesLoaded();

    // Handle if its done or not
    if(currentDataSize < totalDataSize) {

        // Get percentage
        percent = (currentDataSize / totalDataSize) * 100;
        percent = Math.round(percent);

        // Update the message
        stPanelProps.setMessage(percent + "% loaded");

    } else {

        // Kill this event
        _root.onEnterFrame = null;
```

```
            // Start executing again
            _root.nextFrame();
        }

    } // end onLoad event

} else {

    // Load the topics back onto the screen
    showTopics();

} // end "topicsLoaded" if statement

// parseTopics function
// This function parses the incoming XML document and
// builds the topics list
function parseTopics() {

    // Get the data from the ServerData object
    var dataIn = this.getDocIn();

    // if the transaction worked or not
    if(!wasSuccessful(dataIn)) {

        // Attach the error panel
        _root.attachMovie("ErrorPanel", "topicsErrorPanel",
errorPanelDepth); // this goes at the end of the preceding
→ code line

        // Configure the panel
        topicsErrorPanel.setMessage(errorMessage);
        topicsErrorPanel.centerClip();

        // Return out of this function
        return;

    } // end wasSuccessful() if statement

    // Create the topics container movie clip
    _root.createEmptyMovieClip("topics", clipDepth++);
```

continues on next page

```
    dataNode = findDataNode(dataIn);

    topicsNode = dataNode.firstChild;
    topicNodes = topicsNode.childNodes;

    top = 0;
    width = 660;
    for(i = 0; i < topicNodes.length; i++) {
        topicNode = topicNodes[i];
        topicChildren = topicNode.childNodes;

        id = topicNode.attributes.ID;
        name = topicChildren[0].firstChild.nodeValue;
        description = topicChildren[1].firstChild.nodeValue;
        numThreads = topicChildren[2].firstChild.nodeValue;
        createDate = topicChildren[3].firstChild.nodeValue;

        backColor = (i % 2)? 0xE9E9E9 : 0xD9D9D9;
        tempTopic = createTopic(_root.topics, i, width,
backColor,
id, name, description);// this goes at the end of the
→ preceding
// code line
        tempTopic._y = Math.round(top);// added rounding
        top += Math.round(tempTopic._height);// added rounding
    }

    topicPane.setScrollContent(topics);
    //topicPane._visible = true;

    // Kill the panel
    stPanelProps.unloadMovie();

    // Set the topicsLoaded var
    topicsLoaded = true;

} // end parseTopics function

// buildGetTopics function
// This function builds a 'Get Topics' transaction
function buildGetTopicsTransaction() {
```

```
    // Build a basic 'Get Topics' transaction
    getTopicsRequest = buildBaseRequest("GetTopics");

    // Return the xml object
    return getTopicsRequest;

} // end buildGetTopics function

// createTopic function
// This function creates a single topic in the topics clip
→ function createTopic(container, depth, width, color, id,
→ title,
description) {// this goes at the end of the preceding code
→ line
    name = "topic_" + depth;
    container.createEmptyMovieClip(name, depth);
    topic = container[name];
    topic.id = id;

    topic.createTextField("title", 2, 0, 0, width, 0);
    topic.title.text = title;

    with(topic.title) {
        multiline = true;
        wordWrap = true;
        border = false;
        autoSize = "center"; // was center
        selectable = false;
        embedFonts = true;
    }

    topic.titleformat = new TextFormat();
    with(topic.titleFormat) {
        color = 0xcc0000; // deep red
        font = "Genetica";
        bold = false;
        leftMargin = 3; // testing
        size = 10;
    }

    topic.title.setTextFormat(topic.titleformat);
```

continues on next page

```
    yPos = topic.title._height + topic.title._x;

    topic.createTextField("description", 5, 0, yPos, width, 0);
// was ("description", 3, 0, yPos, width, 0);
    topic.description.text = description;

    with(topic.description) {
        multiline = true;
        wordWrap = true;
        border = false;
        autoSize = "left"; // was center
        selectable = false;
        embedFonts = true;
    }

    topic.descriptionformat = new TextFormat();

    with(topic.descriptionformat) {
        color = 0x000000; // black
        font = "Standard";
        bold = false;
        leftMargin = 3; // testing
        size = 8;
    }


topic.description.setTextFormat(topic.descriptionformat);

    height = Math.round(topic._height);
    height = Math.round(topic._height);

    topic.createEmptyMovieClip("background", 1);
    topic.background.color = color;
    with(topic.background) {
        beginFill(color);
        lineTo(width, 0);
        lineTo(width, height);
        lineTo(0, height);
        endFill();
    }
```

continues on next page

```
        // Handle
        topic.background.onRelease = function() {

                // Hide everything unique to the topics screen
                _root.hideTopics();

                // Set the topic ID
                _root.topicID = this._parent.id;

                // Set the topic title
                _root.topicTitle = this._parent.title.text;

                // Play click audio
                _root.click.start(0,0);

                // Move the playhead to the ShowThreads label
                _root.gotoAndPlay("ShowThreads");
        }

        // fire this before return topic (since this is temp.
        → reference)
        topic.background.onRollOver = function(){
            _root.click.start(0,0);
            this._alpha = 30;
        }
        topic.background.onRollOut = function(){
            this._alpha = 100;
        }

        // return the newly created topic
        return topic;

    } // end createTopic function

    // showTopics function
    // This function shows the already loaded topics again
    → function showTopics() {

        // Turn the topics clip back on
        topics._visible = true;
```

continues on next page

```
        // Set the scroll panes contents again
        topicPane.setScrollContent(topics);

    } // end showTopics function

    // hideTopics function
    // This function hides the topics panel
    function hideTopics() {
        // Hide the topics clip
        topics._visible = false;

    } // end hideTopics
```

Because the code is so heavily commented, you should clearly see what's happening in the ActionScript, so I won't cover everything. You'll see the now familiar loading process and also the parsing function for the XML document containing the topics data.

Scan down the code until you come to the line that reads `// Create the topics container movie clip`. This is where the formatting beauty of Flash MX comes into full play. Following this line, using only ActionScript, an empty movie clip is created with the instance name of `"topics"`.

"But wait, that movie clip isn't associated with the ScrollPane component," you might be thinking to yourself. We take care of that in the code a bit later. We create the empty movie clip, fill it with content, and afterward associate it with the ScrollPane. You'll see this come together in a few minutes.

The XML data is evaluated and the length of XML topics title data is determined, and those titles are then turned into data with movie clips and duplicated one after the other, with alternating background colors. To clarify, here's the code where this actually takes place:

```
backColor = (i % 2)? 0xE9E9E9 : 0xD9D9D9;
tempTopic = createTopic(_root.topics, i, width, backColor,
→ id, name,
→ description); // this goes at the end of the preceding
code line
tempTopic._y = Math.round(top);// added rounding
top += Math.round(tempTopic._height);// added rounding
```

The rounding has been introduced because the system employs pixel fonts and to maintain their crisp appearance, the interior MCs must reside on integer pixel values (whole numbers.) It's my personal opinion that non-anti-aliased text (like traditional HTML fonts) is ultimately easier to read as body copy. Each developer has his own style and techniques to deploy dynamic data in his applications, but using pixel fonts (you can buy some great ones at www.miniml.com) should greatly benefit your users.

Formatting Text Objects = Power

It's impossible to plan a message board system in which you predetermine the dimensions of dynamic textual objects where multiple data items will be presented. In Flash 5, you had to stack text fields manually or use `attachMovieClip` to nest textual data together in a semi-presentable fashion. You just didn't know how much text someone was going to enter into certain fields, so you had to take you best guesstimate and hope that the user conformed to your system. Depending on how much content he entered, sometimes your resulting displayed layout would look nice, and other times it could look horrible. With MX, you can now make your system conform to your user—you'll notice that the topics titles are stacked neatly, one atop the other, even if one of the topic titles were to run 3 lines deep. Text objects can now be treated just like a movie clip—and that brings with it a lot of customized power. The system can dynamically accommodate entries of any size while maintaining a professionally presentable format. In this way, Flash behaves like traditional HTML tabling, but to a higher and more controllable degree.

The text formatting for the Title text field is achieved with the following ActionScript:

```
topic.titleformat = new TextFormat();
    with(topic.titleFormat) {
        color = 0xcc0000; // deep red
        font = "Genetica";
        bold = false;
        leftMargin = 3; // testing
        size = 10;
    }
    topic.title.setTextFormat(topic.titleformat);
```

The declared font, Genetica, is actually a Linkage name to a font symbol (Genetica) that was created in the Library. In this way, the dynamically created text field can be given a font to associate with it in the display of text data.

Creating a Font Symbol for ActionScript

To create a new font symbol in the Library, from the Library, choose New Font, and you are presented with a dialog box where you give your font symbol a name, choose available fonts loaded on your system, and have a choice of Bold and Italic. The name you give the font symbol does not itself become a Linkage name—it's just a name like those you give to graphics, and so forth. Once you have created a new font symbol in the Library, right-click on the symbol in the Library and choose Linkage. Give the font symbol a Linkage name, and you can choose to export for ActionScript (in first frame or when first encountered), export for runtime sharing, and so on. The identifier you give the symbol enables you to reference and use the font symbol with ActionScript.

With Flash 5 you would need to set the font for a text field (static, dynamic, or input) while authoring. With Flash MX, you can associate a font with text fields created with ActionScript, on-the-fly, as our application does. You could set up multiple fonts for easy OOP implementation. In fact, the topics are set up in the manner. The following code sets the text formatting for the topic title descriptions:

```
with(topic.descriptionformat) {
        color = 0x000000; // black
        font = "Standard";
        bold = false;
        leftMargin = 3; // testing
        size = 8;
    }

topic.description.setTextFormat(topic.descriptionformat);
```

The Linkage "`Standard`" is actually mapped to the actually font Standard 07_53 (**Figure 3.7**).

Using Different Weights of the Same Font

If you want to use two fonts (such as a normal weight and a bold weight) in one dynamically created text field, you cannot use HTML formatting (`<b>`)—you need to use `setTextFormat` to do this, combined with format objects.

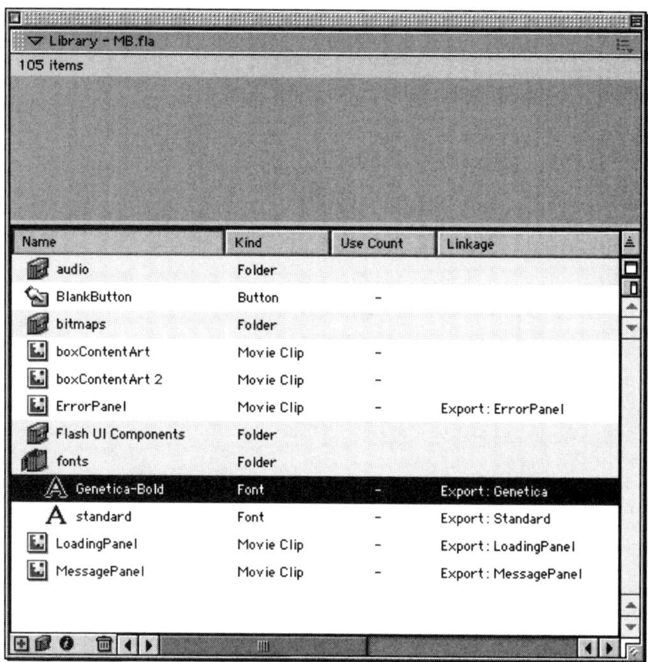

***Figure 3.7** Font Linkage in the Library: The Linkage of the font Standard 07_53 as "Standard"—the names need not match as the relationship has already been set in the font symbol itself.*

In Flash MX, movie clips can have button events associated with them. In the topics list you see when using the application, you'll notice that rolling over the titles will produce an audio cue and a change in the background color. For each topic title and description, the background is set by dynamically created (drawing API) movie clips with the instance name `background`. The `rollOver` is achieved by associated events with the `background` movie clips like so:

```
topic.background.onRollOver = function(){
        _root.click.start(0,0);
        this._alpha = 30;
    }
    topic.background.onRollOut = function(){
        this._alpha = 100;
    }
}
```

On a `rollOver`, the function executes by playing the previously instantiated audio object, and reducing the `_alpha` value of the background clip to 30%. Upon `rollOut`, the `_alpha` is set back to 100%. See how much easier and more OOP this is than conventional Flash 5 methods? To play audio in a traditional Flash 5 button, you would need to actually place the audio event within the `rollOver` state of the button and do the `_alpha` manipulations by hand. But here we are using a movie clip as a button—created dynamically with ActionScript—and we can easily assign different values for anything to them. This is something Flash 5 simply can't do, and it's very powerful.

To reiterate, we are triggering functions on the button event associations with each background movie clip instance. Macromedia has certainly moved in the right direction with this kind of added functionality (compared to Flash 5). You can dynamically create movie clips now that can be influenced and also serve as a button. That's just another example of how Flash has become much more object-oriented in terms of development.

While the individual topics title containers are being constructed, the `topics` movie clip is set invisible; once the construction is completed, the movie clip is made visible. This is set up using two functions, one for each state of visibility:

```
function showTopics() {
    // Turn the topics clip back on
    topics._visible = true;
    // Set the scroll panes contents again
    topicPane.setScrollContent(topics);
} // end showTopics function

// hideTopics function
// This function hides the topics panel
function hideTopics() {
    // Hide the topics clip
    topics._visible = false;
} // end hideTopics
```

The `topics` movie clip is associated with the ScrollPane (instance name of `topicPane`) with this line of ActionScript:

```
topicPane.setScrollContent(topics);
```

In this way the collective set of individual topic titles that are contained inside the `topics` movie clip can now be scrolled using the ScrollPane component. Remember that the ScrollPane can only manage the manipulation of a single loaded SWF, a movie clip, or JPEG. The code actually allows for the creation of a nested system of individual movie clips to be associated with a single, larger all-encompassing movie clip, which in turn can be manipulated (scrolled up or down) as needed.

ShowThreads, ShowMessages, Frames 20 and 30

The display of topics, threads, and messages (**Figure 3.8** and **Figure 3.9**) are almost identical in their code implementation. Please go ahead and peruse the ActionScript that enables their functionality (Frame 20, Frame 30). You will find the code for those functions is very similar to that of ShowTopics (frame 10). The ScrollPane and text formatting again reigns supreme in the data display.

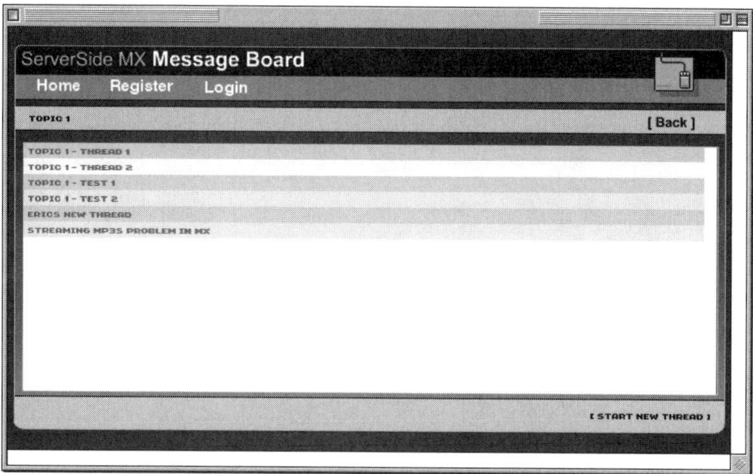

Figure 3.8 *User can select a thread.*

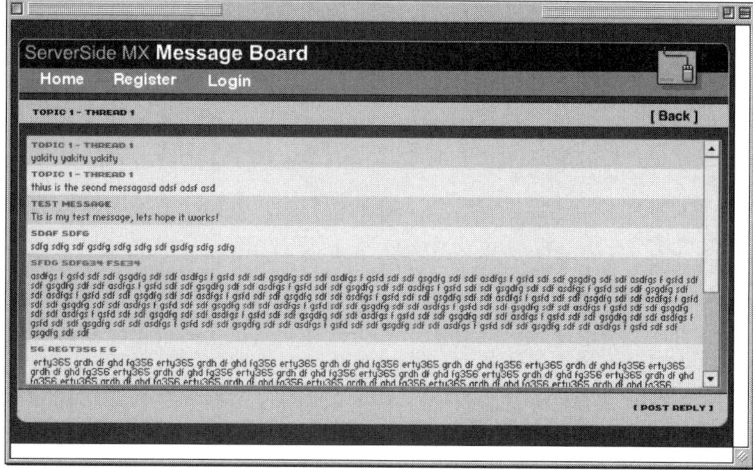

Figure 3.9 *The display of threads and messages is very similar in ActionScript as the display of topics.*

We'll move ahead in the FLA to frame 40 where a user can choose to log in (if he's already registered with the message board system.) A login attempt without a previous registration simply produces an error (and the system displays this error).

Login, Frame 40

On frame 40 ("Login"), you'll find a login panel on the Stage composed of two input fields: Username and Password (**Figure 3.10**). Notice that the text fields are not associated directly with variable names but with variable name instances. Remember, text fields can now be treated as movie clips.

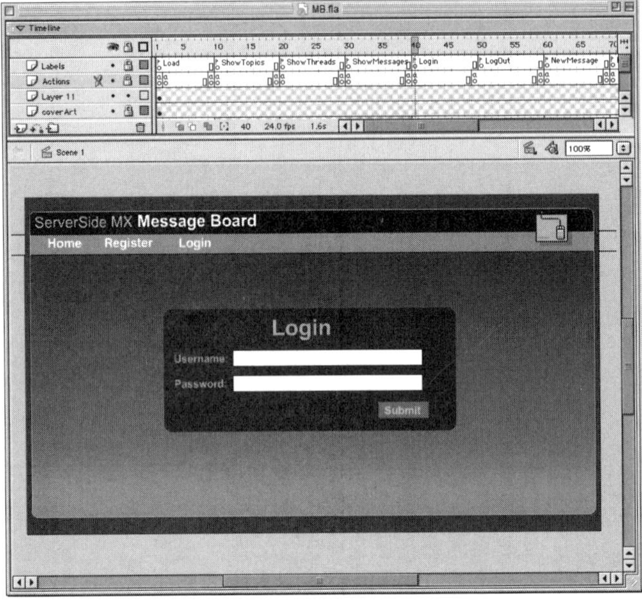

Figure 3.10 *The Login process involves an interface panel with two input fields.*

Several functions are defined here on frame 40: `loginUser()`, `parseLoginResults()`, and `buildLoginTransaction(username, password)`.

There is a button to submit (to process the entered data), and the code on this button is as follows:

```
on(press) {
    // Handle sending the login information
    loginUser();
}
```

On frame 40 itself, you'll find the code that defines the `loginUser` function and the ActionScript to handle the validation of the information submitted. After a proper login has taken place, the user is notified of a proper login and is then sent to the topics view ("ShowTopics"). If the user enters information that does not match data in the database, the message board gives the user an error message. The commented code follows:

```
// loginUser function
// This function is used to log the user into the chat
function loginUser() {
    // build the login transaction
    var loginRequest = buildLoginTransaction(username.text,
password.text); // this goes at the end of the preceding
→ code line// set the document to send to the server
    sd.setDocOut(loginRequest);
    // set the document you want to contain the response
    sd.setDocIn(new XML());
    // set the call back for when its done
    sd.onLoad = parseLoginResults;
    // execute it
    sd.execute();
} // end loginUser function

// parseLoginResults function
// This function is used to parse the login
// results from the server
function parseLoginResults() {
    // Get the data from the ServerData object
    var dataIn = this.getDocIn();
    // if the transaction worked or not
    if(!wasSuccessful(dataIn)) {
        // Attach the error panel
        _root.attachMovie("ErrorPanel", "loginErrorPanel",
errorPanelDepth);// this goes at the end of the preceding
→ code line
        // Configure the panel
        loginErrorPanel.setMessage(errorMessage);
        loginErrorPanel.centerClip();
        // Return out of this function
        return;
    } // end wasSuccessful() if statement
```

continues on next page

```
    // Attach the message panel
    _root.attachMovie("MessagePanel", "loginMessagePanel",
messagePanelDepth);// this goes at the end of the preceding
→ code line
    // Configure the panel
    loginMessagePanel.setMessage("You have logged in
    → sucessfully.
Press 'OK' to contiue");// this goes at the end of the
→ preceding
// code line
    loginMessagePanel.setButtonText("OK");
    loginMessagePanel.centerClip();
    // Redirect the user when the panel is closed
    loginMessagePanel.messagePanelClose = function() {
        gotoAndPlay("ShowTopics");
    }
} // end parseLoginResults function

// buildLoginTransaction function
// This function creates the XML document for a new user
function buildLoginTransaction(username, password) {
    // Build a basic 'Create User' transaction
    var createUserRequest = buildBaseRequest("Login");
    // Get the data node
    var dataNode = findDataNode(createUserRequest);

    // Username XML code
    // Create the Username node
    var usernameNode = createUserRequest.createElement
    → ("Username");
    // Create the Username text node
    var usernameValue = createUserRequest.createTextNode
    → (username);
    // Append the usernameValue node to the usernameNode
    usernameNode.appendChild(usernameValue);
    // Append the usernameNode to the dataNode node
    dataNode.appendChild(usernameNode);

    // Password XML code
    // Create the Password node
    var passwordNode = createUserRequest.createElement
    → ("Password");
```

```
    // Create the Password text node
    var passwordValue = createUserRequest.createTextNode
    → (password);
    // Append the passwordValue node to the passwordNode
    passwordNode.appendChild(passwordValue);
    // Append the passwordNode to the dataNode node
    dataNode.appendChild(passwordNode);
    // return the finished XML document
    return createUserRequest;

} // end buildLoginTransaction function
```

NewMessage, Frame 60

In order to get your information into the database to participate, the NewMessage part of the application (**Figure 3.11**) will collect your subject line and body message. If you have not logged in to the system, trying to start a new thread or reply to a post will result in an error message letting you know that you have forgotten to login. If you never registered, it would be time to do so.

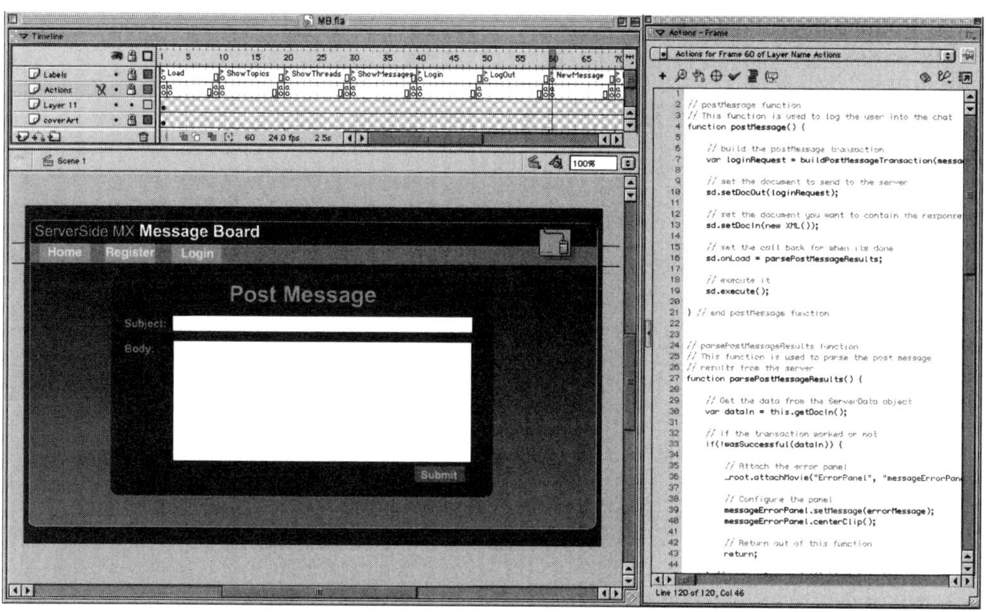

Figure 3.11 *The NewMessage module in the message board application.*

Several functions are defined at this point: `postMessage()`, `parsePostMessageResults()`, and `buildPostMessageTransaction(subject, body)`. `postMessage()` is the main function in this section, and the other two functions are nested within it, so that upon calling `postMessage()`, all functions execute and process.

Please pay special attention to the commenting in the ActionScript because it really goes a long way guiding you to its functionality.

The following code is on the submit button:

```
on(press) {
    // Post the message
    postMessage();
}
```

The ActionScript for the posting of a new message (on frame 60):

```
// postMessage function
// This function is used to log the user into the chat
function postMessage() {
    // build the postMessage transaction
    var loginRequest = buildPostMessageTransaction
    → (messageTitle.text,
messageBody.text);// this goes at the end of the preceding
→ code line
    // set the document to send to the server
    sd.setDocOut(loginRequest);
    // set the document you want to contain the response
    sd.setDocIn(new XML());
    // set the call back for when its done
    sd.onLoad = parsePostMessageResults;
    // execute it
    sd.execute();
} // end postMessage function

// parsePostMessageResults function
// This function is used to parse the post message
// results from the server
function parsePostMessageResults() {

    // Get the data from the ServerData object
    var dataIn = this.getDocIn();
    // if the transaction worked or not
    if(!wasSuccessful(dataIn)) {
```

```
        // Attach the error panel
        _root.attachMovie("ErrorPanel", "messageErrorPanel",
errorPanelDepth);// this goes at the end of the preceding
→ code line
        // Configure the panel
        messageErrorPanel.setMessage(errorMessage);
        messageErrorPanel.centerClip();
        // Return out of this function
        return;
    } // end wasSuccessful() if statement
    // Attach the message panel
    _root.attachMovie("MessagePanel", "messageMessagePanel",
messagePanelDepth);// this goes at the end of the preceding
→ code line
    // Configure the panel
    messageMessagePanel.setMessage("Your message has been
    → posted
sucessfully.\nPress 'OK' to contiue");// this goes at the
→ end of the
// preceding code line
    messageMessagePanel.setButtonText("OK");
    messageMessagePanel.centerClip();
    // Redirect the user when the panel is closed
    messageMessagePanel.messagePanelClose = function() {
        gotoAndPlay("ShowThreads");
    }
} // end parsePostMessageResults function

// buildPostMessageTransaction function
// This function creates the XML document for a new message
function buildPostMessageTransaction(subject, body) {
    // Build a basic 'Post Message' transaction
    var postMessageRequest = buildBaseRequest("PostMessage");
    // Get the data node
    var dataNode = findDataNode(postMessageRequest);
    // Subject XML code
    // Create the usernameNode
    var subjectNode = postMessageRequest.createElement
    → ("Subject");
```

continues on next page

```
    // Create the Subject text node
        var subjectValue = postMessageRequest.createTextNode
        → (subject);
    // Append the subjectValue node to the subjectNode
        subjectNode.appendChild(subjectValue);

        // Body XML code
        // Create the Body node
        var bodyNode = postMessageRequest.createElement("Body");

        // Create the Body text node
        var bodyValue = postMessageRequest.createTextNode(body);

        // Append the bodyValue node to the bodyNode
        bodyNode.appendChild(bodyValue);

        // Message XML code
        // create the messageNode
        var messageNode = postMessageRequest.createElement
        → ("Message");

        // Add the attributes
        messageNode.attributes.TopicID = topicID;
        messageNode.attributes.ThreadID = threadID;

        // Append the subjectNode to the messageNode
        messageNode.appendChild(subjectNode);

        // Append the bodyNode to the messageNode
        messageNode.appendChild(bodyNode);

        // Append the messageNode to the dataNode
        dataNode.appendChild(messageNode);

        // return the finished XML document
        return postMessageRequest;

    } // end buildPostMessageTransaction function
```

Please refer to the backend process diagram (Figure 3.2) at the beginning of this chapter. You can see how the postMessageRequest transaction is processed. For that matter, having the diagram handy will help you understand the processing of different types of requests throughout the entire system.

Register, Frame 70

In order to properly log in, a user needs to first register an account (**Figure 3.12**) within the message board system. This allows for the entry of a username and password, which are stored in the database for future queries. Registration also requires a proper email address to be entered, and a response to an input text box asking whether the email address should be available to others viewing posts and so forth made by this registrant. For now the field should contain "Yes" or "No"—you could provide radio buttons, or similar selection methods for this if you wish to customize the application. Users who don't register or log in receive an error message (**Figure 3.13**).

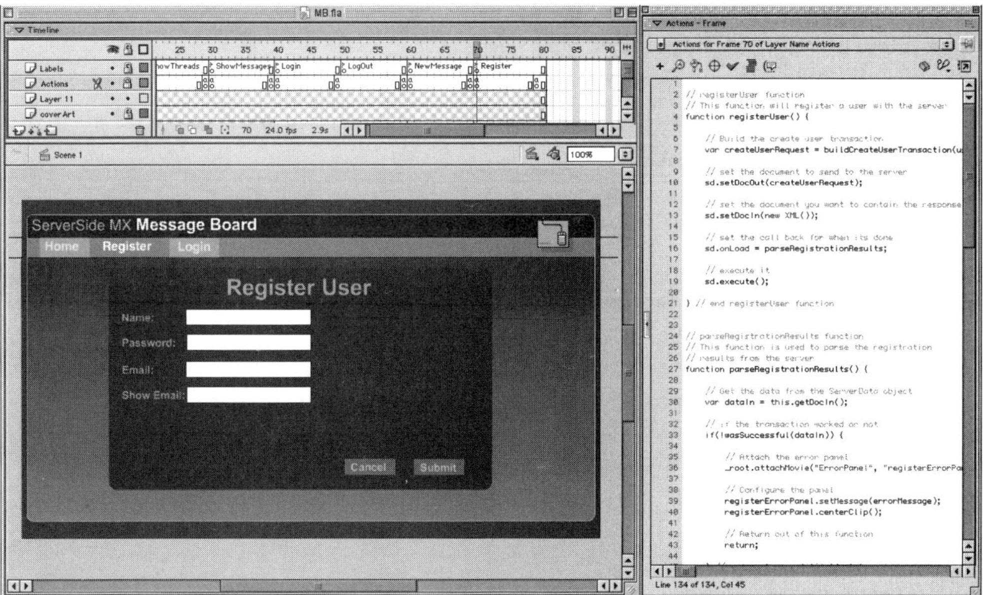

Figure 3.12 *A Flash form collects data and registers a new user to allow for the posting of threads and replies to messages.*

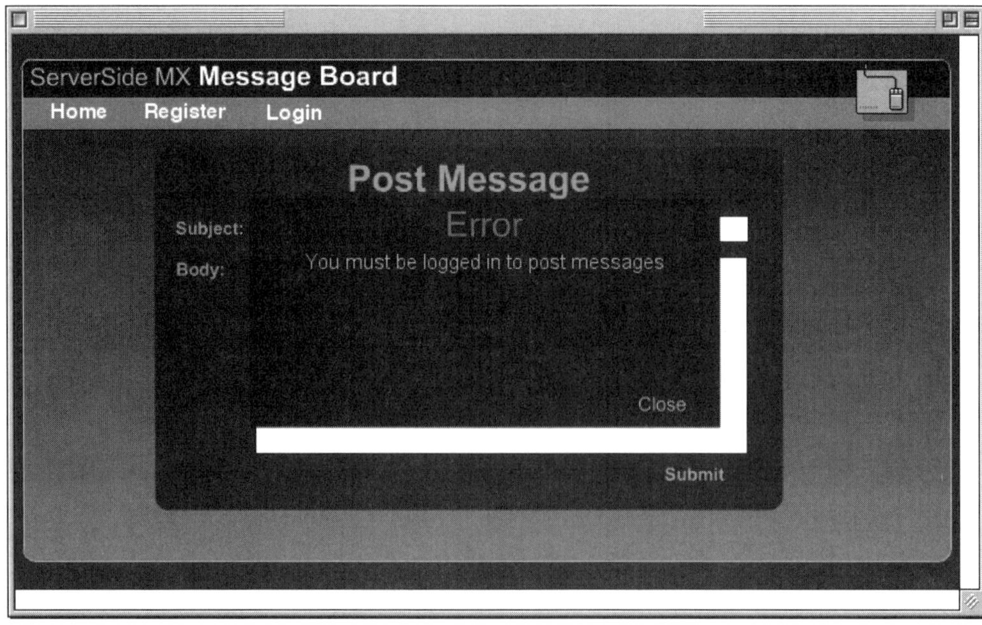

Figure 3.13 *A user who hasn't registered or logged in gets an error message when trying to interact with the message board system.*

The following code is used to register a user in the database. This process involves several functions that run sequentially. The first step is to call `buildCreateUserTransaction` and pass in the needed data. This function builds the XML document needed to register a user. Once we have that document, we send it to the server and use `parseRegistrationResults` to determine whether the transaction was successful. At this point, the application is able to proceed.

```
// registerUser function
// This function will register a user with the server
function registerUser() {

    // Build the create user transaction
    var createUserRequest = buildCreateUserTransaction
    → (username.text,
 password.text, email.text, showEmail.text);// this goes at
→ the end
// of the preceding code line

    // set the document to send to the server
    sd.setDocOut(createUserRequest);
```

```
    // set the document you want to contain the response
    sd.setDocIn(new XML());

    // set the call back for when its done
    sd.onLoad = parseRegistrationResults;

    // execute it
    sd.execute();

} // end registerUser function


// parseRegistrationResults function
// This function is used to parse the registration
// results from the server
function parseRegistrationResults() {

    // Get the data from the ServerData object
    var dataIn = this.getDocIn();

    // if the transaction worked or not
    if(!wasSuccessful(dataIn)) {

        // Attach the error panel
        _root.attachMovie("ErrorPanel",
"registerErrorPanel",
errorPanelDepth);// this goes at the end of the preceding
→ code line

        // Configure the panel
        registerErrorPanel.setMessage(errorMessage);
        registerErrorPanel.centerClip();

        // Return out of this function
        return;

    } // end wasSuccessful() if statement

    // Attach the message panel
    _root.attachMovie("MessagePanel",
"registerMessagePanel",
```

continues on next page

```
messagePanelDepth);// this goes at the end of the preceding
→ code line

    // Configure the panel
    registerMessagePanel.setMessage("You have registed a new
    → account
sucessfully. Press 'Log In' to contiue");// this goes at
→ the end of
// the preceding code line
    registerMessagePanel.setButtonText("Log In");
    registerMessagePanel.centerClip();

    // Redirect the user when the panel is closed
    registerMessagePanel.messagePanelClose = function() {
        gotoAndPlay("Login");
    }


} // end parseRegistrationResults function


// buildCreateUserTransaction function
// This function creates the XML document for a new user
function buildCreateUserTransaction(username, password,
→ email,
showEmail) {// this goes at the end of the preceding code
→ line

    // Build a basic 'Create User' transaction
    var createUserRequest = buildBaseRequest("CreateUser");

    // Get the data node
    var dataNode = findDataNode(createUserRequest);


    // Username XML code
    // Create the Username node
    var usernameNode =
createUserRequest.createElement("Username");

    // Create the Username text node
    var usernameValue = createUserRequest.createTextNode
    → (username);
```

```
// Append the usernameValue node to the usernameNode
usernameNode.appendChild(usernameValue);

// Append the usernameNode to the dataNode node
dataNode.appendChild(usernameNode);


// Password XML code
// Create the Password node
var passwordNode = createUserRequest.createElement
→ ("Password");

// Create the Password text node
var passwordValue = createUserRequest.createTextNode
→ (password);

// Append the passwordValue node to the passwordNode
passwordNode.appendChild(passwordValue);

// Append the passwordNode to the dataNode node
dataNode.appendChild(passwordNode);


// Email XML code
// Create the Email node
var emailNode = createUserRequest.createElement
→ ("Email");

// Create the Email text node
var emailValue = createUserRequest.createTextNode(email);

// Append the emailValue node to the emailNode
emailNode.appendChild(emailValue);

// Append the emailNode to the dataNode node
dataNode.appendChild(emailNode);


// ShowEmail XML code
// Create the Email node
var showEmailNode = createUserRequest.createElement
→ ("ShowEmail");
```

continues on next page

```
        // Create the Email text node
        var showEmailValue = createUserRequest.createTextNode
        → (showEmail);

        // Append the showEmailValue node to the showEmailNode
        showEmailNode.appendChild(showEmailValue);

        // Append the showEmailNode to the dataNode node
        dataNode.appendChild(showEmailNode);


        // return the finished XML document
        return createUserRequest;

    } // end buildCreateUserTransaction function
```

Summary

This supplied message board is ready to deploy as-is, right now. All you would need to do is to change information in the `MCProperties.xml` file, place it on the appropriate sever environment, and away you go! However, as a challenge, you could add some additional functionality to the system to make it even better:

- Users may edit their own posts, but not other user's posts.
- Develop an icon system associated with the Registration process (users could choose from a list of icons that would "brand" their posts.) You could even allow for the upload of JPEGs that users could use as their own personal icons.
- You could display more personal information about participants, such as their location, number of posts they have made in their entire history of using the message board, multiple email addresses, and so forth.
- Create an admin panel with which you could password-protect internal message board functions. This would allow you to quickly and easily create new topic areas, delete controversial posts, edit controversial posts, move posts to different topics (if unrelated to the current topic under which it currently resides), deploy a team of admins, each could control their own topic.

- You could display currently logged-in members and allow for private emailing (within the system itself).
- Each topic could have its own related chat room interface, so that an admin, or other users could speak more freely about certain topics. The transcripts could be made available as a download or as part of an email newsletter system to which users could subscribe.

These are just some ideas for you. Let your imagination run wild, and don't discount using Flash MX for anything. With fast XML parsing, default MX components, dynamic movie clip and text field creation, and text field formatting, Flash MX is ready for center stage where interactive applications are concerned. It has the ability to deliver powerful applications—take advantage of that, and enjoy the supplied message board!

4: Avatar Chat

by Jobe Makar

Chances are that at some point in your Internet career you have visited a chat room (also just called a chat). Most popular chats are well liked because they build what is called a community. An Internet community is a place where you feel welcome and a place where you can make a difference. Communities are usually developed by saving information about each user and giving each user some way to show his or her own personality through a profile, something other users can view to get a little information about you.

Some experimental chats are now giving each user a personality by changing how the chat takes place: they use characters that can walk around! These characters are usually animals, aliens, or monsters, so they don't even come close to truly representing how a person looks, but they do add a new aspect to communication. You can walk toward another person in the chat and then start up a conversation! You know who might be interested in your conversation by seeing which characters are nearby).

In this chapter I show you how to create such a chat, an *avatar chat* (**Figure 4.1**). I only use one character as an example and I don't collect any information from the users, because this is only an introduction to building avatar chats (also known as character chats).

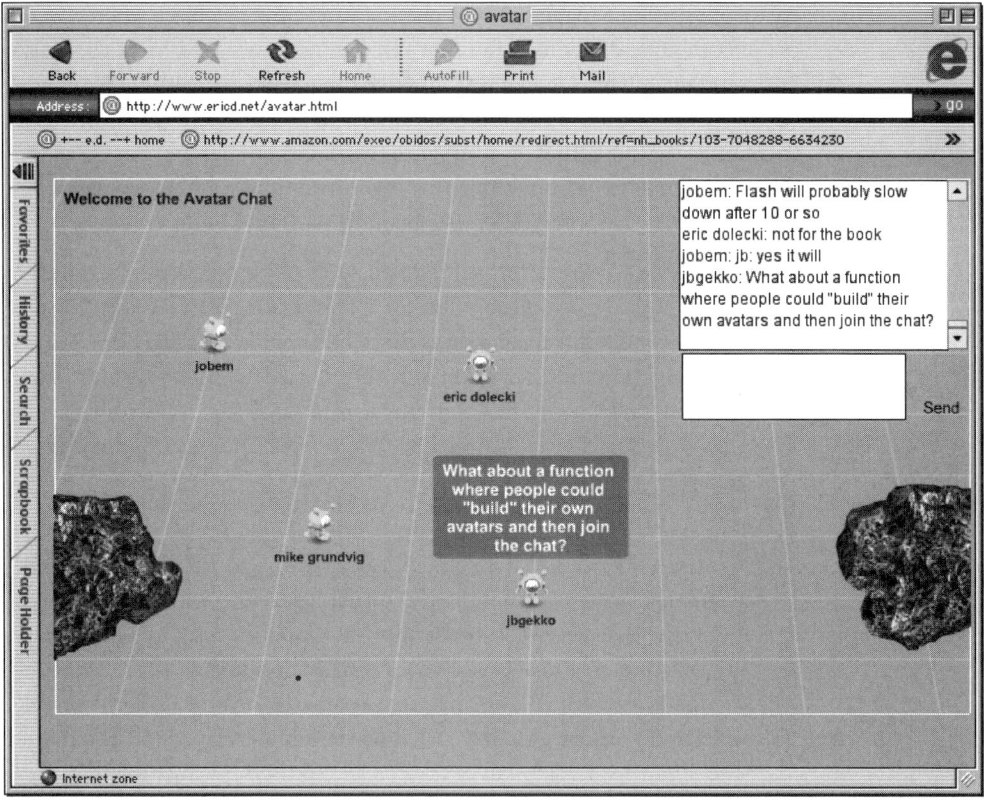

Figure 4.1 *This is a working version of the avatar chat.*

Introducing the Avatar Chat

Before we discuss how to construct an avatar chat, I want to take you on a feature-tour of the avatar chat created in this chapter. Also, I will mention other information that you should review so that you may fully understand what we are doing throughout the chapter.

Chat Basics

To understand how to create an avatar chat, you must first comprehend the basics of creating a regular chat. A chat, as you know, is a place where several people can go and talk to each other through text messages. Most chats also give you the ability to send a text message directly to one person. So, how do they work? Without too much thought you can probably figure out that there must be something on a server that is smart enough to hook all of these users together—something that is the brains controlling who gets what messages and when. There are two primary ways to do this:

1. **Use server-side scripting, like an ASP page, as the controller.** This is not a very good solution for many reasons. The bandwidth used with this method versus what is described next is very high. Also, the speed and power of the server-side script can often times be poor. For just a few users connected at a time this solution is not horrible, but for a real chat system that is intended to support hundreds of user, this is not a viable option.
2. **Use a socket server as the controller.** The concept of a socket server is not hard but it is difficult to explain. A socket server is a piece of software (often written in Java, Visual Basic, or C++) that runs on the server. It listens on a specific port for connections. Flash has the ability to connect to a socket server over a specific port. Once this connection is established information is easily sent to and from the server and at very fast speeds. The socket server knows who connects to it and when. It keeps track of all of the connected users, what room they are in, and their user names. The "ElectroServerAS Object" appendix provides all the details of how socket servers work. Read it now, so that you'll fully understand everything in this chapter.

The front end (for us, this is Flash) connects to the socket server and then the user is prompted to log in. Logging in can mean entering a user name and a password and then having this verified with (or submitted to) a database, or it can just give the user a temporary name to which he is referred while in the chat. After you log in to most chats, you are presented with a screen that has a large window showing conversations (chats) and a text field in which you can type messages. There's usually a way for you to move into a specific room where you see different users.

Avatar Chat Features

In the avatar chat that we develop in this chapter, there's only one room and everyone is in that room. After logging in, the user is taken to a new screen (**Figure 4.2**) where his character appears. The user name appears below his character. The user also sees characters for all the other users in the chat with their names below their characters. There are two text fields on the right side of the screen. The larger one, at the top, is the chat window, which displays the contents of the chat. Every message received is displayed here. The smaller text field below is for sending messages. To the right of that is a button marked "send". When pressed the contents of the message field are sent. When a chat message is received, in addition to appearing in the chat box, it appears over the head of the character that represents the user who sent the message. The characters can walk to new positions. When a user double clicks anywhere on the screen that user's character will then walk to that position.

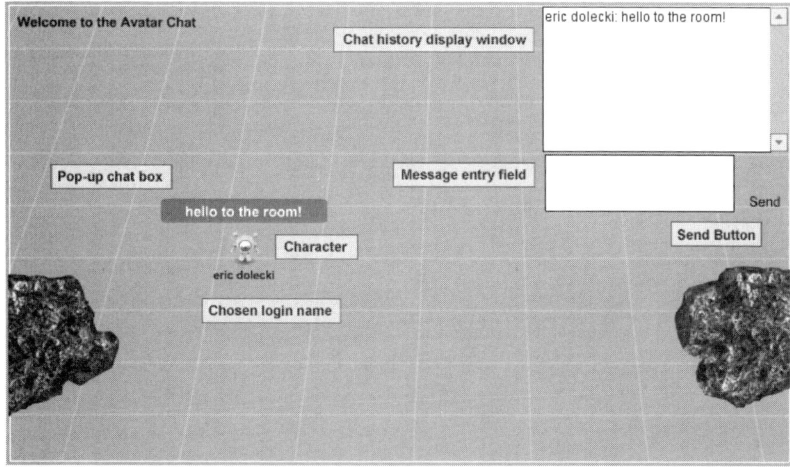

Figure 4.2 *Here are the different components of our avatar chat.*

The ElectroServer

There is one more thing that needs to be mentioned about all of this: the `ElectroServerAS` object. The socket server that we connect to with this chat is called ElectroServer, a copy of which can be found on the CD-ROM (see Appendix B to learn about it and how to set it up).

Flash talks to the socket server by sending and receiving various XML formatted packets of information. There are several different types of packets that you can send and receive, and it can be very difficult and time consuming to write ActionScript that understands all of these packets. Luckily, you don't have to because I wrote the `ElectroServerAS` ActionScript object. This object enables you to easily talk to the ElectroServer socket server, and makes sending a chat message as easy as this line of ActionScript:

```
ElectroServer.sendMessage("Hello World!!");
```

There are more than 40 methods, properties, and events for the `ElectroServerAS` object. Read Appendix B to learn about these methods and how to use the object. Fortunately, using the `ElectroServerAS` object is very easy, and it can help you create chats and multiplayer games in very little time (we'll use it again in Chapter 5, "Multiplayer Game").

Appendix B provides you with the definitions of the `ElectroServerAS` actions and also shows you how to install these actions into your Actions panel in Flash (**Figure 4.3**), so that you don't have to remember the names or syntax for all of the actions— just use the Actions panel!

To recap, the avatar chat in this chapter:

- Has a Flash front end
- Connects to the ElectroServer socket server (provided on the CD-ROM)
- Uses the `ElectroServerAS` object (covered in Appendix B)
- Only has one character (can be extended by you to have more characters)
- Only uses one room (can be extended by you to use any number of rooms)

In the rest of this chapter we'll discuss the architecture of the Flash file, the ActionScript needed to get the characters to walk around, and how to hook the Flash file up to ElectroServer.

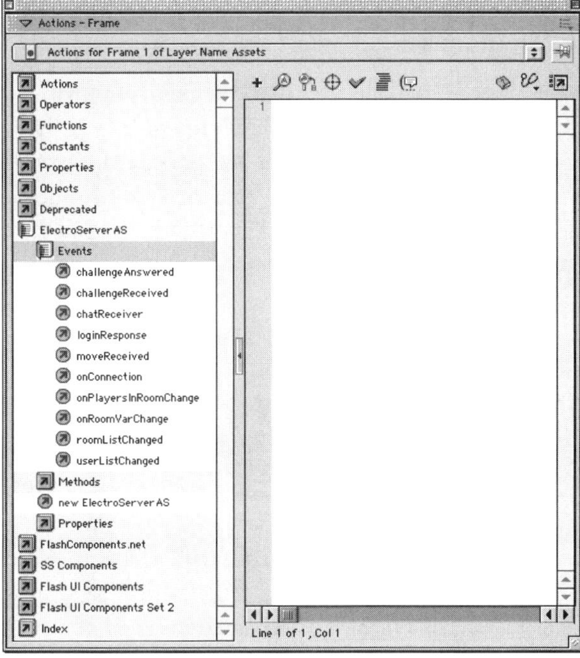

Figure 4.3 *When you install the ElectroServerAS object you can easily access its actions from the Actions Panel.*

Programming the Environment

This section covers pretty much everything in the avatar chat except the multiuser aspects such as logging in, chatting, and other server-Flash interactions, which are covered in the next section. I discuss the different parts of our chat and talk about the structure and ActionScript involved in creating them, namely the character and the pop-up text box for the character.

Alien Autopsy: Deconstructing the Character

Let's start this deconstruction with looking at the structure of the character movie clip. In directory chapter 4 find the file `character.fla` and open it. Immediately you see three layers: Character Actions, Actions, and Assets. The Character Actions layer contains all of the actions that are needed to control the character's movements. The Actions layer contains all of the remaining actions, such as initializing the character. In later files, this layer will also contain all of the actions needed to handle the chatting. The Assets layer contains a movie clip, which has an instance name of chat.

Inside the chat movie clip you only see one layer that contains one movie clip. This movie clip has no instance name but it has a library name of alien and a linkage identifier of alien. As you know, we do not need to keep a copy of a movie clip on the stage to use `attachMovie()`, but we do so to enable better loading in the final file. In the Linkage Properties, Export in first frame is unchecked. If checked, the clip must load before frame 1 is loaded, which defeats the purpose of a loader. If unchecked, as it is here, then it is loaded when a copy of the movie clip is found on the stage. We have a copy of the alien movie clip on the stage so that we can make use of this feature. There is a clip event on this movie clip to set its visibility to `false` when that frame is visited. This is so it does not get in the way visually.

Double-click the alien movie clip to inspect what is inside. There are three layers: Dialog, Character, and Shadow. The Dialog layer contains a movie clip with an instance name of `box`. This is where the individual chat messages will be displayed, which is explained in the next section. Also in that layer is a text field with an instance name of `username` that is used to display the user name of the user that the character represents. The Character layer contains the character (the alien) and has an instance name of `character`. The Shadow layer contains a shadow graphic.

Double-click the `character` instance in the Character layer. In the timeline you see 16 frame labels (**Figure 4.4**). The alien has been rendered in eight angled positions. There is a frame label showing the alien standing at each angle (`stand_1` through `stand_8`) and a frame label showing the alien walking, at each angle (`walk_1` through `walk_8`), hence the total of 16 frame labels. A `stop()` action is on each frame label to keep the timeline from playing. Scrub to a walk frame and double-click the movie clip in that frame. You can see that there are six frames in each walk movie clip. Notice that there are only four unique walk movie clips even though there are eight directions. For each direction the movie clip can be flipped horizontally to work for the opposite direction. This is a very simple trick that saves development time and file space.

Generate an SWF from this file. You'll hear a popping sound that indicates a character has been created and you will see it on the screen. Move your mouse around and watch the character rotate to face your mouse. Double-click anywhere on the screen and the character will walk there. Notice that while the character is walking, it doesn't rotate to face your cursor and that you cannot give it a new destination (that is, your double-clicking goes unnoticed).

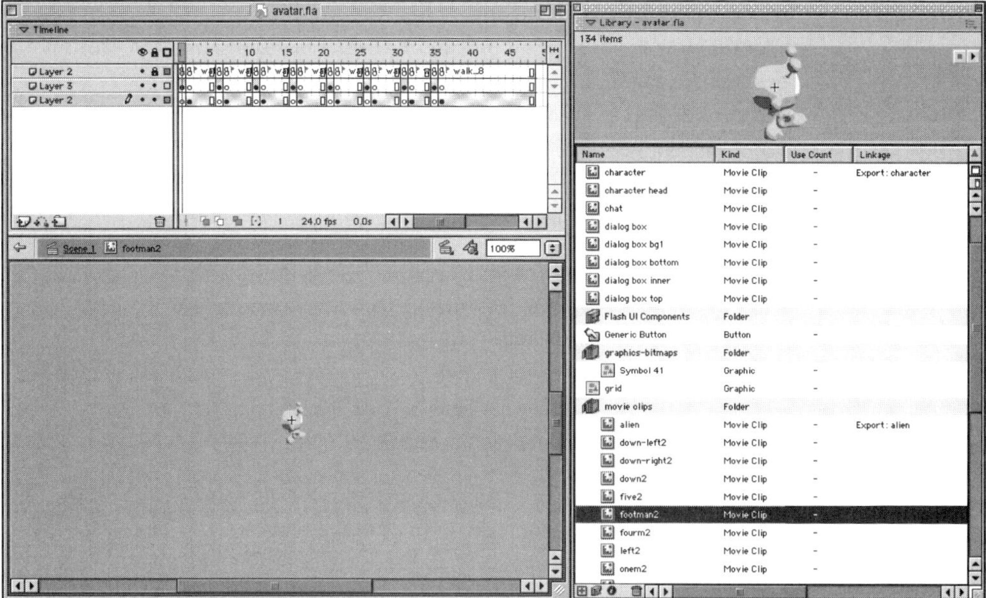

Figure 4.4 *There are two frames for each of the 8 possible angles of the character: one frame for standing still and one for walking.*

Scripting the Action

Now that you have a good idea about what the character is programmed to do, let's look at the ActionScript that it takes to accomplish this. Here are the features that you saw when testing the SWF:

- The character is created.
- The character has a user name listed below it.
- The character rotates to face the mouse.
- When the user double-click, the character walks to that position.

ActionScript's `udpatePerson()` creates all characters that will appear on the screen. ElectroServer calls this function when a new person (including the user) has entered the room. The `updatePerson()` function is also called when a user double-clicks somewhere to move his character—it instructs an existing character to walk to the new position or, if necessary (such as for a new user), creates the character at that position.

In the completed file (later in the chapter), the `initializeMe()` function gives the user's character a randomized initial position and then sends a message out saying that the user has just created a character. Because we aren't connected to ElectroServer in this example file and therefore can't accept instructions from it, we call the `updatePerson()` function from `initializeMe()` to add the character to the stage. Here is the ActionScript for the `initializeMe()` function:

```
function initializeMe() {
    var myCharacter = 1;
    var x = 50+random(500);
    var y = 50+random(300);
    var val = myCharacter+"|"+x+"|"+y+"|0|1";
    updatePerson(name, val);
}
```

This function is called when the user wants his character to be created. The second line of ActionScript sets a variable called `myCharacter` with a value of 1, because we're only using one character in this example. If you decide to extend this application to use more than one kind of character, you would insert a screen that lets a user choose which character he wants to use. The value of `myCharacter` then needs to store the character number that the user chose, which is passed to all other users so that their system knows which character to create.

The next two lines of code build a random position on the stage. Then a variable called `val` is created to store a concatenated string of five pieces of information:

1. The character number (1 in this case)
2. The character's X position
3. The character's Y position
4. The character's angle position
5. The integer position (1 through 8) in which the character is facing

In the final file this string is sent to the server and stored as a server variable, but for now we send it to the `updatePerson()` function, which uses this information to build the character with the correct user name in the correct position.

Here is the updateUser() function:

```
function updatePerson(name, val) {
    var temp = [];
    temp = val.split("|");
    if (people[name] == null) {
        //create the person
        people[name] = {};
        if (name == ElectroServer.username) {
            me = people[name];
        }
        people[name].character = temp[0];
        people[name].x = Number(temp[1]);
        people[name].y = Number(temp[2]);
        var angle = Number(temp[3]);
        var number = Number(temp[4]);
        people[name].username = name;
        //add character
        chat.attachMovie("alien", name, ++chat.depth);
        people[name].clip = chat[name];
        var clip = people[name].clip;
        initializeCharacter(name);
        clip._x = people[name].x;
        clip._y = people[name].y;
        clip._xscale = 50;
        clip._yscale = 50;
        clip.username.text = name;
        enter = new Sound();
        enter.attachSound("enter");
        enter.start();
    } else {
        //person already exists, so update
        //set end position
        var endX = Number(temp[1]);
        var endY = Number(temp[2]);
        var angle = Number(temp[3]);
        var number = Number(temp[4]);
        var clip = people[name].clip;
        clip.move(endX, endY, angle, number);
    }
}
```

The updatePerson() function uses a people object that stores information about each user. The function has two major branches that it can execute code in. If a reference to this user has not yet been created in the people object (that is, this is a new user) then the first branch of the conditional statement is entered, otherwise this is considered an update and the second branch of the conditional is entered. Let's inspect each branch separately. The first branch handles the ActionScript needed to:

- Create the new object reference for this user on the people object.
- Extract the five pieces of information from the val string passed in.
- Add a new instance of the character on the stage using attachMovie().
- Scale and position the character on the stage.
- Play a sound so that everyone in the room knows that a new character has just appeared.

There is one more thing that happens in this branch of the function: the initializeCharacter() function is called. It adds to the character all of the clip events needed to intercept the mouse-down events and to control the rotation and walking. We'll discuss this function in more detail in a minute.

The second branch in the updatePerson() function handles extracting the information from the val string and then instructing the character to move by invoking its move() method, which we'll discuss a little later in the chapter.

The initializeCharacter() Function

The ActionScript explained so far covers the basic initialization of a character (adding the movie clip and creating an object). The initializeCharacter() function is what gives each character the ability to rotate and walk. Also, if the character shown is the one that represents the user, then the character can also listen for double-clicking on the screen. Here is the initialize Character() function:

```
function initializeCharacter(name) {
    path = people[name];
    path.speed = 5;
    path.locked = false;
    path.angleSpan = 360/8;
    path.clip.ob = path;
    path.clip.move = move;
    if (name == ElectroServer.username) {
```

```
            path.myCharacter = true;
            path.clip.onMouseMove = mouseMoved;
            path.clip.onMouseDown = mouseGotClicked;
        }
    }
```

When this function is called, the user name of the character being created is passed in. A reference to the object that stores the information about that user is created and is called `path`. A variable called `speed`, which represents the speed at which the character walks when instructed to walk, is set on the object.

A variable called `lock` is also set on the object. This variable is used only by the character that represents the user. If the `lock` variable is `false`, the character rotates to follow the user's mouse and listens for clicking on the screen. If `lock` is `true`, the character won't follow the mouse or listen for clicks. The variable is set to `true` when the character is walking so that it can reach its destination without acting odd along the way (following the mouse).

The variable called `angleSpan` is the amount of degrees that each of the eight rotations covers. Remember that the character has eight rotation frames, and we need a way to know which of the rotation frames to display. The `angleSpan` variable helps us figure this out (you'll see how this works a little later in the chapter).

The next line creates a reference, called `ob`, to the object on the movie clip itself. This allows the movie clip of the alien to talk to the object that represents it. Then we create a `move()` function on the movie clip. It gets called when it is time to instruct a character to walk to a new position.

A conditional statement checks to see if the name passed in is equivalent to the user's user name. If it is, then we know that this character needs some extra abilities: to rotate with the mouse and to listen for clicking. A variable is set on the object called `myCharacter`. If it is `true` then the character is the one that represents the user.

The next two lines of ActionScript define `onMouseMove` and `onMouseDown` event handlers, which take care of rotating the character and listening for clicks.

In the `initializeCharacter()` function we set one function—or 3 functions if the character is the user—onto the character clip.

The move() Function

Let's take a look at some of the functions just introduced. The first, `move()`, is the one that every character has. Here it is:

```
function move(endX, endY, angle, number) {
    //Store the information passed in
    this.ob.endX = endX;
    this.ob.endY = endY;
    this.ob.angle = angle;
    this.ob.number = number;
    //Calculate the x and y speed at which to walk
    this.ob.xmov = this.ob.speed*Math.cos(this.ob.angle);
    this.ob.ymov = this.ob.speed*Math.sin(this.ob.angle);
    //Create variables that store your starting position
    this.ob.startX = this.ob.x;
    this.ob.startY = this.ob.y;
    //Send the character to the correct walking frame
    this.character.gotoAndStop("walk_"+number);
    //Lock it so there can be no input
    this.ob.locked = true;
    //Create an onEnterFrame event to move the character
    this.onEnterFrame = function() {
        //Update the position
        this.ob.x += this.ob.xmov;
        this.ob.y += this.ob.ymov;
        this._x = this.ob.x;
        this._y = this.ob.y;
        //Check to see if the character has arrived at the
        → destination
        if ((this.ob.endX-this.ob.startX)/Math.abs
        → (this.ob.endX-
            this.ob.startX) != (this.ob.endX-this.ob.x)/
            → Math.abs(this.ob.endX-
            this.ob.x) || (this.ob.endY-this.ob.startY)/
            → Math.abs(this.ob.endY-
            this.ob.startY) != (this.ob.endY-this.ob.y)/
            → Math.abs(this.ob.endY-
            this.ob.y)) {
            this.ob.x = this.ob.endX;
            this.ob.y = this.ob.endY;
            this._x = this.ob.x;
```

```
                this._y = this.ob.y;
                this.character.gotoAndStop("stand_"+
                → this.ob.number);
                //Unlock the character if it is yours
                if (this.ob.myCharacter) {
                    this.ob.locked = false;
                    this.mouseMoved();
                }
                this.onEnterFrame = null;
            }
        };
    }
```

The ActionScript in this function has been commented at each major event. When information is received from the server (or faked as in this file) to tell a character to move, the `move()` function is called. The information passed into the function is the destination x and y position, the angle at which to walk, and an integer that represents one of the eight possible angles of rotation of the character. The ActionScript stores each of these pieces of information on the object that represents this character. The x and y speeds at which the character should walk are calculated and stored on the object as `xmov` and `ymov`. The starting position of the character is stored, to be used later to determine if the character has reached the destination.

The character is sent to the appropriate walk frame. This is done but concatenating `number` with `"walk_"`, where the `number` variable represents a number (1 through 8) of the frame angle that the character should display. Next, the `locked` variable is set to `true`. Then an `onEnterFrame` event is set on this movie clip so that the character's position can be updated every frame and we can check to see if it has reached its destination. The first four lines of ActionScript in the `onEnterFrame` event serve to update the position of the character in memory and then to update the position of the movie clip itself.

We use an `if` statement to check whether the character has reached or gone past its destination. This `if` statement looks more complicated than it really is. It simply checks to see if the sign of the difference of the current x position and the destination position has changed, or if the sign of the difference between the current y position and the destination y position has changed. For instance, if `startX` is 10 and `endX` is 90, the sign of this difference (90 – 10 = 80) is positive; if the current position is 92, the sign of the difference (90 – 92 = -2) is negative, and the character has reached or just passed its destination. When the `if` statement evaluates to is `true` the position of the character is updated so that it appears at the coordinates `endX` and `endY`. The `onEnterFrame` event is then set to `null` so that it no longer executes.

The next time the move() function is called the onEnterFrame event will be created again and this whole process will occur until the character has reached its destination.

Wow, that was a big function. Luckily the next two are much smaller. Next we look at the function mouseMoved().

The mouseMoved() Function

The mouseMoved() function is called when the user's mouse moves and is only on one character, the user's. Here it is:

```
function mouseMoved() {
    updateAfterEvent();
    if (!this.ob.locked) {
        var mx = this._parent._xmouse;
        var my = this._parent._ymouse;
        var xDiff = mx-this._x;
        var yDiff = my-this._y;
        var angle = Math.atan2(yDiff, xDiff);
        var realAngle = angle*180/Math.PI;
        if (realAngle<0) {
            var realAngle = realangle+360;
        }
        var number = Math.ceil(realAngle/this.ob.angleSpan);
        this.character.gotoAndStop("stand_"+number);
        this.ob.angle = angle;
        this.ob.number = number;
    }
}
```

Every time the mouse moves this function checks to see if the object that represents the user is locked (locked or true). If it is then it does nothing else, if not then it continues. The x and y position of the mouse are temporarily stored as mx and my. By taking the difference between the mouse's x position and the character's position, and the mouse's y position and the character's y position, we can determine the angle that mouse makes with the user's character (imagine an imaginary line drawn through his character and to his mouse). This angle is found by using the method of the Math object called atan2(), or *arctangent*. The angle is in radians and in the next line we set a variable called realAngle with the value of the angle converted to degrees. This angle should go between 0 and 360 degrees, but for some reason (that I found by testing) it comes in from 0 to 180 and -180 to 0 when you test this out and show the output with a trace in the output window. This is a total of 360 (-180 to 180) and is valid, but I like to work with angles that exist between 0 and 360 so the 'If' statement acts as a filter to convert the negative angles into positive ones. We then calculate the number of the frame that the character should be on (1 through 8) by using the realAngle and the angleSpan variables and rounding this comparison up. The final three lines of ActionScript set the angle of the character and then store the angle and the number.

The mouseGotClicked() Function

mouseGotClicked() is the final function on the frame in the Character Actions layer and, as its name implies, it's called when the mouse is clicked. It stores the time of the click, and the next time the mouse is clicked, the function checks to see the difference in time from the first click to the second. If the time difference is small enough (500 milliseconds), a double-click is recognized, and a move is sent. Here is the ActionScript:

```
function mouseGotClicked() {
    if (!this.ob.locked && !_root.chat.offlimits.hitTest
    → (_root._xmouse, _root._ymouse)) {
        this.lastClicked = this.now;
        this.now = getTimer();
        if (this.now-this.lastClicked<500) {
            var mx = this._parent._xmouse;
            var my = this._parent._ymouse;
            if (this.ob.endX != mx && this.ob.endY != my) {
                this.ob.endX = mx;
                this.ob.endY = my;
                _root.moveMe();
            }
        }
    }
}
```

The first thing that happens in this function is the if statement, which checks for two things. The first is something that we have seen already, the locked variable. If the character is locked, we do nothing else; if it isn't locked, we check the second condition, which invokes the hitTest() method of the movie clip object. hitTest() returns a value of true if the mouse is over a movie clip with an instance name of offlimits and false if it is not. (We don't have the movie clip in this file, so hitTest() returns false.

In the final file we place an invisible movie clip called offlimits over the chat window so that people can't click and have their characters walk onto the chat window. This is a very simple way to keep the characters in a reasonable area.

We then check the difference between click times. If it's less than 500 milliseconds, then it was a double-click and we continue in the code. The position of the mouse is stored as mx and my. We immediately check to make sure that mx and my are not the same as the current position of the character, because if they are we do not need to move anywhere. If they are not the same, everything is good and we continue in the code. We store the values endX and endY (from the mouse position) and then call the function in the root called moveMe(). The moveMe() function, in the final file, sends a message to the server saying that the character has moved. In our example file, of course, it sends the message directly to the updatePerson() function.

You have now seen all of the ActionScript needed to add a new character and to move it around on the stage. Next we look at the ActionScript involved with the pop-up chat box.

The Pop-up Chat Box

When a chat message is received, two things happen: the chat message appears in the text field on the right side of the screen (not in the file in this section, but in the final file) and a pop-up chat box appears over the head of the character that sent the message. The pop-up chat box, which displays for about five seconds and then disappears, has a dynamic height based on the amount of text sent. In this section we discuss how this is done.

Open chat_box.fla in the chapter 4 directory. This file is identical to the previous example file with one addition: the button seen in the bottom left side of the stage. Generate an SWF from this file, and click the button. A chat box appears above the character (**Figure 4.5**), stays for about five seconds, and then goes away. Close the SWF and open the Actions panel to look at the ActionScript on the button:

```
on(release) {
    chat[name].box.update("Hello cruel world!")
}
```

This action simply calls an update() method on an instance of the chat box called box. Let's look at that movie clip. Open the library and find a movie clip called dialog box. This is the movie clip that is given an instance name of box in the character. Double-click this library item to inspect its contents. There are two layers in this movie clip, Actions and Graphics. The Actions layer, which we'll inspect soon, contains all of the ActionScript needed to handle the chat box functionality. The Graphics layer contains one movie clip that also has an instance name of box. Inside that movie clip are three movie clips—top, middle, and bottom—that make up the top, middle, and bottom of the chat box. These movie clips are separate so that we can scale the middle movie clip with the size of the text and then place the top and the bottom movie clips to add the rounded borders.

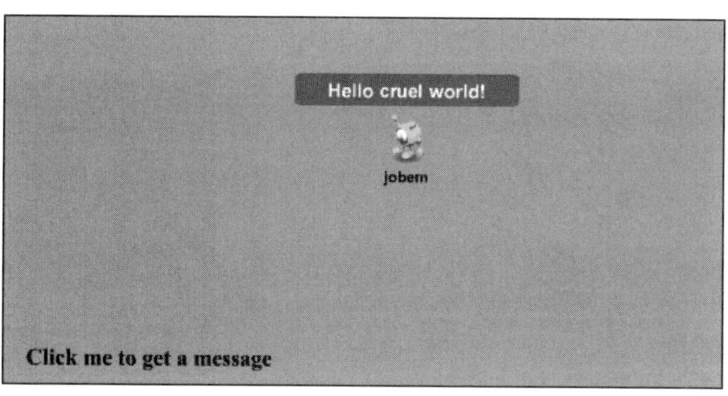

Figure 4.5 *When a chat message comes in, it appears over the head of the user who sent it.*

Now let's look at the ActionScript in the Actions layer. There is nothing mysterious happening or new here: scaling and positioning movie clips, creating a text field with ActionScript, and using setInterval() to call a function after a certain amount of time.

Through a series of four functions we can dynamically create the text field that displays the chat text, places it, sizes the background graphics to fit, and then sets a timer to turn off the chat box after 5 seconds. Here is the ActionScript:

```
_visible = false;
function update(newval) {
    if (newval != "" && newval != undefined && newval != null) {
        _visible = true;
        createText(newval);
        startTimer();
    } else {
        clearInterval(displayInterval);
        _visible = false;
    }
}
```

continues on next page

```
function startTimer() {
    seconds = 5;
    clearInterval(displayInterval);
    displayInterval = setInterval(update, 1000*seconds);
}
function createText(content) {
    field = "dialog";
    this.createTextField(field, 1, 10, 0, 290, 0);
    this[field].text = content;
    this[field].multiline = true;
    this[field].wordWrap = true;
    this[field].border = false;
    this[field].autoSize = "left";
    this[field].selectable = false;
    this[field].embedFonts = true;
    this.fieldFormat = new TextFormat();
    this.fieldFormat.color = 0xffffff;
    this.fieldFormat.font = "arial";
    this.fieldFormat.bold = true;
    this.fieldFormat.size = 25;
    this.fieldFormat.align = "center"
    this[field].setTextFormat(this.fieldFormat);
    sizeBG();
}
function sizeBG() {
    box.middle._yscale = this.dialog._height;
    box.middle._yscale = this.dialog._height;
    box.bottom._y = this.dialog._height;
    this._y = _parent.character._y-30-this._height;
}
```

The first line of ActionScript, `_visible = false`, makes it so that we do not see the chat box when it is loaded. We don't want to see it until it is needed. To make a chat message appear, the `update()` function is called and a message is passed in. If the message, `newval`, is not empty, the `createText()` and `startTimer()` functions are called, and the chat box is set visible so that we can see it. The `createText()` function creates the text field and calls the `setBG()` function (which stands for set background). The `setBG()` function scales the middle movie clip and places the entire chat box at an appropriate height. The `setTimer()` function calls set up a `setInterval()` event that calls the `update()` function after 5 seconds and passes in nothing. Since nothing is passed in, the `update()` function sees this as a time to "turn off" and sets the visibility to `false`. That's it! The chat box uses a series of very simple functions to work in the way that you have seen.

How the Chat Works

Now that you know everything about how the character works, it's time to talk about the chat. With the `ElectroServerAS` object, creating the chat is an easy thing. (If you have not read Appendix B yet, now would be a good time—or at least be prepared to flip to that section as a reference.) Also, in order to test this chat you must be able to start the ElectroServer socket server on your own computer. This is explained in Appendix A, "Multiuser Servers."

Tour of the File

Open `avatar.fla` in the chapter 4 directory. This file looks slightly different than the ones that we have already looked at. There is a pre-loader on the first few frames. Move to the frame labeled `done loading` and double-click the movie clip that has an instance name of `chat` in that frame. This movie clip contains all of the graphic assets. Notice that there are four frame labels in this timeline. Let's look at each individually.

- **`failed`**—This frame simply contains the text `Connection Failed`. When a connection to the server is attempted but does not succeed, this frame is displayed.
- **`login`**—This is the frame where the user enters his user name and then attempts to log in to the server.
- **`login failed`**— As the name implies, when a login is not a success, this frame is displayed. There is a text field on the frame that displays the reason why the login attempt did not succeed. Also on that frame is a button that says `Try Again`. When clicked, the user is taken to the login frame.
- **`chat`**—This frame is where the user will spend most of his time when connected to the chat. There are grid lines in it that give the chat a 3D feel to go with the 3D nature of the character. On the right side of the screen is a chat box text field with an instance name of window. A scroll bar component is attached to this window so that the user can easily scroll through the contents of the chat. We have given the scroll bar component an instance name of `bar` so that we can reference it with ActionScript. When a new chat message comes in and is displayed in the chat field, the scroll bar height adjusts automatically, and moves to the bottom so that the most recently added text is always showing. There is another text field on this frame and it has an instance name of `message`.

This is where the user types his chat message. When he's ready to send it, he can either press the Enter key on his keyboard or click the Send button. Here's the ActionScript on the Send button:

```
on (release, keyPress "<Enter>") {
    if (message.text != "" && message.text != undefined) {
        _root.chatSend(message.text);
        message.text = "";
    }
}
```

This ActionScript simply checks to make sure that the text field has some contents before attempting to send the message. If the message is not blank, the `chatSend()` function on the root is called, and the message is passed in. Once the message is sent, the message field is erased. We discuss the `chatSend()` function shortly.

There are two movie clips that look like rocks in this frame as well. One has an instance name of `rock1` and the other `rock2`. We give them instance names because we are going to use them while z-sorting. Z-sorting is the process that occurs to make movie clips appear to be at the correct depth. If a character should be behind `rock1`, for example, then we change the depth using `swapDepths()` to show this. This process is discussed later in this chapter.

The ActionScript

Before you continue, I recommend you start ElectroServer on port 1024 (see Appendix A for information on this) and test the chat. You can open more than one copy of the SWF file to log in more than one person. Play with all of the features to get a good feel for everything that is going on (**Figure 4.6**).

Notice that there is an `#include` action at the top of the frame in the Actions layer that includes `ElectroServerAS.as`. This is the file that contains all of the ElectroServerAS object definitions and must be included for things to work properly.

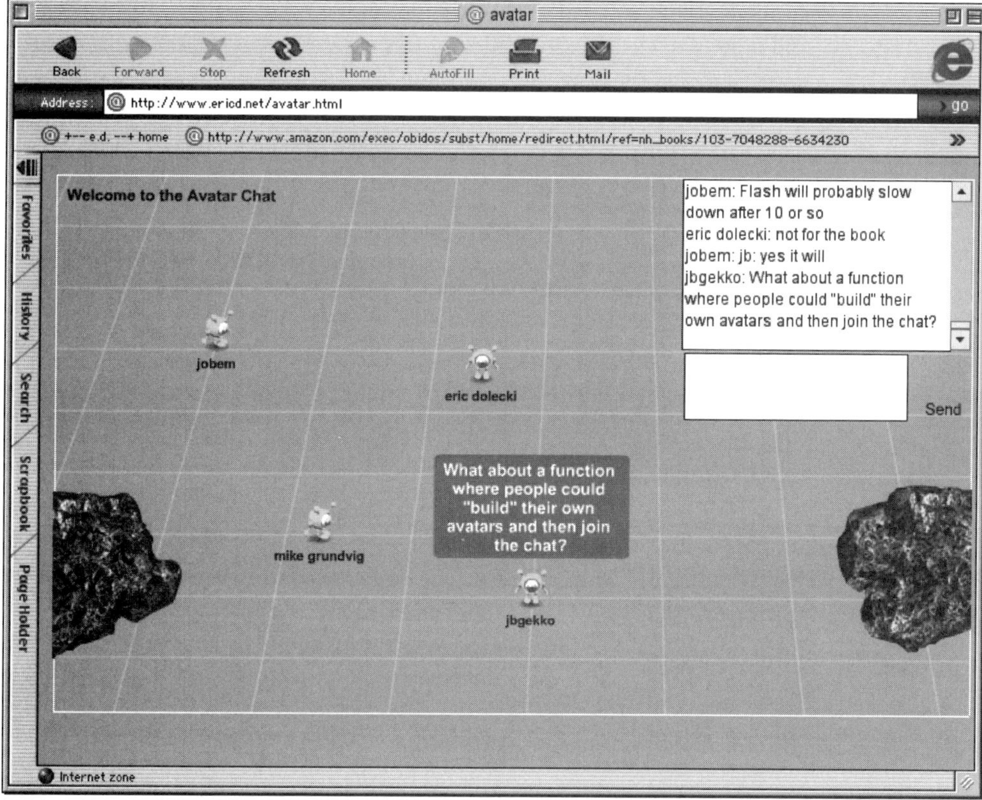

Figure 4.6 *This is the avatar chat in action.*

Using the ElectroServerAS object we can do things like send messages, change server variables, and define event handlers to be called when a message arrives or when a user updates a position. Here is the ActionScript that we use to define all of the event handlers and the initial properties of the ElectroServerAS object:

```
ES = new ElectroServerAS();
ES.IP = "localhost";
ES.PORT = 1024;
ES.onConnection = this.connectionResponse;
ES.loginResponse = this.loginResponse;
ES.chatReceiver = this.messageArrived;
ES.onRoomVarChange = this.roomVariablesChanged;
ES.connectToServer();
```

In the first line we create a new instance of the ElectroServerAS object and call it ES. We set some properties on this object such as the IP that it should connect to and the port. The port should match the port on the ElectroServer socket server properties file. Then we define event handlers for all of these events (explained in Appendix B). Finally, we connect to the server by invoking the connectToServer() method.

Now let's look at each of the four event handlers. Here's connectionResponse():

```
function connectionResponse(success) {
    if (success) {
        chat.gotoAndStop("login");
    } else {
        chat.gotoAndStop("failed");
    }
}
```

It is very simple. When called, a true or false value is passed in. If true, the connection is a success and the user is told to log in; otherwise the connection fails and the "failed" frame label is displayed.

Here is the loginResponse:

```
function loginResponse(success, reason) {
    if (success) {
        chat.gotoAndStop("chat");
    } else {
        chat.gotoAndStop("login failed");
        chat.reason.text = reason;
    }
}
```

This event is fired when a response is received from the server after the user has attempted to log in. The first parameter, success, contains either true or false. If true, the login attempt succeeds and the user is sent to the "chat" label. If false, the attempt fails and the user is sent to the "login failed" label, and the reason parameter contains a string saying why the login was not a success.

Now let's look at messageArrived(). Here is the ActionScript for this function:

```
function messageArrived(info) {
    var from = info.from;
    var body = info.body;
    var msg = from+": "+body+newline;
```

```
        chat[from].box.update(body);
        chat.window.text = ES.addToHistory(msg);
        chat.bar.setScrollPosition(chat.window.maxscroll);
        chatSound = new Sound();
        chatSound.attachSound("chat");
        chatSound.start();
    }
```

This function is called when a chat message is received. The `info` parameter is a reference to an object. This object contains three properties: `from`, `type`, and `body`. The `from` property is the user who sent the message, and `body` is the message itself. The `type` property, which we are not using, is either `"public"` (the message is meant for the entire room) or `"private"` (the message is meant for the user). We did not include a way to send private messages in this file (although it isn't difficult), so in our case it will always be `public`. We then make the pop-up chat box appear over the head of the character who sent the message, add the message to the chat field and to the chat history, and set the scroll position to its maximum. Finally, we play a sound as an aural indication that a chat message has been received.

You'll recall that the ElectroServer socket server gives us the capability to create variables on it in the current room. Whenever a variable is created, modified, or deleted everyone in the room is informed via the `onRoomVarChange` event. We store the position of each character with server variables. This makes things very easy for us. When the user clicks to move, his own server variable is updated and then everyone is informed. When the user leaves the chat, his variable is automatically deleted from the server and everyone in the room is informed of that, too, so his character is removed. Here is the ActionScript for the `roomVariablesChanged()` function:

```
function roomVariablesChanged(ob, type, varName) {
    if (type == "list") {
        for (var i in ob) {
            updatePerson(i, ob[i]);
        }
    } else if (type == "update") {
        updatePerson(varName, ob[varName]);
    } else if (type == "delete") {
        deletePerson(varName);
    }
}
```

As previously mentioned, this function is called when a room variable is created, updated, or deleted. Also, when the user first enters a room, the VariablesChanged() function is called. There are three parameters passed in. The first one, ob, is an object that contains all of the room variables. The next parameter, type, is a string value saying what kind of room variable event this is, "list", "update", or "delete". "list" means that the user has just entered the room and he is getting all of the variables. In this case we loop through every property on the object and call the updatePerson() function for each to create all of the characters. "update" means a variable has just been created or modified, and we call the updatePerson() function. "delete" means that the variable has been deleted from the server and so we must remove the person from the screen by calling deletePerson(). Here is the deletePerson() function:

```
function deletePerson(name) {
    chat[name].removeMovieClip();
    delete people[name];
}
```

This function is very simple. It removes the character movie clip and then deletes the object that represented that movie clip off of the people object.

Notice that the ActionScript in the moveMe() function is slightly different than it is in character.fla. In character.fla we call the updatePerson() function from moveMe(), but here we invoke the createVariable() method of the ElectroServerAS object. This creates the variable on the server that then fires the onRoomVarChange event that then calls the updatePerson() function. So the updatePerson() function is still called as a result of the moveMe() function, but it occurs after a few other things take place.

The initializeMe() function here is also different than the one in character.fla. It joins the user to a room and creates a variable on the server.

Now let's look at the rest of the functions, the ones that handle logging in, sending a message, and z-sorting.

```
function login(username) {
    ES.login(username);
}
```

This function is called from the "login" frame and a user name is passed in. It just calls the login() method of the ElectroServerAS object.

Here is the function that sends a chat message:

```
function chatSend(info) {
    ES.sendMessage(info, "room");
}
```

This function is very simple. A string is passed in and then it calls the sendMessage() method of the ElectroServerAS object. The message is then sent to the server and broadcast to everyone in the room.

Here is the function that handles z-sorting:

```
function sortClips() {
    for (var i = 0; i<zSort.length; ++i) {
        zSort[i].swapDepths(zSort[i]._y);
    }
}
```

Whenever a movie clip is created using the updatePerson() function, a reference to it is added to the zSort array. This function is called twice a second (set up using setInterval() in the udpatePerson() function). The z-sorting done here is very easy. The instances rock1 and rock2 are in the zSort array too. This z-sorting gives the world a more 3D feel. A character that appears to be behind another one will be swapped to a lower depth.

That's all of the ActionScript in this file. In this section you've seen a practical use of the methods and properties contained within the ElectroServerAS object.

Summary

In this chapter you've learned the basics of creating an avatar chat. You can very easily extend the functionality of this chat. You can add hot-spot areas (such as doorways, stairs, and so forth) where a user is teleported to another room. The other rooms can have their own set of graphics. You can enable private messaging by allowing a user to click on another character and then send that character a message. Good luck!

5: Multiplayer Game

by Michael Grundvig

Computer games have always been popular. I'm sure when the first CRT lit up some joker in the back thought, "Man! I bet that could play some mean games!" Over the years, first video games, then computer games have risen to play larger and larger roles in our society. Today, game consoles are little less than computers without keyboards and floppy drives. Many of the most popular games have gone so far as to become household names—Mario Brothers, Quake, and so forth.

Few things have changed computer games as much as the Internet. With the ability to connect players of a game with other players all over the world has come a host of new features, the largest of which is multiplayer gaming. Many games today enable users to play against other human players over the Internet. The astounding rise of multiplayer gaming can be attributed to one thing: it's fun. No matter how intelligent or capable a games' AI, it just can't compare to the entertainment value of fragging John from down the hall or Masako from Tokyo.

Flash has not been forgotten in this gaming boom. There are many excellent Flash games all over the Internet. Often one of the first things people attempt to use Flash for is to make a game. While single-player Flash games are quite common, their multiplayer counterpart is strangely lacking. This chapter is an attempt to help address that.

In this chapter we build an online multiplayer game called "Sea Commander." This game is similar to the old Milton Bradley *Battleship* board game that you may have played before. If you have never played Battleship, the basic idea is to sink your opponent's ships. You each have a board where you can place your ships on a grid that the other player can't see. You then take turns "shooting" at each other by calling out the coordinates of your shot. If you hit one of his ships, he tells you that it was a hit. When you sink a ship, your opponent tells you which ship was sunk. The game is over once either player's ships have all been sunk. In our game, we will automate the process of shooting and marking the shot for the player. We'll build it using the demo version of ElectroServer, a Java-based socket server designed for use with Flash, and the `ElectroServerAS` object.

Multiplayer Game Concepts

As far as Flash is concerned, there are only three realistic ways to do Internet-based multiplayer games: polling, the `XMLSocket` object, or Flash Communication Server.

Polling

Polling is the process of having an application request an update from the server again and again. This is most commonly done using any of the objects that support loading external data like `XML.load()` or `XML.sendAndLoad()`.

With polling, the client makes an HTTP request and the application server responds with the expected results. This requires you to have server-side code written in various languages (APS, PHP, ColdFusion, Java, and so on) that understand the specific details of what you are trying to accomplish.

The downside of polling is that the client is making the request for the data. It doesn't know if data exists or not, it just has to ask. To put this into an analogy, imagine you are driving with your friends to Las Vegas. Your friends ask you every 10 minutes, "Are we there yet?" and you always respond, "No." When you actually get there, you just wait until they ask again before you can respond, "Yes." Thus polling is very inefficient. It doesn't allow the server to notify the client that the data it's waiting for is ready.

In our little analogy, you can see that you might have arrived in Las Vegas right after the last question, but wouldn't be able to tell them until they asked again. Polling introduces latency in all communication. The simple solution seems to be just asking faster, right? Well yes, that does reduce the latency but it also increases the amount of work being done with no gain.

The biggest advantage of polling is that it's simple. Polling does not require knowledge of the more complicated languages that XMLSocket does. In polling, you don't have to use a separate socket server. A plain application server running any number of languages will suffice.

Flash Communication Server

Flash Communication Server is a new technology from Macromedia that's built into the newest version of the Flash player. It is essentially a high-performance socket server that supports the concept of server-side scripting and has a lot other bells and whistles. We won't use Flash Communication Server for our multiplayer game because we want to showcase several technologies in this book, but we do use it for the multiple-communication application in Chapter 8.

XMLSocket

The other option for multiplayer Flash games is `XMLSocket`. `XMLSocket` allows the server to directly notify the client when something has happened. If you were to take our Las Vegas analogy, your friends would sit quietly in the back for the entire trip. Once you get to Vegas, you would tell them you have arrived and that would be the end of it.

The biggest disadvantage of `XMLSocket` is its complexity. This isn't to say that it's particularly hard, just that it's more complicated then the polling solution. `XMLSocket` makes a socket connection to a remote server. You will need to either write or use an existing server to use `XMLSocket`. Many languages can be used to write a server—C++, Java, Visual Basic, C#, to name a few—but these languages are significantly more complicated then Flash's ActionScript.

Another disadvantage is that you need to be able to keep your socket server running at all times if you expect other people to play your game online. You can run these servers on your local computer, but that's probably not fast enough for a production website. Typically, people will get a dedicated server or an account with a hosting company that lets them run user applications. Unfortunately, both of these options cost money.

In this chapter we will use `XMLSocket` as we did in Chapter 4, "Avatar Chat." We will be able to modify the chat code from the last chapter to support the new functionality of a multiplayer game. Specifically this means adding the ability for a user to challenge another user to a game. Fortunately, both the ElectroServer and the ElectroServer ActionScript object (`ElectroServerAS`) have been tuned for multiplayer game development. They both support features that make it easier for you to build and test online games. The two appendixes in the back of this book discuss these features so we won't go into them in depth here.

Introducing The Game: Sea Commander

Sea Commander is a full-featured multiplayer game (**Figure 5.1**). While it certainly isn't the next Quake, we worked hard to develop a non-trivial example to illustrate the concepts involved. Before we get into the multiplayer aspects of the game, it's important to cover some of the concepts involved. These concepts are not specific to this game so you can reuse this code in other projects without any problems.

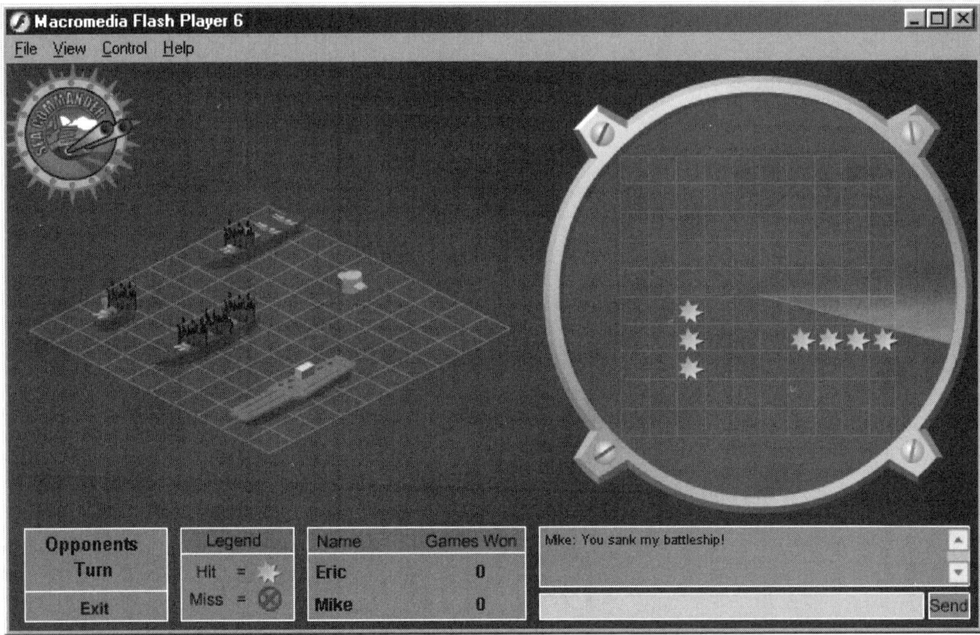

Figure 5.1 *Our multiplayer game in action.*

Isometric World

The portion of the Sea Commander game that represents your ships uses an isometric perspective. Isometric views are used in a lot of games due to their overall simplicity. For example, the older Ultima games, XCOM, Civilization 2, as well as XCOM and many Real Time Strategy games use it. An isometric view is rather hard to explain. The best way to think of it is to take a square, rotate it 90 degrees, and then shrink it vertically (**Figure 5.2**).

Isometric views have one *very* convenient aspect to them: the artist can render fewer sprites as a whole. Specifically, you can reuse images very easily as **Figure 5.3** shows.

With one image, we create both a left and a right view of the ship. If we had another image of the ship facing away from us, we could use the same trick and end up with four views of the ship from only two images. This is even more useful in Flash because you only need to load one image for each of the two views and flip it horizontally in code, like this:

```
myObject._xscale -= myObject._xscale * 2;
```

This works for many different types of objects and enables you to dramatically speed up development time.

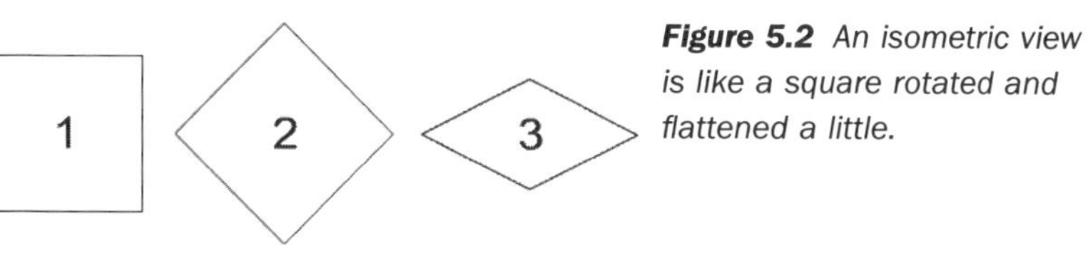

Figure 5.2 *An isometric view is like a square rotated and flattened a little.*

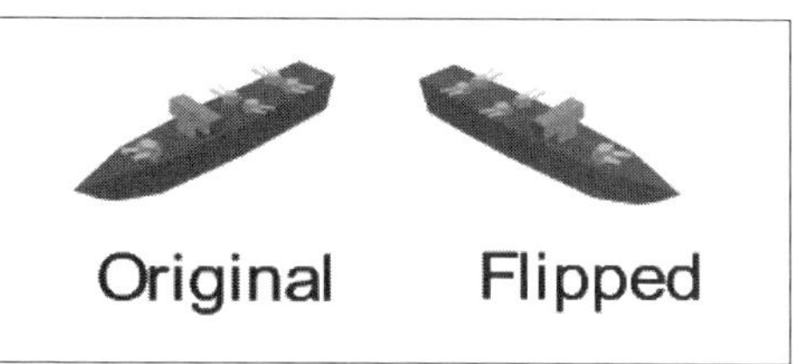

Figure 5.3 *The original image (left) can be flipped horizontally to create a different view (right).*

Placing Objects in an Isometric World

Placing objects in an isometric world is a little bit tricky. I won't get into the gory details of it but I will show the basic method used. **Figure 5.4** shows the game screen used for placing ships. Before we start though, I want to thank Jobe Makar for all the isometric code used for this project. Other people have done similar things, but I have found his isometric code to be extremely elegant and simple to use. I guess that's what a Master's degree in physics gets you!

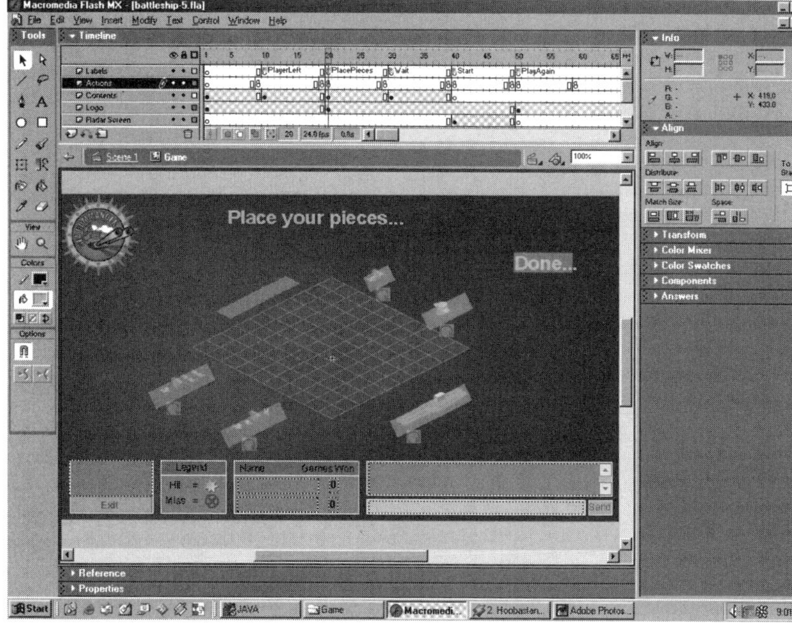

Figure 5.4 *The screen used for placing your ships.*

An isometric view is really a 3D view shown on a two-dimensional screen. Normally when you use Flash, you are using a two-dimensional grid of coordinates for movie clips: _x this and _y that, and so forth. To use an isometric view, you need to make a virtual 3D world in memory. This really means no more then just making sure every object you want displayed has x, y, and a z coordinates. The other thing you need to do is use a function to place objects. If you place them yourself, they will not be positioned correctly. The first thing to do is initialize your isometric world:

```
yAng = 45;
xAng = 30;
sinY = cosY=Math.sin(yAng*Math.pi/180);
cosX = Math.cos(xAng*Math.pi/180);
sinX = Math.sin(xAng*Math.pi/180);
```

Once that has executed, you can use this function:

```
function placeObject(name) {
    name._x = (name.z*sinY)+(name.x*cosY);
    name._y = (name.y*cosX)-(((name.z*cosY)-(name.x*sinY))
    → *sinX);
}
```

Whenever you need something placed on the screen, you need only set its isometric coordinates and call `placeObject` on it. For example:

```
root.attachMovie("myObject", "myObject2", 100);

myObject2.x = 0;
myObject2.y = 0;
myObject2.z = 0;
placeObject(myObject2);
```

Notice that the `placeObject` function takes a reference to the object itself. This allows the objects to be in different timelines, but still be placed correctly. It also makes it more convenient for objects to place themselves, like this:

```
placeObject(this);
```

From the Screen to an Isometric World

Now that we have covered taking movie clips and displaying them on the screen using an isometric world, we need to talk about how to take an object from the screen and translate it to its correct isometric coordinates. At first glance, you may not see a reason for doing this, but in reality it's quite useful. In Sea Commander, we need to allow people to drag their ships around and place them. Dragging items in Flash uses the _x and _y coordinates built in, but at some point you need to translate those back to x, y, and z coordinates. The following function does that for you:

```
function screenToIso(fx, fy) {
    zp = (fx/cosY-fy/(sinY*sinX))*(1/(cosY/sinY+sinY/cosY));
    xp = (1/cosY)*(fx-zp*sinY);
    point = new Object();
    point.x = xp;
    point.y = 0;
    point.z = zp;
    return point;
}
```

There are several important things to note about this function. The first is that it returns a point object. Macromedia does this itself, so this should seem familiar. The second is that this function automatically assumes the y coordinate to be 0. This is because you are translating two coordinates, fx and fy, into three. You have to assume at least one coordinate to do that. In this case, we assume the y coordinate, which defines the "altitude" of something. You could easily make that a variable as well, based on your needs.

Sorting Depths

One thing that many isometric engines fail to do properly is sort the depth of objects. You need to sort the depth to ensure that objects don't overlap in a way that isn't possible. To solve this problem, we use a function that looks like this:

```
function sortDepth(name) {
    var a = 1000; // max x dimension, a constant
    var b = 1000; //max z dimension, a constant
    var c = (a * (b-1)) + a; //total depths per y
    var n = (c * Math.abs(name.y)) + (a * (Math.abs
    → (name.z)-1)) + name.x;
    name.swapDepths(Math.ceil(n));
}
```

This depth sorting routine is rather unique. It uses the idea that a single depth exists for all objects in an isometric world and with just a single object; it is able to determine the correct depth. This makes the routine blazingly fast because it does not have to interrogate other objects and determine this objects relationship to them.

Multiplayer Guts

By now, we have covered all the basic ideas needed to really get into the game. You have a good understanding of the isometric engine and how it is used. As this chapter is meant to build off the avatar chat application in Chapter 4, we won't be covering all the basics again. If you haven't read that chapter yet, this would be a good time to do so to get a better understanding of multiplayer basics before we continue.

Just as in the last chapter, we will be using the `ElectroServerAS` object along with the ElectroServer socket server. This book's appendixes cover both of these in much more detail

For the rest of this chapter, we will walk through all the major pieces used to build the game. Each of these pieces is broken down with a partial listing of the code used and an explanation of its importance.

The Gathering Place

In every multiplayer game, you have to have a gathering place (**Figure 5.5**). That is, a place where everyone can get together to play the game. People need to be able to find each other and challenge others to the game. As anyone who plays *StarCraft* on BNet can tell you, it also serves as a prime place to brag about your triumphs or whine about your defeats.

In the last chapter, Jobe walked us through building an avatar chat, but we'll be using a straight chat for this game, because that makes it easier for the user to challenge other users. It is a sophisticated, fully functional chat supporting rooms, user lists, private messages, and more. It serves as a lightweight showcase for the `ElectroServerAS` object and is the perfect place to launch people into our game.

As the last chapter went into details about how to connect to the server and log you in, we are only going to cover the specific changes.

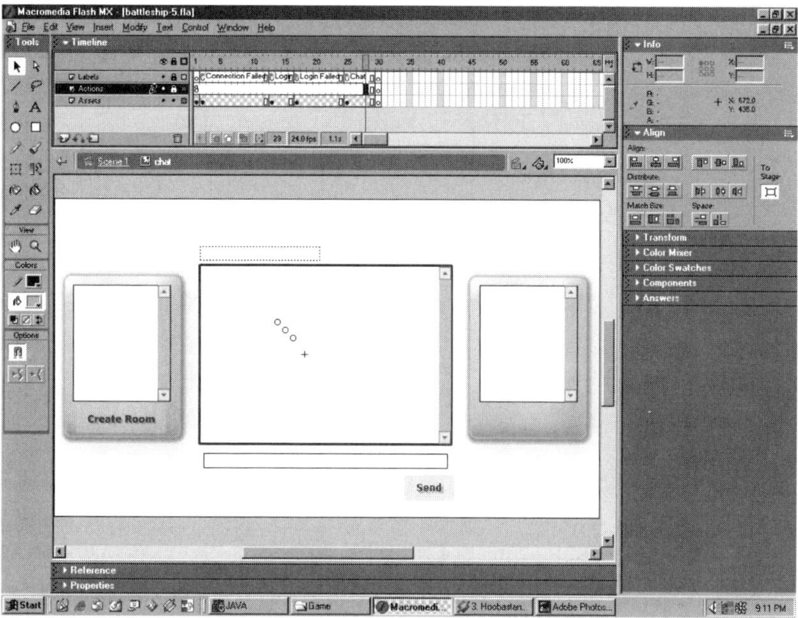

Figure 5.5 *The chat interface in the Flash environment.*

Find SeaCommander.fla in the Chapter 5 folder on the CD-ROM. When you first open the file you will see that it has a pre-loader from frames 1 through 7. The real code begins on frame 8 where all the major chat functions are initialized. Here is the code that starts it all:

```
//New the ElectroServer object
ES = new ElectroServerAS();

// Set the initial values
ES.ip = "localhost";
ES.port = 1024;

// Set all the event handlers
ES.onConnection = this.connectionResponse;
ES.loginResponse = this.loginResponse;
ES.chatReceiver = this.messageArrived;
ES.roomListChanged = this.roomListChanged;
ES.userListChanged = this.userListChanged;
ES.challengeReceived = this.challengeReceived;
ES.challengeAnswered = this.challengeAnswered;
```

continues on next page

```
ES.challengeCancelled = this.challengeCancelled;
ES.onConnectionRefused=this.connectionRefused;

// Actually make the connection
if (!ES.isConnected) {
    // If we are not already connected
    ES.connectToServer();
} else {
    // If we are already connected
    ES.joinRoom("Lobby");
    chat.gotoAndStop("Chat");
    chat.room.text = "Lobby";
}
```

Notice toward the end that a "chat" reference is used. This is the actual chat room movie clip. Browse through that clip; it contains all the graphics and buttons needed for a chat. Go back to the main timeline on frame 8 and we can walk through the code used. The first thing to do is request for the ElectroServerAS object, called ES in the code, to connect to the chat server. That code causes the onConnection event to be fired. In this case, we are forcing it to call connectionResponse, which looks like this:

```
function connectionResponse(success) {

    if (success) {
        chat.gotoAndStop("Login");
    } else {
        chat.gotoAndStop("Connection Failed");
    }
}
```

Simply put, this code tells the chat movie clip to move to either the "Login" screen or "Connection Failed" screen. Assuming you connected properly, the next thing you do is log in. On this screen of the chat movie clip, there is a button that, once clicked, calls this function on the root:

```
function login(username) {
    ES.login(username);
}
```

This function asks the server to log a user in. The server has an event for this as well, called loginResponse. We have overridden that event with a function by the same name that looks like this:

```
function loginResponse(success, reason) {
    if (success) {
```

```
        ES.joinRoom("Lobby");
        chat.gotoAndStop("Chat");
        chat.room.text = "Lobby";
    } else {
        chat.gotoAndStop("Login Failed");
        chat.reason.text = reason;
    }
}
```

Because no two users are allowed to have the same username, the server responds with either a success or failure Boolean, along with reason. This function just forwards the chat movie clip to a screen that lets you try a new username if your first was not accepted. If your username was good, this function logs you into a room called `"Lobby"` and forwards the chat movie clip to the `"Chat"` label.

At this point, you are now able to chat normally. There are a variety of house-cleaning functions that have to be used to keep the room list, user list, and chat windows up to date. For instance, when the user list changes, this function is executed:

```
function userListChanged(userList) {
    var path = chat.userList;
    var enabled = path.getEnabled();
    path.setEnabled(true);
    path.removeAll();
    path.setChangeHandler("personClicked", _root);
    for (var i = 0; i<userList.length; ++i) {
        path.addItem(userList[i].name);
    }
    path.setEnabled(enabled);
}
```

Likewise, for the room list:

```
function roomListChanged(roomList) {
    var path = chat.roomList;
    path.removeAll();
    path.setChangeHandler("roomClicked", _root);
    for (var i = 0; i<roomList.length; ++i) {
        var name = roomList[i].name;
        var item = name+"("+roomList[i].total+")";
        path.addItem(item, name);
    }
}
```

One of the most critical functions is the one that handles incoming messages from the server. It looks like this:

```
function messageArrived(info) {
    var from = info.from;
    var body = info.body;
    var type = info.type;
    if (type == "public") {
        var msg = formatFrom(from)+": "+formatBody(body)+
        → "<br>";
    } else if (type == "private") {
        var msg = formatFrom(from)+"[private]: "+
        → formatBody(body)+"<br>";
    }
    chat.window.htmlText = ES.addToHistory(msg);
    chat.bar.setScrollPosition(chat.window.maxscroll);
}
```

This function takes in a message and formats it using the `formatFrom` function, which just wraps HTML code around a given message and returns it all as a string. This string is then displayed. Sending a message is equally simple:

```
function chatSend(info) {
ES.sendMessage(info, "room");
}
```

The last and arguably the most important thing we need to worry about is how people challenge each other to games and accept or decline challenges from other people.

To send a challenge, you need only click on a person's name in the user list. The following function is called automatically:

```
function personClicked(path) {
    var name = path.getValue();
    if (name != ES.username) {
        chat.popup.gotoAndStop("Waiting");
        chat.userList.setEnabled(false);
        ES.challenge(name, "Sea Commander");
    }
}
```

The `ES.challenge` code could accept any game name you specify. This is intentional, enabling your chat to support multiple games. In this case we've hard coded it to `"Sea Commander"`.

The person you challenge receives a challenge request from you, and the ES object checks to see if he is already in a game. If he is in a game, the ES object replies automatically and declines the request. If he is not in a game, the following function is called automatically:

```
function challengeReceived(from, game) {
    var msg = from+" has just challenged you to a game of
    → "+game+"!";
    chat.userList.setEnabled(false);
    chat.popup.gotoAndStop("Challenged");
    chat.popup.msg.text = msg;
}
```

As you can see, it just pops up a dialog and gives him the opportunity to accept or decline. Based on his choice, one of these next two functions are executed:

```
function acceptChallenge() {
    chat.userList.setEnabled(true);
    chat.popup.gotoAndStop(1);
    ES.acceptChallenge();
    this.gotoAndStop("Game");
}

function declineChallenge() {
    chat.userList.setEnabled(true);
    chat.popup.gotoAndStop(1);
    ES.declineChallenge();
}
```

Both of these functions are quite self-explanatory. They just enable the user list again, remove the popup, and send either an accept or decline response. If the user is accepting a challenge, the play head is advanced to the "Game" label. This is something you would change if you wanted multiple games available to your chat. You would want to make some reference to what game to forward, possibly even loading in the SWF for the game dynamically. Upon receiving this response, the challenger executes the following function:

```
function challengeAnswered(response) {
    if (response == "accepted") {
        _root.gotoAndStop("Game");
    } else if (response == "declined") {
```

continues on next page

```
            chat.popup.gotoAndStop("Declined");
            chat.popup.msg.text = "The challenge has been
            ➥ declined.";
        } else if (response == "autodeclined") {
            chat.popup.gotoAndStop("Declined");
            chat.popup.msg.text = "The challenge has been
            ➥ automatically declined.";
        }
        chat.userList.setEnabled(true);
    }
```

Notice that this function also forwards the play head to the "Game" label if the user who was challenged accepted. At this point, both the users are in the game proper.

While there is more code used for the chat, we have covered everything you need to follow it. The chat also supports creating and joining rooms, sending private messages, and more.

Waiting for Players to Join

At this point, both players are ready to play the game. They have accepted the challenge and are trying to meet in the designated location. Part of the underlying guts of ElectroServer is that all games take place in private rooms. You as the developer don't need to understand how that is accomplished, just know that when people play, they are hidden from everyone else on the server. This is important because it takes time for people to join the rooms.

If one player is using a cable modem and the other is on a dial-up connection, the cable modem user almost certainly will beat the other person into the game. So you have to wait. A simple solution might be just to wait a variable amount of time and then start the game, assuming that they have joined in the interim. Well, that would work assuming you waited long enough *and* if they didn't get disconnected from the server somehow via closing or crashing the browser or losing their connection to the Internet.

This is a big problem and not one of the easier ones to solve. One of the easier solutions—and the one we will use for this game—is to set a room variable for each player who enters the room and then watch for when they are all set. To learn more about room variables, take a look at ElectroServerAS object appendix. The code to handle this is shown here:

```
function roomVarChanged(ob) {
    if (ob.player1 == "here" && ob.player2 == "here") {
        locked = false;
        if (!initializedYet) {
            initializedYet = true;
            game.gotoAndPlay("PlacePieces");
        }
    } else {
        locked = true;
        if (initializedYet) {
            game.gotoAndStop("PlayerLeft");
        }
    }
}

function iAmIn() {
    var name = "player"+ES.player;
    var val = "here";
    ES.createVariable(name, val);
}
```

When you initially join a room, the function `iAmIn` is executed. This sets a room variable that the fires off the function `roomVarChanged`. If both players are in the room, this function will call `startGame` and we can move onto the next section.

Placing the Pieces

Once both players are in the room, it's time for them to place their pieces. Both players can do this at the same time, but all pieces must be placed before the game can begin.

The first thing to think about is how we will represent the ships in memory. There is a surprisingly simple method that handles this for us. Specifically, you create a two-dimensional array the size of the playing grid. Every ship takes up several positions in the grid. So in the `onClipEvent(load)` method, you just place something along the lines of

```
placementGrid = [[], [], [], [], [], [], [], [], [], []];
```

And you have your grid. When we get into the code that actually illustrates placing your ships, you'll see this grid used a great deal. Now we have a grid that represents our ships' placement, but we also need a grid to send to our opponent when we are ready to play. For convenience reasons that will become clear when we show how to take shots, a ship's position in the placementGrid is actually a reference to the ship itself. This means you can't send the placementGrid directly to your opponent because the ElectroServerAS object internally uses Branden Hall's WDDX ActionScript implementation and that is unable to send movie clips. Attempting to send the placement grid results in errors. The solution is quite simple; just create a second grid like this:

```
sendToOpponentGrid = [[], [], [], [], [], [], [], [], [], []];
```

This grid is then populated with empty strings to represent the position of ships. This makes for a lightweight object to send to your opponent and is quite simple to implement.

We discussed the code necessary to do isometric views earlier in the chapter and this is where it really comes into play. You'll notice that in the game movie clip, we have a movie clip called isoBoard. If you look at the ActionScript on that object, you see a large for statement that loops over the five ships, sets many of their initial variables, and creates many of the functions they need to perform properly. Covering each ship is a button with the following code:

```
on(press) {
    startDragging();
}

on(release, releaseOutside) {
    stopDragging();
}
```

As you can see, clicking the mouse on the ship simply calls the startDragging function just as letting up on the mouse calls stopDragging. The startDragging function is detailed here:

```
ship.startDragging = function() {
    if(this.dragEnabled) {
        this.xOffset = this.p._xmouse-this._x;
        this.yOffset = this.p._ymouse-this._y;
        this.run = this.drag;
    }
};
```

Seems to be pretty simple, but then it doesn't actually do that much work, the real work is done in the drag method. The only thing to really notice about the startDragging function is that it creates xOffset and yOffset variables on the ship. These variables are used to offset the point where you clicked from where you are placing the ship. This is necessary to position the ship correctly on the grid. Here's the drag method:

```
ship.drag = function() {
        this.sortDepth2();
    this._x = this.p._xmouse - this.xOffset;
    this._y = this.p._ymouse - this.yOffset;
    if (this.useHighlight) {
        this.updateISOCoords();
        this.p.highlight.x = this.round(this.x) * this.p.size;
        this.p.highlight.y = this.round(this.y) * this.p.size;
        this.p.highlight.z = this.round(this.z) * this.p.size;
        this.x = Math.round(this.p.highlight.x / this.p.size);
        this.z = Math.round(this.p.highlight.z / this.p.size);
        if (this.orientation == "vertical" && this.x>=0 &&
        → this.x<=9 && this.z<=0 && this.z>=-10+this.cells) {
            this.p.highlight._visible = true;
            this.p.highlight.showCells(this.cells);
            this.p.highlight._xscale = Math.abs
            → (this.p.highlight._xscale);
                    this.p.placeObject(this.p.highlight);
        } else if (this.orientation == "horizontal" &&
        → this.x>=0 && this.x<=10-this.cells && this.z<=0 &&
        → this.z>=-9) {
            this.p.highlight._visible = true;
            this.p.highlight.showCells(this.cells);
            this.p.highlight._xscale = -Math.abs
            → (this.p.highlight._xscale);
            this.p.placeObject(this.p.highlight);
        } else {
            this.p.highlight._visible = false;
        }
    } else {
        this.updateISOCoords();
        this.x = this.round(this.x)*this.p.size;
        this.y = this.round(this.y)*this.p.size;
        this.z = this.round(this.z)*this.p.size;
        this.p.placeObject(this);
    }
};
```

Whew! That is one big function! Fortunately, it's pretty straightforward. Let's break it down, shall we? The first thing is to execute the sortDepth2 function. We talked about this concept in the ISO section earlier in the chapter. The code then sets the ship's current position to your current mouse position. For reference, this.p is equal to the ship's _parent value. Which, in this case, is the isoBoard movie clip. The next couple of lines call updateISOCoords, which takes the new x and y position of the ship and runs it against the screenToISO function, which we talked about earlier. After it gets the isometric coordinates, it sets them to the ship as this.x, this.y, this.z. The next few lines of code display the highlight movie clip and position it properly on the grid. The large if statement is only used to handle showing the highlight if it is fully on the grid and not partially off.

We also mentioned a stopDragging function earlier. It is detailed here:

```
ship.stopDragging = function() {
        if(this.dragEnabled) {
        this.sortDepth2();

            if(this.placed) {
            if (this.placedOrientation == "vertical") {
                for (i=0; i < this.cells; i++) {
                this.p.placementGrid[this.gridX]
                → [this.gridY + i] = null;
                }
            } else {
                for (i=0; i < this.cells; i++) {
                    this.p.placementGrid[this.gridX + i]
                    → [this.gridY] = null;
                }
            }
            this.placed = false;
        }

        this.p.highlight._visible = false;
        this.run = null;
        this.updateISOCoords();
        this.x = this.round(this.x)*this.p.size;
        this.y = this.round(this.y)*this.p.size;
        this.z = this.round(this.z)*this.p.size;
        this.p.placeObject(this);
        this.success = this.p.placeShip(this);
        if (!this.success) {
```

```
            this._x = this.startingX;
            this._y = this.startingY;
            this.updateISOCoords();
        }
    }
};
```

Ouch, another big function. Much of it is similar to the startDragging function, particularly the placement code. Let's go ahead and break this one down. The first thing this code does is sort the depth of the ship. This ensures the ship is positioned properly in relation to everything else on the grid. The next big step is to clean up the old placement of the ship. Once the ship is placed, we set this.placed to equal true, and we have to walk through the placementGrid and set all references to it to null.

Once the old position has been cleaned up, if it needed to be, we place the ship down. We do this by updating its ISO coordinates and then calling the ISO function placeObject on it.

At this point, we have to determine if the ship is overlapping any other ships if it is on the board completely. We do this by calling the placeShip function on the isoBoard movie clip. I won't go into the code for this function here because it's essentially a series of if and for statements that look through the placement grid and ensure that there is nothing already placed there. Internally, this function places the ship if the way is clear. The function returns either true or false based on whether the passed position is open.

If the placeShip function returns false, we immediately set the ship back to its starting position, which lies off the grid. If it returns true, we are finished placing that ship and can continue.

When you have placed all your ships, you click the Done button to continue. This button calls the lockBoard function, which looks like this:

```
function lockBoard() {
    // Check to see if all pieces are placed
    done = true;
    for(i = 1; i <= 5; i++) {
        if(!this["ship" + i].placed) {
            done = false;
        }
    }
```

continues on next page

```
        // remove the rotate buttons and stop the dragging
        if(done) {
            for(i = 1; i <= 5; i++) {
                this["ship" + i].dragEnabled = false;
                this["ship" + i].rotateClip._visible = false;
            }
        }

        // Return the results
        return done;
    }
```

This function is quite simple. It just loops over all the ships and ensures they are all placed and then loops over them again, turning off their rotate buttons and making it so you can no longer drag them.

If the `lockBoard` function returned `true`, then the button continues on and executes this code:

```
    if(done) {
        myBoardDone = true;
        var obj = new Object();
        obj.action = "PlacePieces";
        obj.placementArray = isoBoard.sendToOpponentGrid;
        sendMove(obj);

        if(theirBoardDone) {
            gotoAndPlay("Start");
        } else {
            gotoAndPlay("Wait");
        }
    }
```

This code is simple but does a great deal. It first sets a variable called `myBoardDone` to `true`. This variable is used later when we receive the other player's ships positions, as we'll see in a moment. The next step is to build an object with an action member variable that has a value of `"PlacePieces"` and another variable called `placementArray` with a value of my `sendToOpponentsGrid`. Once that's done, we call the `sendMove` function, which we get to in the next section.

To tie this all together, we need to look at the `moveReceived` function for a moment. When either side sends its `PlacePieces` information, the `moveReceived` function is called. Inside that function is the following snippet of code along with other bits we will get to in the next section:

```
    action = obj.action;
    if(action == "PlacePieces") {
        theirGrid = obj.placementArray;
        theirBoardDone = true;
        if(myBoardDone) {
            gotoAndPlay("Start");
        }
```

This code gets the action and checks to see if it is `"PlacePieces"`. If it is, then it sets the variable `theirGrid` to the `placementArray` the other player passed us. We then set `theirBoardDone` to be `true` and check to see if `myBoardDone` is `true`. If it is, both boards are done and we can proceed into the game proper.

At this point, you should have a good feel for how the pieces are positioned and a good idea of how the rest of the game will continue.

Making a Move

Making a move in the game is more complicated then you might initially think. There are a lot of little things that have to be taken into account, which we will get into in a moment.

The lion's share of the code for the game resides in three places: the `PlacePieces` frame, on the `isoBoard` movie clip and on the grid movie clip inside of the radar clip. When you finish placing your pieces, you are taken to the `"Ready"` frame, which is where the game actually takes place. The code looks like this:

```
isoBoard._x = -150;
if(myTurn) {
    panel.turn.text = "Your Turn";
} else {
    panel.turn.text = "Opponents Turn";
}
```

Not much there. All this code does is tell you if it's your turn and move the `isoBoard` clip over to the left of the screen. This code actually references a Boolean called `myTurn`. The variable `myTurn` is available to tell you if the next move is yours or not. It is created on the `PlacePieces` frame with this:

```
if(ES.player == 1) {
    myTurn = true;
} else {
    myTurn = false;
}
```

Now that we know whose turn it is, we can move on to actually taking a shot. There are really two distinct pieces to taking a shot. First the person actually shooting takes their shot, and then the person actually receiving the shot updates his display appropriately. We will split these up into two steps to facilitate discussion.

Taking the Shot

Taking a shot is quite simple for the user, but the code goes through several steps to actually handle it. When the grid clip loads initially, it executes this code:

```
currDepth = 100;
g = _parent._parent;
```

To take a shot, you need only click on the grid within the radar screen. Clicking on the grid executes the following code:

```
// This handles actually taking the shot
this.onRelease = function() {
    if(g.myTurn) {
        var xPos = Math.ceil((this._xmouse + 1) / 20) - 1;
        var yPos = Math.ceil((this._ymouse + 1) / 20) - 1;

        // Determine if this spot has already had a shot
        var alreadyShot = g.alreadyShot(xPos, yPos);
        if(alreadyShot) {
            g.playSound("AlreadyShot");
            return;
        }

        // Determine if it was a hit or not
        var hit = g.takeShot(xPos, yPos);
        if(hit) {
            markShot("hit", xPos, yPos);
        } else {
            markShot("miss", xPos, yPos);
        }

        // Create the object to actually send to the opponent
        var obj = new Object();
        obj.action = "Fire";
        obj.x = xPos;
        obj.y = yPos;
```

```
            // Send the object and prepare for the opponents turn
            g.sendMove(obj);
            g.myTurn = false;
            g.panel.turn.text = "Opponents Turn";
        }
    }
```

Seems like a lot, but its pretty straightforward. When you click on the grid, the onRelease event executes. This event checks to see if it is your turn or not before doing anything else. If it is your turn, we mathematically determine which grid squares you are in with these lines:

```
var xPos = Math.ceil((this._xmouse + 1) / 20) - 1;
var yPos = Math.ceil((this._ymouse + 1) / 20) - 1;
```

From there, we check the alreadyShot function on the PlacePieces frame:

```
function alreadyShot(x, y) {
    var shot = myShotGrid[x][y];
    if(shot != null) {
        return true;
    } else {
        return false;
    }
}
```

This function just checks the myShotGrid array we created earlier and determines if there is a value in it. If you have already shot there, the function returns a Boolean and we play a sound; if not, we continue on.

Now that we know you haven't shot there before, we can take the shot itself. This involves calling the takeShot function on the PlacePieces frame. This function and the isHit function, which it calls, are as follows:

```
function takeShot(x, y) {
    var hit = isHit(x, y);
    if(hit) {
        myShotGrid[x][y] = "hit";
    } else {
        myShotGrid[x][y] = "miss";
    }

    return hit;
}
```

continues on next page

```
function isHit(x, y) {
    var hit = theirGrid[x][y];
    if(hit != null) {
        return true;
    } else {
        return false;
    }
}
```

The function takeShot immediately calls isHit to determine if the shot actually hit an opponents ship. Remember in the last section where we talked about the opponent sending his array of ship positions to us? Well, this is what it is for. It allows us to check to see if we hit or not without actually contacting the opponent and waiting for a response.

Now that we know if we hit or not, the takeShot function updates the myShotGrid array with the information and returns if it was a hit or not.

Back in our code on the grid movie clip, we use the information from takeShot and call the markShot function telling it to mark as either a hit or a miss. The markShot function looks like this:

```
function markShot(target, gridX, gridY) {
    if(target == "hit") {
        var clip = "HitClip";
    } else {
        var clip = "MissClip";
    }
    currDepth++;
    var newClip = "clip" + currDepth;
    this.attachMovie(clip, newClip, currDepth);
    var c = this[newClip];
    c._x = (gridX * 20) + 10;
    c._y = (gridY * 20) + 10;
}
```

This function just takes the hit or miss clip and attaches it to the grid at the correct location. Once we have done all this, we can finally send the move information to our opponent:

```
var obj = new Object();
obj.action = "Fire";
obj.x = xPos;
obj.y = yPos;
g.sendMove(obj);
```

At this point, we just need to reset everything for our opponent's turn:

```
g.myTurn = false;
g.panel.turn.text = "Opponents Turn";
```

As soon as this code executes, ElectroServer sends the move to the other client and we start handling the second part of taking a shot, receiving the shot.

Receiving the Shot

Receiving the shot is much more complicated than taking the shot—we have to watch to see if the shot has sunk a ship or if it hits a ship, we have to have an animation play, and so on. When writing games, you'll find that animation always complicates something that should be quite simple.

Receiving a shot begins where? You guessed it, in the `PlacePieces` frame. It specifically involves the `moveReceived` function. We first talked of this function in the `PlacePieces` section because setting your board is actually your first move in this implementation. This time, we are going to use it to handle a shot. The code in question looks like this:

```
} else if(action == "Fire") {
        myTurn = true;
    panel.turn.text = "Your Turn";
    var x = obj.x;
    var y = obj.y;
    isoBoard.dropBomb(x, y)
```

The first thing this does is update the display to tell you it is now your turn. With that done, it pulls out the x and y grid coordinates of the shot and passes them along to the `dropBomb` method on the `isoBoard` movie clip. When `dropBomb` is first called, it executes the following code:

```
bombDepth++;
this.attachMovie("Bomb", "bomb" + bombDepth, bombDepth);
b = this["bomb" + bombDepth];
b.x = gridX * size;
b.y = -100;
b.z = - gridY * size;
b.rate = 1;
placeObject(b);
```

This code is actually quite simple; it creates a `Bomb` movie clip on the stage at the correct isometric location exactly 100 pixels above the grid. From there, the code adds a dynamic `onEnterFrame` event with this code:

```
b.onEnterFrame = function() {
    // Done falling
    if(this.y >= -10) {
        // See if it was a hit
        var ship = placementGrid[gridX][gridY];
        // If a hit
        if (ship != null) {
            var explosion = placeExplosion(b.x, b.z);
            ship.hits.push(explosion);

            // If the ship is maxed out
            if(ship.hits.length >= ship.cells) {
                ship.sunk = true;
                ship._alpha -= 50;
                for(i = 0; i < ship.hits.length; i++) {
                    ship.hits[i]._alpha -= 50;
                }
                _parent.sendMessage("You sank my " +
                → ship.name + "!");
                _parent.isGameOver();
            }
        } else {
            placeSplash(b.x, b.z);
        }
        this.unloadMovie();
    }
    this.y += this.rate;
    this.rate++;
    placeObject(this);
}
```

I've left some of the comments in to make the code easier to discuss. The majority of it is designed to handle when the bomb actually hits the bottom. After the large `if` statement, you will notice the following code:

```
this.y += this.rate;
this.rate++;
placeObject(this);
```

This code is the reason the bomb speeds up as it falls. The rate variable is increased by one every frame. Once the bomb gets with 10 pixels of the grid, it starts executing the large `if` statement. Within that statement, we first try to get whatever variable exists at the current grid square in our placement grid. You'll recall from the PlacePieces section that a grid square in the placementGrid contains a reference to a ship or it is null. If it is null, we need only place the splash and be done with it. If it is not null, we place an explosion on that spot.

Once we have the explosion created, we add the explosion to the hits array on the ship. We then check to see if the length of the hits array is as large as the ship is. If it is, we know this ship is sunk and we flag the ship as sunk, fade it down a bit, and fade down all of its flames by looping over the hits array. At this point, we send a message to the other player informing him of the ship that was sunk.

The last piece of code in this function is a call to isGameOver, which leads us right into our next section.

Winning

With all of these convoluted functions, you'd think winning would be more complicated than it really is. The entire function is outlined here:

```
function isGameOver() {
    var over = true;
    for(var i = 1; i<=5; ++i) {
        var ship = isoBoard["ship"+i];
        if(!ship.sunk) {
            over = false;
        }
    }

    if(over) {
        sendMessage("You jerk! You won!");

        var obj = new Object();
        obj.action = "YouWin";
        sendMove(obj);

        var curScore = parseInt(panel.theirScore.text);
        panel.theirScore.text = curScore + 1;

        playAgainMessage = "You Lost!";
        gotoAndPlay("PlayAgain");
    }
}
```

This function starts out by looping over all the ships to see if any are not flagged as sunk. If they are all flagged, we send a message to our opponent congratulating them. It looks like this:

```
sendMessage("You jerk! You won!");
```

This is probably more complimentary than the messages users will send after they realize they have lost. After this message, we build an object that has an action of `"YouWin"`. When we send this object to our opponent; his `moveReceived` code will execute the following:

```
} else if(action == "YouWin") {
    var curScore = parseInt(panel.myScore.text);
    panel.myScore.text = curScore + 1;

    playAgainMessage = "You Won!";
    gotoAndPlay("PlayAgain");
}
```

This code just updates the scores in the panel and sends you to the `PlayAgain` frame. From there you have the option of starting all over again if you want.

Conclusion

By now, you should have a firm understanding of the code used to build your own multiplayer game in Flash using the ElectroServer and its related objects. You can see how much work it really is and I bet you can also see why there are not a great deal more multiplayer games in Flash.

While it is a lot of work, I think the tradeoffs are worth the extra effort. The game is so much richer for being multiplayer as to make it almost an entirely new experience. Without playing other people you would get tired of the AI very quickly and the game would get stale. With multiplayer, you are assured a long life for your game and people will keep coming back to try their hand against others.

This game is only a rudimentary version. There are many features you can use to extend it and make it an even better game: different weapons, different play modes, more music and sound effects, more control over the game play, and so on.

Finally, I want to mention that if you don't actually enjoy making the game or at least find it interesting, it's likely that other people won't enjoy playing your game, either, so whatever else you do, have fun!

6: Instant Messenger

by Michael Grundvig

Just a few years ago your telephone may have been tied up for hours up by a sister chatting with her friends. Today, if you have a computer in the house, chances are that your sister is instant messaging. Instead of making separate phone calls, she can communicate with all her friends at the same time. She can chat with people who share the same interests, without ever actually meeting them. Instant messaging is a phenomenon and it's not going to dissipate anytime soon. It's incredibly popular—so much so, Apple is even making iChat part of its OSX operating system! Instant messengers are so well liked because they are incredibly easy to use. If you can type, you can participate. You can communicate with anyone around the world.

When we sat down to decide on which applications to create for this book, an instant messenger was one of the first on the list. Flash MX makes building such an application far easier than it was in Flash 5 because of additional ActionScript and data-aware components. You could easily integrate a Flash Instant Messenger into your Web site, allowing others to interact there in real time. You can communicate immediately with visitors without needing to use email at all. You can brand and extend your messenger any way you want to—much different than using someone else's application with its set user interface and its own branding. And you can't integrate other messengers into your own site or application—they are standalone applications.

Our Flash Messenger

This messenger uses Java and XML in its implementation. You'll see that come together later. We put together a simple instant messenger with some of the basic features you find in traditional messaging applications:

- Account creation
- Group management
- Ability to add/remove friends
- Friend listing
- Activity status icons
- Messaging

To speed development, our example messenger uses HTML pop-up windows for specific pieces of the user interface (individual chat windows, dialog boxes, and so on). On your own, however, you could integrate all the pieces into a single Flash application by using `LoadMovie()` or `LoadMovieNum()`. That's up to you. The system is extremely extensible—allowing you to manipulate it easily for your own uses. We've included two new skinned components for you as well: a blue scrollbar and a blue pushbutton. You can find these in the FLA for this application.

A Quick Overview of the IM

When you launch the instant messenger, you are presented with a welcome screen, which includes three buttons: Login, New User, and Help.

Login

Clicking the Login button produces a JavaScript pop-up window with input fields for username and password. In the main window, a connection is made through the new `localConnection` function. When you click the Login button in the login pop-up window, it calls the method `localConnection.send()` to call the login function in the main window. It supplies the window with the username and password. If there is an error during the login process, the main window opens the login window again, and using `localConnection.send()`, calls a function to set an error message in a text field below the Login button.

New User

Clicking the New User button at the welcome screen produces a JavaScript pop-up window, with a new user interface. No `localConnection` is needed here, because the pop-up window is independent.

Help Button

The Help button walks you through a quick tutorial showing you how to get up to speed quickly by using the Next and Previous buttons.

Now let's move on to more of the interesting aspects of the instant messenger.

After Login

After you have logged in, you are presented with a main interface. The heart of the main interface is the contact list, which uses a separate class called `ContactList`. You can drag all contacts in the contact list into different groups. You can also expand and contract the groups for ease of use. When you find a contact with whom you want to chat, click on his name and a chat window opens. Like the login window, this uses `localConnection`; however it's a little more complicated with the chat windows because most likely more than one chat window is open (each with a separate contact). To allow for this, each window is assigned a special ID, which it uses to communicate with the main window. When a new chat window is opened, it calls a function in the main window communicating that it is connected. The main window then sends the unique ID, which is used for future communications.

Updates

Updates are requested from the server at regular intervals. There are two different updates that the server may send. The first is `ChangeState`, which is sent when a contact in your contact list changes its state. The other is `SendMessage`, which is sent when a message is sent to you. When a `sendMessage` update is received, if the contact who sent the message has a chat window open, then the contact moves to the top of the contact list and displays a flashing message symbol. When you click on the contact, the flashing message symbol disappears, and a chat window with the message from that contact opens.

Getting Started

The instant messenger is a big application. There is a lot of code involved in it. There's too much for us to cover it in any detail in this chapter, so let's go through the most important pieces. We'll start with the concepts the application uses and then progress to the code itself.

To the Server and Back Again

The IM is primarily a client-server application just like many of the other applications in this book. You first connect to the server and log in. From there, you send messages back and forth talking with the server. As previously mentioned, the two possible messages are `ChangeState` and `SendMessage`.

There are several possible ways for a Flash MX application to talk with a server. Chapter 5, "Multiplayer Game," covers these in detail. For this application we'll use the concept of polling. Briefly, polling involves the client asking the server every so often if there is anything new for it. The server always replies either yes or no. If there is data for the client, in the form of `ChangeState` or `SendMessage`, the server sends that along with the response. The client repeats this process for as long as it is connected. The client initiates the process by logging into the server so that the server knows it needs to start listening to this specific client as well as all the others that could connect.

With so many methods for building an IM available to Flash MX, someone will invariably ask, "Why polling?" Quite simply, polling is based on HTTP, and HTTP is not usually blocked by firewalls. Most of the other possible solutions are usually socket based and therefore stand a good chance of being blocked by corporate firewalls.

Communicating with the Server

Before we get to the code, we need to look at what the client and the server can send back and forth to each other. For the rest of the chapter, we call these transactions.

There are a *lot* of transactions in this application. I mean it. Tons! There are transactions for every task that you can possibly accomplish. Transactions exist for creating a new group, editing a group name, adding a friend, moving a friend, logging on, logging off, and so forth. Because of the sheer volume of transactions, we'll discuss only a few of the larger ones.

A *transaction* is a single complete task that contains a request and a response. Both the server-side code and the client are built around this concept. Because the client and the server are written in different languages and reside in different locations, it's necessary to decide on a common format that both sides can use to communicate. XML is perfect for this.

As we've discussed in previous chapters, code reuse is a big part of this book. To accomplish this, we tried hard to standardize the data formats we're using everywhere, so the transaction XML documents' basic design will appear very familiar to you.

Login

The `Login` transaction is really quite simple. It is used to log a user into the system. As you can see, the transaction only contains a unique name to identify it and the username/password pair:

```
<Request>
    <TransactionType>Login</TransactionType>
        <Data>
        <Username>bob</Username>
            <Password>mypass</Password>
        </Data>
</Request>
```

The server responds to this request with one of two possible documents, `Success` or `Error`. If the request is successful, you get the following response:

```
<Response>
    <Status>Success</Status>
        <Data>
```

```
            <Message>The transaction completed successfully
            → </Message>
        </Data>
    </Response>
```

There are several possible errors that can be returned. Assuming, for example, the username doesn't exist, you would see:

```
<Response>
    <Status>Error</Status>
        <Data>
        <Message>Username is not found</Message>
        </Data>
</Response>
```

And if the password were incorrect, the following would be returned:

```
<Response>
    <Status>Error</Status>
        <Data>
        <Message>Invalid password</Message>
        </Data>
</Response>
```

CreateUser

The CreateUser transaction is used to register a new user in the system. The transaction request contains the username, password, and an email address for the new user:

```
<Request>
    <TransactionType>CreateUser</TransactionType>
        <Data>
        <Username>bob</Username>
            <Password>mypass</Password>
            <Email>bob@aol.com</Email>
        </Data>
</Request>
```

The server tries to create a user once it receives this request. As with all transactions, there are several possible responses: success, or one of the general errors —failing to access the database, a server error, and so on. The success response looks like this:

```
<Response>
    <Status>Success</Status>
        <Data>
        <Message>The transaction completed successfully
        → </Message>
    </Data>
</Response>
```

LoadContactList

Once a user has created an account and logged in, the first thing he needs to do is retrieve his contact list, using the LoadContactList transaction. (A new user's list returns empty, since no contacts have yet been created, but we keep the code simple by having every user call the list.) The server stores this information in the database and returns it upon request. The user sends the server a simple document that looks like this:

```
<Request>
    <TransactionType>LoadContactList</TransactionType>
        <Data />
</Request>
```

The server responds in kind with this document:

```
<Response>
    <Status>Success</Status>
        <Data>
        <Groups>
            <Group ID="19">
                <Name>Authors</Name>
                <Friends>
                    <Friend ID="12" State="online">
                        <Name>Sean</Name>
                    </Friend>
                    <Friend ID="34" State="offline">
                        <Name>Mike</Name>
                    </Friend>
                </Friends>
            </Group>
            <Group ID="134">
                <Name>Budies</Name>
                <Friends>
                    <Friend ID="234" State="online">
```

```
                        <Name>Scott</Name>
                    </Friend>
                </Friends>
            </Group>
        </Groups>
    </Data>
</Response>
```

This document has a lot of content in it. Specifically, it contains all the groups in the user's contact list, and specifies all the users in each group. It's important to note that the IDs of both the groups and the users are passed because while people like seeing the names, the server-side code expects the database IDs to be used because they guarantee uniqueness.

SendMessage

Once the contact list loads, we can send messages to other users. To do that, you use the `SendMessage` transaction, specifying the `friendID` of the person to whom you want to send the message and then specifying the message itself. The `friendID` is actually the `userID` on the users table of the database. Remember that you received the IDs of all your friends when you executed the `LoadContactList` transaction. This is important because when you receive a message, it includes the sender's friendID. The sendMessage XML looks like this:

```
<Request>
    <TransactionType>SendMessage</TransactionType>
        <Data>
        <FriendID>1</FriendID>
            <Message>Yo</Message>
        </Data>
</Request>
```

Upon receiving this request, the server responds with the standard all-clear message:

```
<Response>
    <Status>Success</Status>
        <Data>
        <Message>The transaction completed successfully
        → </Message>
    </Data>
</Response>
```

GetUpdates

Thus far, we've covered how the client tells the server what to do, but we haven't discussed how the server actually tells the client whether there is a message waiting for it, or if a friend has changed status, and so forth. This is the key to the entire instant messenger application. Here's the trick: the server *can't* tell the client that there is a message waiting. Because the IM is built around polling, the client has to request this information from the server, hence the `GetUpdates` transaction. The client sends this deceptively simple XML document as the request:

```
<Request>
    <TransactionType>GetUpdates</TransactionType>
        <Data />
</Request>
```

And the server responds with an XML document that can contain multiple updates. The basic document looks like this:

```
<Response>
    <Status>Success</Status>
        <Data>
        <Updates></Updates>
    </Data>
</Response>
```

This response is a bit special in that it contains multiple parts that can exist in any order. This is necessary because a single update can contain messages from other users and status changes all in one.

There are two different types of updates available. The first is `ChangeState`, which is used to signify if a friend just came online or went offline. It looks like this:

```
<Update>
    <Type>ChangeState</Type>
        <Data>
        <FriendID>10</FriendID>
            <NewState>Offline</NewState>
    </Data>
</Update>
```

The other update is SendMessage. This state is used when someone else has sent a message to you. It looks like this:

```
<Update>
    <Type>SendMessage</Type>
        <Data>
        <FriendID>10</FriendID>
            <Message>hi!</Message>
    </Data>
</Update>
```

Now the GetUpdates response can have multiple updates at one time inside of it. Here is an example that contains the two we showed previously:

```
<Response>
    <Status>Success</Status>
        <Data>
        <Updates>
            <Update>
            <Type>ChangeState</Type>
                <Data>
                <FriendID>10</FriendID>
                    <NewState>Offline</NewState>
             </Data>
            </Update>
            <Update>
            <Type>SendMessage</Type>
                <Data>
                <FriendID>10</FriendID>
                    <Message>hi!</Message>
            </Data>
            </Update>
        </Updates>
    </Data>
</Response>
```

Into the Code!

Let's take a look at how the client actually connects to the server. Copy the Chapters/chapter_6 folder from the CD-ROM to your workspace. Open `mainWindowWelcome.fla` (**Figure 6.1**) in Flash MX and let's dig in!

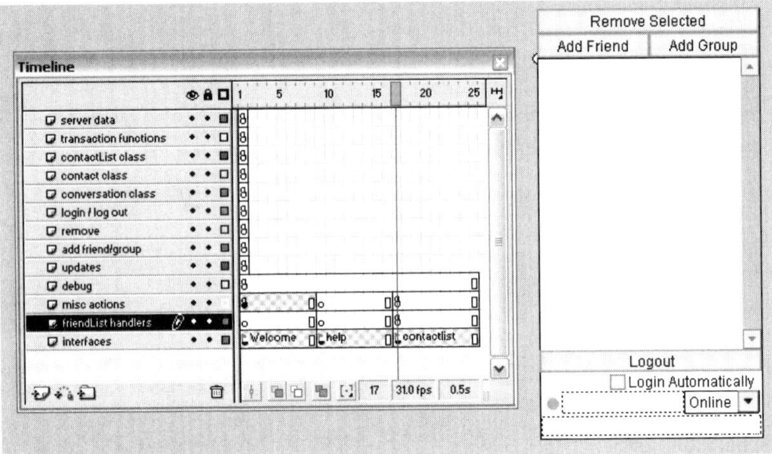

Figure 6.1 *Names of layers indicate their content.*

You'll immediately notice no fewer than 13 layers dedicated to ActionScript. Instead of lumping all the scripts into one frame where applicable, we've broken out specific functionality into layers for easy viewing. The names of the layers should make it evident what type of scripting is contained within them.

Server Data

The layer that we are currently interested in is called "server data". It contains the code that actually handles the communication with the server. Just as we did in the other chapters, we're using the `ServerData.as` object to hide the specific implementation details from us. With that in mind, the first thing we need to do is include the appropriate file and then configure it properly. The code to do this looks like the following:

```
#include "ServerData.as"

_global.server = new ServerData();
```

```
server.setMethod(server.SEND_AND_LOAD);
server.setLanguage(server.JAVA);
server.setURL("http://123.123.123.123:8080/flash/tran");
```

All we do is set the parameters that the ServerData object needs. Specifically, we create a new instance of the object and place it within the global scope. We then tell it what method to use and what language it would be communicating to. Finally, we set the URL to the Transaction Controller on the server. Of course, you need to change this information to point to your own server to get this application to work.

The next thing you see in this layer is a function called sendToServer, which is used to handle actually sending data to the server from the client. This function just simplifies the process and allows us to avoid duplicating code. Here it is:

```
_global.sendToServer = function (theXML, callBack,
getUpdates) {

    debug.print(theXML);

    // if this isn't a getupdates request
    if (getUpdates) endUpdates();

    // set the document to send to server
    server.setDocOut(theXML);

    // set the xml to receive as the reply from server
    server.setDocIn(new XML());

    // get the callback arguments from the arguments
    server.callBackArgs = arguments.slice(2);

    // store the callback function
    server.callBack = callBack;

    // set the callback function
    server.onLoad = function (success) {

        debug.print(this.getDocIn());

        // check to see if there is an incoming doc
        if (success) {
```

continues on next page

```
// start updates
      startUpdates();

      // call the callback function
      this.callBack.apply(this, this.callBackArgs);

      } else {

      // call the server error function
      onServerDisconnect();

      }
   }

   // send the document
   server.execute();
}
```

Okay, now that may seem like a lot of code initially but it is pretty heavily commented. Let's walk through it to see what it does. This method does quite a bit for us in regard to working with the server. We initially call it, pass in the XML document we want to send and the function we want to call to handle the response from the server, and finally tell it whether this is an update request.

The very first line of the function passes the XML document to the `debug` object. (We've left this in so you can see how to debug various transactions.) The very next line is a tricky one—it determines whether `endUpdates()` should be called. The `endUpdates` function turns off the `setTimeout` call that executes the `requestUpdates()` function. Make sense? I didn't think so. As mentioned earlier, when the client polls the server, it uses the `getUpdates` transaction, which is scheduled to run automatically. Because this transaction also uses the `sendToServer()` function, it needs to identify itself to avoid conflicts. These conflicts can prove very difficult to track down. A good example would be when I send you a message via the client but `getUpdates` is called by `setTimeout` before I receive a response. This causes `sendServerData` to be called again and make it forget my previous message, and the response would be lost. Because of this, when any transaction other then `getUpdates` is called, the `endUpdates` method is called to suspend updates temporarily. After we receive a response from the server, we go ahead and call `startUpdates()` to get the updates scheduled again. This sticky issue is often referred to in other languages as a concurrency issue.

The next couple of lines prep the ServerData object with the data it will use. As we have seen in other chapters, the ServerData object supports the concept of a callback, a function that is called once the server has responded to the data from the client. In the case of this application, the callback might also need parameters sent to it. The next two lines set that up for use later.

At this point, we go ahead and create a new function that is assigned to the onLoad event of the ServerData object. This function works just like any other object that supports onLoad. First, we make another debug call so you can easily trace the data being returned. We then have an if statement that handles whether there was a low-level error while communicating with the server. If there's an error, we call the onServerDisconnect() function. If no error occurs, we turn on startUpdates() again and then execute the callback that we set up earlier in the method. As you can see, this makes for a generic function that all transactions can use.

The onServerDisconnect function basically shuts down the interface and sends a message about the error to the user. Let's take a look at the onServerDisconnect() code, and then go through it in detail:

```
onServerDisconnect = function () {
    var logOutXml = buildLogOutTransaction();

    // send xml
    server.setDocOut(logOutXml);
    server.setDocIn(new XML());
    server.onLoad = null;
    server.execute();

    // end updates
    endUpdates();

    // open the error window
    openBrowserWindow("connectionError.html",
    → "connectionError", 147, 91);

    // show the error
    doMessage("Server Error");

    // logout
    // clear the contact list
    friendsList.removeAll();
```

continues on next page

```
// clear the message
    doMessage("");

    // disable the buttons
    addFriendButton.setEnabled(false);
    addGroupButton.setEnabled(false);
    removeSelectedButton.setEnabled(false);

    // change the logout button
    login.setLabel("Login");
    login.setClickHandler("loginHandler", _root);
}
```

As you can see, that's a reasonably straightforward method. The first few lines of this method simply tell the server that this client is logging out. It's important to note that we do *not* use the `sendToServer()` function. We send the `Logout` transaction directly because if there's a critical failure with the server (such as its going offline or becoming unresponsive), the `sendToServer()` function calls the `onServerDisconnect()` function again and we're stuck in an infinite loop. In short, we send the `Logout` transaction directly so we don't need to care if it's received properly or not. After that, we shut down the update process by calling `endUpdates()`. At this point, we pop up a new window so the user can see the error that occurred. The rest of this function is used to turn off all the current buttons and switch the Logout button back to a Login button.

Transaction Functions

We've talked about some of the most important transactions from a data standpoint, as well as how that data is sent to the server. Now it's time to cover those transactions from a code standpoint.

All of the transactions are on the Transaction Functions layer, which really serves as the brain for the whole application. We'll discuss the same transactions here that we covered earlier in the chapter. Remember, there are actually many more transactions involved in the application. Fortunately, they all follow the same basic structure so you should have no trouble figuring them out after going through this.

We start this layer off by including the `commonTransactionFunctions.as` file. You probably remember seeing this file in other projects. We've used it everywhere because it encapsulates the basic XML structure in several convenient helper methods. Here's how to include it:

```
#include "commonTransactionFunctions.as"
```

That file includes several functions that simplify making a request XML document. We won't go into it in detail here because it's quite straightforward.

Login

The Login transaction simply passes the username and password to the server. It builds a new basic request, adds both the username and password, and returns the XML document back to the caller:

```
_global.buildLoginTransaction = function (username,
→ password) {
    // Build a basic login transaction
    var createLoginRequest = new buildBaseRequest("Login");
    // add the username data to the xml doc
    createLoginRequest.addData("Username", username);
    // add the password data to the xml doc
    createLoginRequest.addData("Password", password);
    // return the finished XML document
    return createLoginRequest.getDoc();
}
```

CreateUser

CreateUser is another simple transaction. We need to only build the basic request and then add in a username, password, and an email address. Once that's done, the XML document is returned to the caller. The code to actually build this transaction is shown here:

```
buildCreateUserTransaction = function (username, password,
email) {
    // create create user transaction
    var createCreateUserRequest = new buildBaseRequest
    → ("CreateUser");
    // add the username to the xml doc
    createCreateUserRequest.addData("Username", username);
    // add the password to the xml doc
    createCreateUserRequest.addData("Password", password);
    // add the email to the xmld oc
    createCreateUserRequest.addData("Email", email);
    // return xml doc
    return createCreateUserRequest.getDoc();
}
```

SendMessage

SendMessage isn't much different from the other transactions. The biggest thing to notice is that we use the friendID, which equates into a userID on the database. Here's the code to create the sendMessage transaction:

```
    buildSendMessageTransaction = function (friendID,
    → message) {
    // create the message transaction
    var createSendMessageRequest = new buildBaseRequest
    → ("SendMessage");
    // add the friendID to the xml doc
    createSendMessageRequest.addData("FriendID", friendID);
    // add the message to the xml doc
    createSendMessageRequest.addData("Message", message);
    // return the xml doc
    return createSendMessageRequest.getDoc();
}
```

GetUpdates

GetUpdates, getting updates from the server, is the simplest of all transactions because it requires no data to be sent other then the name of the transaction itself:

```
buildGetUpdatesTransaction = function () {
    // create the getUpdates transaction
    var createGetUpdatesRequest = buildBaseRequest
    → ("GetUpdates");
    // return xml doc
    return createGetUpdatesRequest;
}
```

LoadContactList

LoadContactList is also a simple transaction. We need only set the transaction name and be done with it:

```
buildLoadContactListTransaction = function () {
    // create the getUpdates transaction
    var createLoadContactListRequest = buildBaseRequest
    → ("LoadContactList");
    // return xml doc
    return createLoadContactListRequest;
}
```

Contact List, Contacts, and Conversations

We've talked a bit about how we send the data to the server and the data itself, so now let's look at how we handle the responses from the server. This process involves using several objects—including `ContactList`, `Contact`, and `Conversation` objects—that all map nicely to the concepts involved.

Let's start with the contact list. The process of actually parsing the contact list takes place in the `parseContactList` function on the "transaction functions" layer. This function does the messy job of parsing the XML and passing the data into the `ContactList` object. It's rather long, so we've ensured that it's heavily documented for you to follow. We'll talk more about this function following the code:

```
parseContactList = function (contactList, friendsArray,
→ xmlDoc) {
    // check to see if the contact list is succesful
    var success = wasSuccessful(xml);
    // if its not, end
    if (!success) return false;
    // get the data node
    var dataNode = _root.findDataNode(xmlDoc);
    // get the groups
    var groups = dataNode.firstChild.childNodes;
    // loop through groups
    for (var i = 0; i < groups.length; i++) {
        // get the name of the group
        var groupName = groups[i].firstChild.firstChild;
        // get the group id
        var groupID = groups[i].attributes.id;
        // add the group id to the groupID object
        groupIDs[groupName] = groupID;
        // add the group to the contact list
        contactList.addGroup(groupName);
        // get the friends in the group
        var friends = groups[i].childNodes[1].childNodes;
        // loop through friends in group
        for (var j = 0; j < friends.length; j++) {
        // get friend id
```

continues on next page

```
            var friendID = friends[j].attributes.ID;
            // get friend name
            var friendName = friends[j].firstChild.firstChild;
            // get the state of the friend
            var friendState = friends[j].attributes.State;
            // make a new contact object
            friendsArray.push(new contact(friendName, friendID,
            → friendState));
            // set up the onMessageReceived handler
            friendsArray[friendsArray.length - 1].onMessageReceived
            → = function (contact) {
                friendsList.moveContactToTop(contact.group,
                → contact);
                 friendsList.update();
            }
            // add the contact to the group
            contactList.addContact(groupName, friendsArray
            → [friendsArray.length - 1]);
            }

        }
        // return true to indicate success
        return true;
    }
```

parseContactList begins by taking a reference to contactList, an array of all the friends in the system, and the XML document to use. If the XML document contains an error for the server, we immediately return false out of it so the interface can handle it properly.

The first real piece of work in this function comes when we start looking over all the groups listed in the XML document. You'll recall from our earlier discussion that all friends are listed in groups and the contact list is made up of groups. The code pulls all the group information out of the XML document and adds it to the ContactList class via the addGroup method. We'll talk about the ContactList class in more detail later.

The next step is to loop over all the friends within a given group. Just as with groups, we get the ID and the name, but we also get the state of the friend from the XML. We take this data and create a new Contact object, and then add the new contact to the friendsArray that was passed into the function. Next we add our own event handler called onMessageReceived to the current contact object. The handler is called when a message from this contact is received. The handler is really quite simple—it just moves the contact to the top of the groups' list of friends and tells the list to update itself. After the handler code comes one line that just calls the addContact method on the ContactList object to ensure the contact list has a reference to this contact.

Now that we have talked about how the data from the XML document is read into the various objects, let's look at the objects themselves, starting with the ContactList class.

ContactList

ContactList is a big class. With all comments and code, the class weighs in at almost 600 lines. Of those 600 lines, more then 250 of them belong to the update() method, which actually creates the movie clips on the screen. Because of its size and the fact that it is so heavily commented, we won't cover it in detail here. Instead, we'll discuss the major methods and how they are used.

addGroup

The addGroup method is used to add a new group to the contact list. Here's the code:

```
contactList.prototype.addGroup = function (groupName) {
    // add the group to the group array
    this.groups.push({name: groupName, contacts: [], open:
    → false});
    // update
    this.update();
    // call the onChange event
    this.onChange();
    // call the onAddGroup event
    this.onAddGroup(groupName);
}
```

This method is quite short and takes only the group name as a string for its arguments list. The first thing addGroup does is create a new object and push it onto the groups array.

It's important to note that there is no separate group object. To keep things simple, we simply use the shorthand syntax that Flash MX provides to create a new object with several variables on it:

name—Just the group name

contacts—An array of all the Contact objects within the group

open—A Boolean indicating whether the group has been expanded in the GUI

Once we have added the group to the array, we call update. This ensures the contact list gets redrawn to represent the changes. Finally we call the onAddGroup event handler.

addContact

The addContact method is used to add a contact to a group and update the contact list display with the new information. The code is shown here:

```
contactList.prototype.addContact = function (group, contact,
→ moving) {
    // store the group in the contact
    contact.group = group;
    // check to see if a group was supplied, if not add
        // to the first group
    if (group == null) {
        groupName = this.groups[0].name;
    } else {
        groupName = group;
    }
    // find group in array
    for (var i in this.groups) {
        // check for group
        if (this.groups[i].name == groupName) {
        // add contacts to group
        this.groups[i].contacts.push(contact);
        // break from loop
        break;
        }
    }
    // call the onChange event
    this.onChange();
    // call the onAddContact event if the contact is not
    → being moved
```

```
        if (!moving) this.onAddContact(group, contact);
    }
```

This method takes a group, a contact object, and a Boolean (the moving variable is of type boolean) that says whether the contact is being moved in the group. We first create a shorthand reference to the group array, and then we get the group name. If the group variable passed in is null, we are adding the contact to the first group—this occurs when you first add a friend to your contact list.

Once we have the group name, we start looping over all the groups, checking to see whether we have the right one. Once the correct one is found, we add the contact to the contacts array inside that group and break from the loop.

At this point, we call the onChange event on our ContactList object. Finally, we check to see if the contact was just moving within the group. If it was, we call onAddContact and pass in the group and the contact.

Opening or Closing a Group

The GUI interface for the IM supports the ability to open or close a group dynamically. As you saw earlier, the group objects all contain a variable called open.

There are several methods that can be used to expand or collapse a group. Depending on the situation, any of them can be used. They all work on the same principle, so we'll cover the most complicated one here:

```
contactList.prototype.toggleExpandCollapse = function
→ (group) {
    // loop through groups to check for group
    for (var i = 0; i < this.groups.length; i++) {
        // check for group
        if (this.groups[i].name == group) {
        // check to see if group is open
        if (this.groups[i].open) {
            // set open to false
            this.groups[i].open = false;
        } else {
            // set open to true
            this.groups[i].open = true;
        }
```

continues on next page

```
            // break from loop
            break;
            }
        }
        // update groups and contacts
        this.update();
        this.onChange();
    }
```

The toggleExpandCollapse method takes a group name as a parameter. The first thing it does is walk through all groups in the array until if finds the one that matches the group name that was passed in. Once it has the match, it checks to see if the group is currently open (`open = true`) or closed (`open = false`). If the group is open, the method closes it; if it's closed, the method opens it; and then the method breaks from the loop.

The final step in this process is to call `update()` and `onChange()`. This method works because the call to `update()` causes the GUI to be redrawn. The `update()` method walks through the groups again and draws them appropriately based on the value of their `open` variable.

There are two other methods that can be used to achieve this result: `expandGroup()` and `collapseGroup()`. If you know the groups' open or closed state already, you can call these instead and get the same result.

update

`update` is the largest single method in the entire application. It's relatively easy to follow, though, with the extensive in-code documentation in the FLA file. We've left out the comments here in the chapter just to keep the code brief. We'll cover the highlights following the code.

The `update` method draws the contact list onto the screen. We make this a lot more elegant by using some of the new Flash MX features.

This method starts out by looping over all the groups in it and running this code against them:

```
var target = this.container.createEmptyMovieClip("group_" +
→ this.groups[i].name, ++num);

target.createTextField("groupName", 1, 12, 0, 110, 20);
target.groupName.selectable = false;
target.groupName.embedFonts = true;
```

```
var groupFormatting = new TextFormat();
groupFormatting.color = 0xff0000;
groupFormatting.font = "Arial";

target.groupName.text = this.groups[i].name;
target.groupName.setTextFormat(groupFormatting);

target.attachMovie("openStatus", "openStatus", 2);
target.openStatus._y = 5;

if (this.groups[i].open) {
    target.openStatus.gotoAndStop(1);
} else {
    target.openStatus.gotoAndStop(2);
}

target._y = Math.round(target._height * num);

target.thisRef = this;
target.group = this.groups[i].name;
```

As you can see, we start by creating a new movie clip and assigning it to a variable called `target`. We add a text field called `groupName`.to the new movie clip, and then we create a `TextFormat` object and apply it to the text field.

Next, we attach a movie clip to the current group to illustrate whether it's expanded. We do this by advancing the newly added clip to the right frame.

The last step is to position the target clip in the contact list and give it access to some of the contact list's values.

The next bit of code adds an `onRelase` handler to the group so that we can expand or contract the group when it is clicked.

```
target.onRelease = function () {
    this.thisRef.toggleExpandCollapse(this.group);
    this.thisRef.selected = this.group;
    this.thisRef.update();
}
```

This function just calls `toggleExpandCollapse` and passes in the current group. Notice that `thisRef` is a reference to the `ContactList` object. Finally, the `update` method on the contact list is called to show the new group state.

The following bit of code is used to set the background color of the groupName text field:

```
if (this.selected == this.groups[i].name) {
    var tempFormat = new TextFormat();
    tempFormat.color = 0xFF9900;
    target.groupName.setTextFormat(tempFormat);
}
```

The next bit of code in this method starts off like this:

```
if (this.groups[i].open) {
for (var j = 0; j<this.groups[i].contacts.length; j++) {
```

This code just checks to see whether the group is currently open and if so, it starts iterating over all the contacts within the group. This is necessary because we need to show the contacts only in an open group.

The following block of code creates the contact graphically. It looks very similar to the previous group code because it does a similar task.

```
target = this.container.createEmptyMovieClip("group_" +
→ this.groups[i].name + "_" + this.groups[i].contacts[j].name,
→ ++num);

target.createTextField("contactName", 1, 12, 0, 110, 20);
target.contactName.selectable = false;
target.contactName.embedFonts = true;

contactFormatting = new TextFormat();
contactFormatting.font = "Arial";
target.contactName.text = this.groups[i].contacts[j].name;
target.contactName.setTextFormat(contactFormatting);

target.attachMovie("status", "status", 2);
target.status._y = 5;
target.status.gotoAndStop(this.groups[i].contacts[j].
→ contactStatus);

target._y = Math.round(target._height * num);
target._x = 15;

target.thisRef = this;
target.contactRef = this.groups[i].contacts[j];
target.groupRef = this.groups[i];
```

This code creates a new movie clip and then creates a new text field within it. This text field has a new TextFormat added to it almost immediately. We then attach a status movie clip to the original clip. status shows whether the person is online. The final steps are to position the clip on the screen properly and add some references to it so it can find the objects it will need later.

This next little bit of code is similar to the group selection code. This determines if a contact has been selected and changes the background of the text field if it has:

```
if (this.selected == this.groups[i].contacts[j]) {
    var tempFormat = new TextFormat();
    tempFormat.color = 0xFF9900;
    target.contactName.setTextFormat(tempFormat);
}
```

There are still two event handlers—onPress and onRelease—on a given contact that we haven't discussed. They follow the same basic model that all other code in this method uses, so we won't go over their code specifically.

The onPress event is called when you click on a contact. It is used to handle actually dragging contacts from group to group. Look in the code and you see that it creates an onEnterFrame event that is used to check whether the contact is dragged over any specific group and then highlights the group accordingly.

The onRelease event is called when you actually drop the contact somewhere. This method removes the onEnterFrame event that was set up in the onPress event. It also handles moving the contact to the new group if necessary.

Whew! That's it for the update method. The ContactList object constitutes much of the code in the instant messenger. There are just a couple more objects left to cover and we'll be finished!

Contact Class

The Contact class is primarily a class for storing data. It has only one method that does real work. You can find the code for this class on the Contact Class layer.

The class itself just manages the user's name, ID, and status. The guts of the Contact class exist in the messageReceived method:

```
contact.prototype.messageReceived = function (message) {
    // check to see if the contact has a conversation
    if (this.conversation != null) {
        // forward message to conversation
        this.conversation.messageReceived(message)
    } else{
        // set status
        this.setStatus("message");
        // store message
        this.message = message;
    }
    this.onMessageReceived(this);
}
```

When a message is received from a user, this method is called. The basic idea is that if a message is received, it's part of a conversation and a given contact object tracks its own conversation. In our implementation of an IM, users can have only one-on-one conversations. This means that a single contact has only one conversation object ever referenced inside of it. If that conversation reference is null, then we go ahead and set the status of the contact to `"message"`. This means that the contact list will show a blinking icon for the contact to signify that you have a message waiting. If the contact object already has a conversation registered with it, it forwards the message onto the `messageReceived()` method of the `conversation` object, which we'll get to next.

Conversation Class

The actual process of handing a conversation takes place in the `Conversation` object. This object acts as an interface between the contact list window and a specific conversation window. Internally, creating a `conversation` class automatically spawns a new window for that conversation.

The `Conversation` class contains a queue of messages from a given contact. This is necessary for two reasons: you can receive multiple messages before you start a conversation and you wouldn't want to lose any, and you can close the conversation window at any time and therefore might not have received the new messages in a conversation.

One of the most important methods inside a single `conversation` object is `messageReceived()`. A `contact` object calls this method when that contact receives a message. Here's the code for this:

```
conversation.prototype.messageReceived = function (message)
{
    if (this.connected) {
        var contactName = String(this.contact.name);
        var contactID = String(this.contact.id);
        var contactStatus =
String(this.contact.contactStatus);

        this.connection.send(this.id + "main",
        → "messageReceived", {name: contactName, id:
        → contactID, contactStatus: contactStatus}, message);

        this.checkMessageId = setInterval(this,
        → "checkMessage", 100, message);

    } else {
        this.queue.push(message);
    }
}
```

The main `if` statement of this method is used to determine whether the object is currently connected. If the conversation is connected via `LocalConnection` to an open conversation window, then the `conversation` object pulls the data needed from the contact object and formats a message to be sent to a method on the open window via a reference to the `LocalConnection` object called `this.connection`. Finally we set a timer to call the `checkMessage` method in 100 milliseconds. That method looks like this:

```
this.checkMessage = function (message) {
    if (!this.connection.connected)
        this.onMessageFailure(this.contact, message);
    clearInterval(this.checkMessageId);
}
```

This is necessary to ensure that the open conversation window received the message. If the `checkMessage` finds an error or is unable to confirm what happened, it calls the `onMessageFailure` event. The final statement in `checkMessage` just clears out the timer so that this method isn't run more then once.

Back in our original messageReceived method, we still have to talk about the other half of the main if statement:

```
this.queue.push(message);
```

That line adds the message into a queue array that ensures no messages are lost when the window isn't open. The next time the window opens; it gets all messages in the queue dumped into it.

The process of actually loading the messages into the window from the queue occurs here:

```
conversation.prototype.doQueue = function () {
    // loop through queue
    for (i = 0; i < this.queue.length; i++) {
        // receive the message
        this.messageReceived(this.queue[i]);
    }
}
```

This method simple calls the messageReceived method for all messages in the queue array.

Summary

An instant messenger is not a trivial application. In this chapter, we've walked through the major client-side pieces that are necessary to build one. We left out the server-side discussion entirely because it would have made the chapter needlessly more complicated. All the server-side code is fully documented and included on the CD-ROM. With an understanding in the appropriate language, you should have no trouble seeing how it was built.

With some experimenting and research, it would be possible to take this skeleton instant messenger to a whole new level. Who knows, you maybe wire it up to Flash Communication Server and add video chat, or use Flash Remoting for some new capabilities. Whatever you choose to do, we hope this sample application helps you!

7: Email Client Application

by Tim K. Chung

Almost everyone in the Internet community has or knows someone who has a Hotmail email address. Email programs like Hotmail and Yahoo offer users a way to send and retrieve messages online via a central location on the Internet. Hence, their popularity is obvious—people from all over the world can communicate with each other simply by logging into a central location.

This chapter explores the architecture and the means of creating a simple email management program using Flash MX, XML, Java, and Microsoft Access. The program handles email by using the person's pre-existing email account.

First, we'll look at a general overview of the application, and then we'll explore the data transactions and see how everything works. The last section of this chapter reviews Flash-specific programming concepts applicable to this application, including prototyping and local connections, and revisits the custom classes created for this application.

Although the technologies used here are specific to the discussion of Flash MX, you will walk away with an understanding of the architecture and be able to adapt other technologies such as ColdFusion, .NET, mySQL, or whatever you so choose to the same process.

Getting Started: Peachmail Joe

To get things started, let's look at the steps that a user goes through in working with a browser-based email management program like Hotmail. We'll call our application Peachmail. Meet Joe, who is a new user to our application.

Joe's Motivation

Summer break! Joe is going on vacation and must leave his computer at home. Realizing he may not have access to his email, he tries to find a solution. A friend tells him about Peachmail, a service that allows him to access his email simply by getting online and accessing Peachmail's Web site.

He decides to check it out.

Joe's Registration

Joe gets home, fires up his machine, and loads up Peachmail's Web site. First, Joe needs to create an account with Peachmail, entering in such details as his username, email address, password, POP server, and SMTP server. Joe selects mejoe to be the username that uniquely identifies him at Peachmail. Now that Joe has an account, he logs into Peachmail.

Joe's Vindication

Joe now has access to these Peachmail services:

- Address Book Services. Joe can add, edit, and remove contacts from his address book.
- Email Services. Joe can view, send, receive, organize, and delete email from his account.
- Account Services. Joe can modify his personal information or, heaven forbid, delete his account.

Joe adds a few friends to his address book and sends out an email letting his friends know he still has access to his email during his vacation:

```
Hey you crazy blokes! It's me Joe! I'm using Peachmail.com
to access my email. It's absolutely brilliant!

Cheers,
Joe
```

Joe then logs out of Peachmail and feeling special about himself, decides to go spend a week's pay on a coffee at Starbucks.

A Closer Look: What Joe Doesn't Know

Behind the scenes, Joe has actually touched three different interfaces of the Peachmail application:

- The front-end, or graphical user interface (GUI). This is what Joe sees when he loads up the Web site. It formats the display area, provides the visuals to Joe's interactions, and sends the commands that Joe triggers to the back-end. It can be anything from an HTML form on a Web page to a Flash program to a Java applet.
- The back-end, or server-side interface. It performs actions based on the front-end's feedback, manages the data that's sent between the front-end and the data storage, and is the "traffic-cop" between incoming and outgoing data. The back-end is typically created using server-side scripting languages, such as Perl, ASP, PHP, or ColdFusion, but can also be developed using more large-scale languages such as Java and C++.

- The data storage interface, such as a text file or a database. This is the data warehouse. The most common databases tend to be Oracle, or MSSQL Server for large-scale operations, and mySQL, postgreSQL, or Microsoft Access for smaller operations.

For our email client application, we'll use Flash MX for the front-end, Java for the back-end, and Microsoft Access for the database. The data being sent and received between the front-end and back-end will be in XML format to accommodate Flash MX's XML data handling routines, as you'll see later. Now let's take a look at what we want our application to do.

Bread and Butter

To quickly summarize the steps Joe went through at Peachmail: he created an account, logged into Peachmail, and sent an email. Using his actions as the base, we can quickly develop a blueprint (**Figure 7.1**) for what we want our application to do.

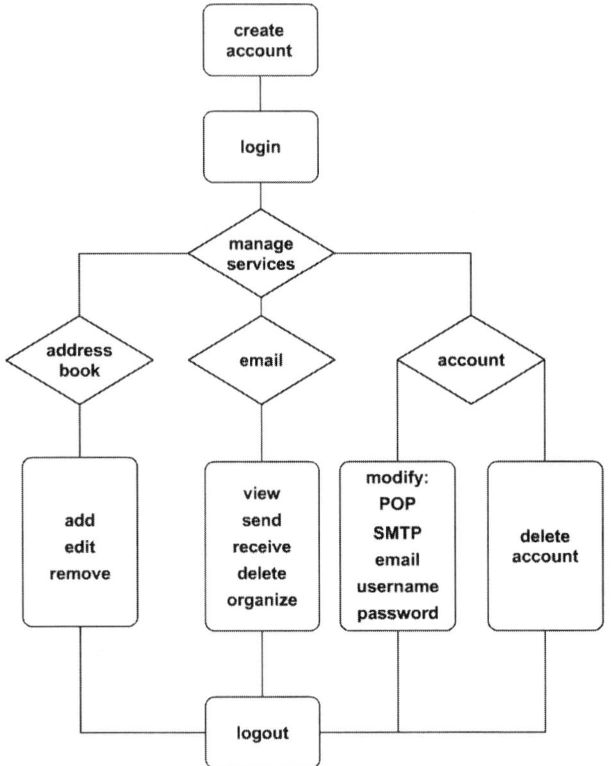

Figure 7.1
The blueprint for our email client application.

This is the ideal functionality for the application. Note that to keep things simple, the following limitations are applied:

- Peachmail does not include account management services, that is, account modification and account deletion.
- Peachmail's address book services do not include an edit function.
- Peachmail is limited to using only one folder to track email; there is no organization tool to allow creation of custom folders and moving messages around.
- Messages are only stored for incoming email.
- Attachments can only be received, not sent.

After we discuss creating the database, we'll look at login and registration, address book services, and email services. We leave it for you, as an exercise, to extend the functionality of Peachmail and include the missing pieces that make up the ideal model in the blueprint.

Now that we have a good idea of what we are going to create, we can focus on the data required for this application to work.

The Data Definition

The first item on the blueprint is creating the account. Because the application is for email management, Joe had to enter his email address, his SMTP server, and his POP server, in addition to the obligatory username and password. We'll lump all this information into a table called Users, and add a UserID number to uniquely identify each registered user. **Figure 7.2** shows the fields in the Users table.

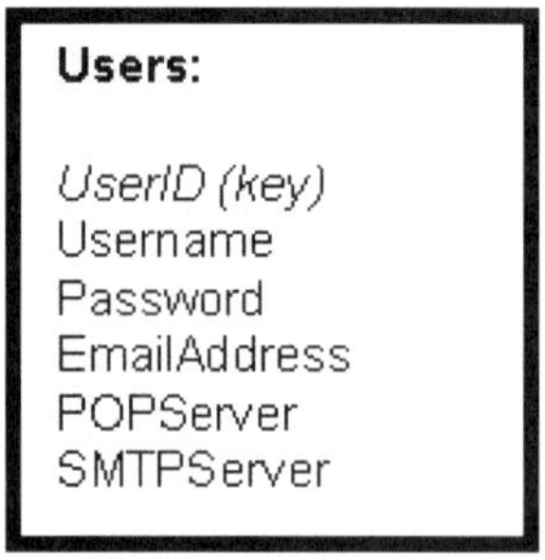

Users:

UserID (key)
Username
Password
EmailAddress
POPServer
SMTPServer

Figure 7.2
The Users table.

When Joe logs into Peachmail, the application checks against the Users table to ensure that Joe is a registered Peachmail user. If Joe makes any changes to his account, the changes are saved to this table.

Once Joe is logged in, he has access to his address book, which is simply a list of names and email addresses that Joe can use to send out email. We need to create a table called AddressBookEntries to store names and email addresses, and add AddressBookEntryID to uniquely number each entry. In addition, we add a UserID field to link to each user, such as Joe, so that we know to which user each address book entry belongs. **Figure 7.3** shows the fields for this table.

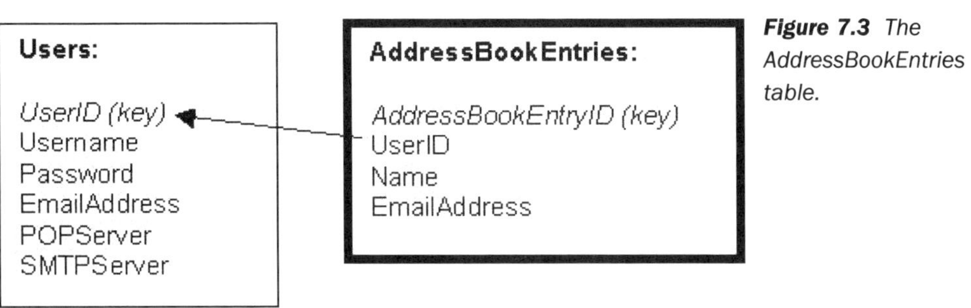

Figure 7.3 *The AddressBookEntries table.*

The core of Peachmail is the email service, which Joe uses to receive and send out email. For this, we need a table called Messages in which to store the email messages that are received. **Figure 7.4** shows the fields in this table.

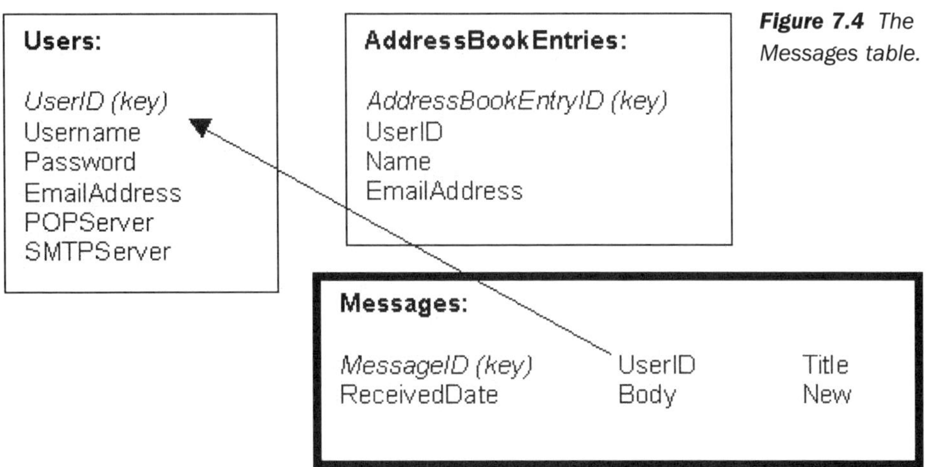

Figure 7.4 *The Messages table.*

Body stores the message, and ReceivedDate records the date when the message is received. Title contains the message subject, and New is used to flag which messages are unread. UserID links the message to a specific user, and MessageID is a number to uniquely identify each message.

To keep messages organized, we want to allow Joe to create folders to store his messages, so we have a simple table called Folders. **Figure 7.5** shows the fields for this table.

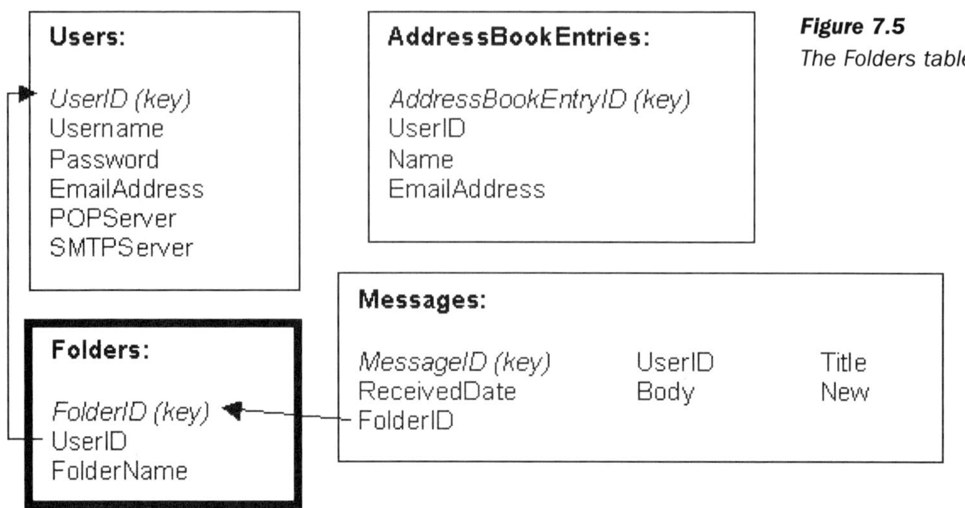

Figure 7.5 *The Folders table.*

Each folder links back to the user through the UserID, and its FolderID is used to link a folder to messages in the Messages table.

Lastly, we want to deal with attachments from email messages, so we have a table for Attachments, and **Figure 7.6** shows its fields.

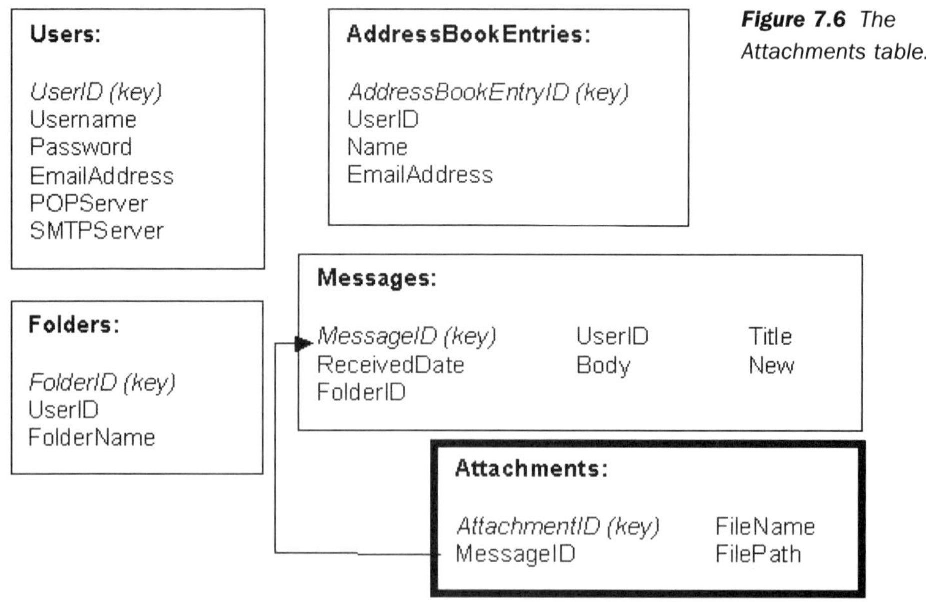

Figure 7.6 *The Attachments table.*

FileName and FilePath combine to identify where the file is stored on Peachmail's server. MessageID links back to a specific message in the Messages list, and AttachmentID is a number to uniquely identify each attachment.

Figure 7.7 shows the final picture, or entity relationship diagram (ERD).

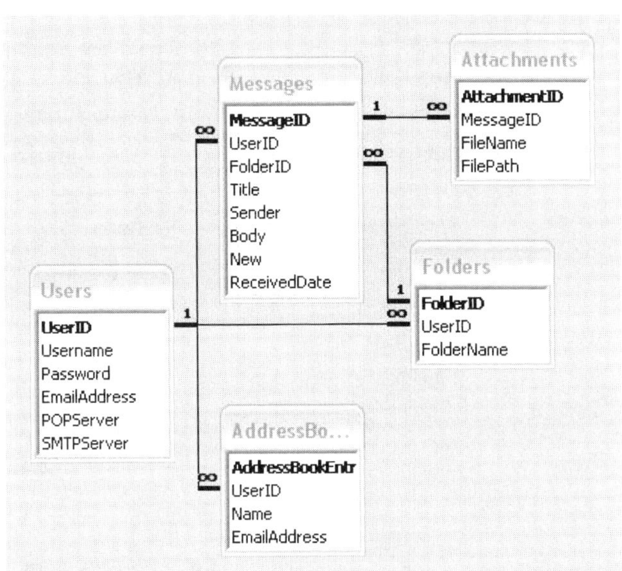

Figure 7.7 *The ERD for the Peachmail data definition.*

Table 7.1 shows the final data definition for Peachmail, including the type of data for each field.

Table 7.1 *Peachmail Data Definition*

TABLE NAME	FIELD NAME	FIELD DATATYPE
Users	UserID	AutoNumber
	Username	Text
	Password	Text
	EmailAddress	Text
	POPServer	Text
	SMTPServer	Text
AddressBookEntries	AddressBookEntryID	AutoNumber
	UserID	Number
	Name	Text
	EmailAddress	Text

continues on next page

Table 7.1 Peachmail Data Definition (continued)

TABLE NAME	FIELD NAME	FIELD DATATYPE
Messages	MessageID	AutoNumber
	UserID	Number
	FolderID	Number
	Title	Memo
	Body	Memo
	New	Yes/No
	ReceivedDate	Date/Time
Folders	FolderID	AutoNumber
	UserID	Number
	FolderName	Text
Attachments	AttachmentID	AutoNumber
	MessageID	Number
	FileName	Text
	FilePath	Text

The next logical step is to create the database using our data definition.

Building Peachmail: the Database

The procedure for creating a database varies from one database program to another, but the skills are basically the same. The more difficult part comes after the creation of the database and actually linking it up to a back-end. Let's quickly walk through creating the database using Microsoft Access, and then we'll have some comments on linking the server to the database.

Creating the Database

When Microsoft Access loads up, select File, New, and then choose to create a new database. When prompted to name the database (**Figure 7.8**), use `peachmail.mdb` for this Microsoft Access Database (`.mdb`) file, and then click Create.

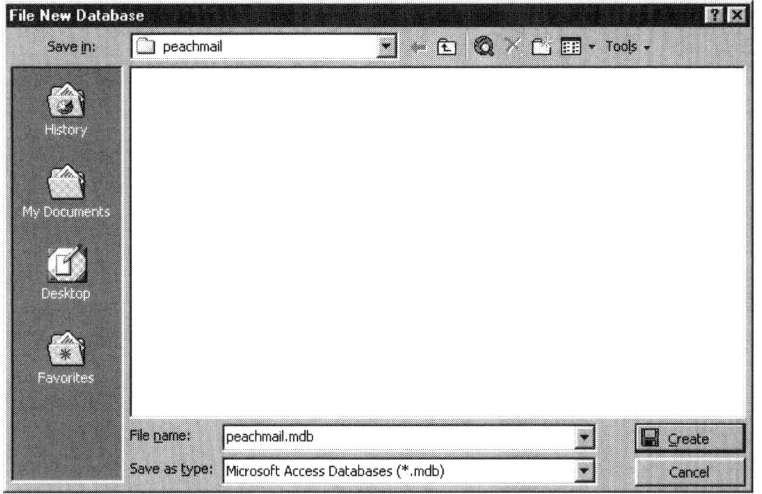

Figure 7.8 Create the Microsoft Access database file.

Create a table in Design view and you are presented with an empty form. Fill in the form for each of the tables listed in our database definition to create the tables. For example, **Figure 7.9** shows what the Messages table would look like.

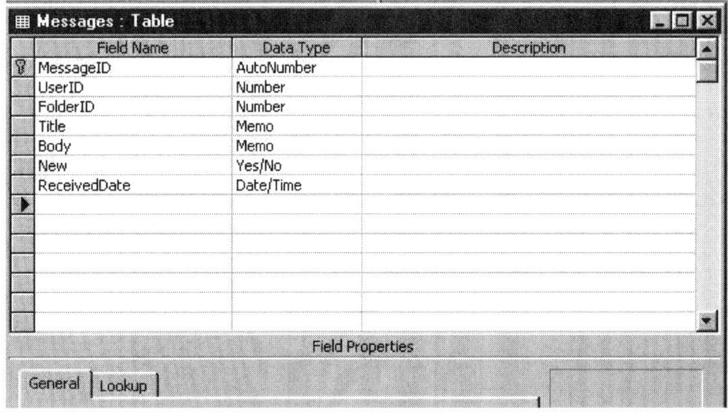

Figure 7.9 Creating the Messages table in Microsoft Access.

Once you've created all the tables, the Peachmail database is complete.

Linking to the Server

To set up the database for linking, use ODBC to create a mapping on the Web host. This mapping is an alias combining the location and filename of the database file on the Web host machine. The server would reference the mapping to link to the database. Because our discussion is focused on Flash, we won't go into too much detail on how to link up Java to the database, but note that a JDBC driver is required for the specific type of database your application will communicate with. For more information on JDBC, consult `http://java.sun.com/products/jdbc/`.

Building Peachmail: Registration and Login

Joe's first action when he arrives at Peachmail is to register for an account. He is presented with a screen to enter his username, password, email address, POPServer, and SMTPServer. Once he enters this information, Peachmail processes the information by sending this data to the server. After Peachmail confirms his account, Joe proceeds to log in. Let's first look at how Flash MX will generate the data to send to Java, and then explore how Flash handles the responses from Java.

The Front-End: Flash MX

Peachmail's first screen (**Figure 7.10**) contains two buttons: Login and New User.

Joe clicks on the New User button and is presented with the Create New User screen. He fills out his details and clicks Create, which triggers Flash to generate the following XML transaction data:

```
<Request>
    <TransactionType>
        CreateUser
    </TransactionType>
    <Data>
        <Username>
            myjoe
        </Username>
        <Password>
            myjoepassword
        </Password>
        <EmailAddress>
            joe@joes_email.com
```

```
            </EmailAddress>
            <POPServer>
                mail.joes_email.com
            </POPServer>
            <SMTPServer>
                smtp.joes_email.com
            </SMTPServer>
        </Data>
    </Request>
```

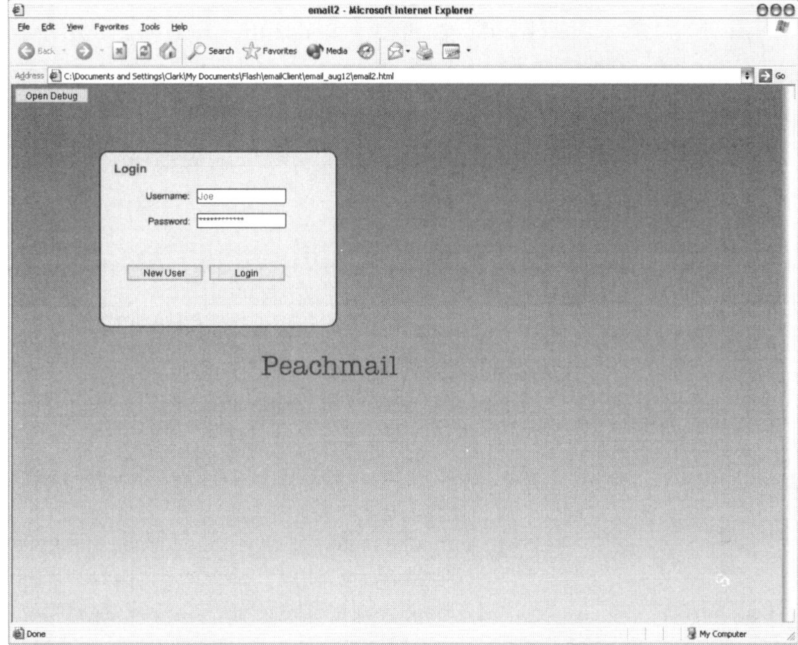

Figure 7.10 *Peachmail's Login screen.*

This is all the information that Peachmail needs to process the registration. Next, Joe is told that his registration is successful and he returns to the main screen and clicks Login. This triggers Flash to generate the login XML transaction data:

```
    <Request>
        <TransactionType>
            Login
        </TransactionType>
        <Data>
```

continues on next page

```
        <Username>
            myjoe
        </Username>
        <Password>
            myjoepassword
        </Password>
    </Data>
</Request>
```

In the Peachmail application are functions named `createHandler` and `loginHandler` for the Create button and Login button, respectively. These button handlers help to generate the preceding XML documents, and pass them to Java for processing.

`createHandler` does the following:

1. Creates the XML new user request from the input fields on the screen.
2. Passes the request to Java.
3. Creates a callback function to test whether the creation was successful.

Here is the ActionScript code for `createHandler`:

```
createHandler = function () {
    message.text = "Creating...";
    // check the two passwords
    if (password.text === passwordRepeat.text) {
        // make the xml
        var createUserXml = buildCreateUserRequest
        → (username.text, password.text, email.text,
        → popServer.text, smtpServer.text);
        // callback
        createUserCallback = function () {
            if (wasSuccessful(this.getDocIn())) {
                // goto the created interface
                gotoAndStop("created");
            } else {
                // show message
                message.text = getError(this.getDocIn());
            }
        }
        // send create user xml
        sendToServer(createUserXml, createUserCallback);
    } else {
```

```
            // make message
            message.text = "Passwords do not match";
        }
    }
```

`loginHandler` does the following:

1. Creates the XML login request from the username and password.
2. Sends the data to Java for processing.
3. Sets up a callback function to check whether the login was successful Here is the ActionScript code for `loginHandler`:

```
loginHandler = function () {
    // make the xml
    var loginXML = buildLoginRequest(username.text,
    → password.text);
    // give a message
    message.text = "Logging In...";
    // check received xml
    loginCallback = function () {
        if (wasSuccessful(this.getDocIn())) {
            // goto email interface
            gotoAndStop("email");
        } else {
            // show error
            message.text = getError(this.getDocIn());
        }
    }
    // send login request
    sendToServer(loginXML, loginCallback);
}
```

Notice how the `loginHandler` and the `createHandler` act similarly—both create a XML request, pass the request to Java, and create a callback function for the Java response, to see whether the request was successful. This create-send-callback action is used in other handlers throughout the Peachmail application.

buildBaseRequest: Creating the XML Request

loginHandler calls a function buildLoginRequest and createHandler calls a function buildCreateUserRequest. Let's take a quick look at the code:

```
buildLoginRequest = function (username, password) {
    // build the request
    var createLoginRequest = new buildBaserequest("Login");
    // add the username
    createLoginRequest.addData("Username", username);
    // add the password
    createLoginRequest.addData("Password", password);
    // return the finished xml doc
    return createLoginRequest.getDoc();
}

buildCreateUserRequest = function (username, password,
→ emailAddress, POPServer, SMTPServer) {
    // Build a basic create user transaction
    var createCreateUserRequest = new buildBaseRequest(
    → "CreateUser" );
    // add the username data to the xml doc
    createCreateUserRequest.addData("Username", username);
    // add the password data to the xml doc
    createCreateUserRequest.addData("Password", password);
    // add the email address
    createCreateUserRequest.addData("EmailAddress",
    → emailAddress);
    // add the servers
    createCreateUserRequest.addData("POPServer", POPServer);
    createCreateUserRequest.addData("SMTPServer", SMTPServer);
    // return the finished XML document
    return createCreateUserRequest.getDoc();
}
```

As you can see, both buildLoginRequest and buildCreateUserRequest create a buildBaseRequest object to form the proper XML document for the respective handler. Along with the addData() method, it creates the XML document mirroring the syntax of the two XML documents Joe created previously, and it returns the XML document to the respective handler.

Here is the constructor for buildBaseRequest and the addData method, along with some helper methods:

```
// buildBaseRequest constructor
function buildBaseRequest(transactionType) {
    // Create the XML Object
    this.doc = new XML();
    // Create the request node
    var requestNode = this.doc.createElement("Request");
    // Create the transaction node
    var transactionNode = this.doc.createElement
    → ("TransactionType");
    // Create the transaction value
    var transactionNodeValue = this.doc.createTextNode
    → (transactionType);
    // Populate the value of the transaction node
    transactionNode.appendChild(transactionNodeValue);
    // Create the data node
    var dataNode = this.doc.createElement("Data");
    // Append the transaction node to the request node
    requestNode.appendChild(transactionNode);
    // Append the data node to the request node
    requestNode.appendChild(dataNode);
    // Append the request node to the parent doc
    this.doc.appendChild(requestNode);
    // Return the completed document
    return this.doc;
} // end buildBaseRequest function

// addData function
buildBaseRequest.prototype.addData = function (newData,
→ value, attributes) {
    // find the data node
    var dataNode = findDataNode(this.doc);
    // create the newData node
    var newDataNode = this.doc.createElement(newData);
    // check to see if a value was specified
    if (value != null)
        // create the value text node
        var valueTextNode = this.doc.createTextNode(value);
    // check to see if attributes were specified
    if (attributes != undefined)
        // loop through the attributes and set them
        for (var i in attributes)
```

continues on next page

```
            // add the attribute
            newDataNode.attributes[i] = attributes[i];
        // append valueTextNode to newDataNode
        newDataNode.appendChild(valueTextNode);
        // append newDataNode to dataNode
        dataNode.appendChild(newDataNode);
    } // end adddata

    // findDataNode function
    // This helper function finds and returns the data node in a
    → transaction xml doc
    function findDataNode(xmlDoc) {
        // Get the children nodes
        var children = xmlDoc.firstChild.childNodes;
        // Get the second child node (the data node)
        var dataNode = children[1];
        // return the node
        return dataNode;
    } // end findDataNode function

    // getDoc function
    // returns the xml doc
    buildBaseRequest.prototype.getDoc = function () {
        // return the xml document
        return this.doc;
    }

    // wasSuccessful function
    // This helper is used to determine if a transaction
    → executed properly or not.
    function wasSuccessful(xmlDoc) {
        // Create an XML object to be sure
        var xmlDoc = new XML(xmlDoc);
        // Parse through and find the status
        var mainNodes = xmlDoc.firstChild.childNodes;
        var statusNode = mainNodes[0];
        var status = statusNode.firstChild.nodeValue;
        // If its an error, find the message
        if(status == 'Error') {
            var dataNode = mainNodes[1];
            var messageNode = dataNode.firstChild;
            errorMessage = messageNode.firstChild.nodeValue;
```

```
        return false;
    }
    // return true if there was no error
    return true;
} // end wasSuccessful function

// getError function
// This helper is used to get the error of an unsuccesful
→ xml doc
function getError(xmlDoc) {
    // Create an XML object to be sure
    var xmlDoc = new XML(xmlDoc);
    // Parse through and find the error
    var mainNodes = xmlDoc.firstChild.childNodes;
    var dataNode = mainNodes[1];
    var messageNode = dataNode.firstChild;
    errorMessage = messageNode.firstChild.nodeValue;
    // return error
    return errorMessage;
} // end getError function
```

sendToServer: Sending XML to Java

Both loginHandler and createHandler use sendToServer() to send XML data to Java, like this:

```
sendToServer(loginXML, loginCallback);
```

Here's a closer look at the sendToServer() function:

```
global.sendToServer = function (theXML, callBack) {
    // set the document to send to server
    server.setDocOut(theXML);
    // set the xml to recieve a reply from server
    server.setDocIn(new XML());
    // get the callback arguments from the arguments
    server.callBackArgs = arguments.slice(2);
    // store the callback function
    server.callBack = callBack;
    // set the callback function
    server.onLoad = function (success) {
        // check to see if there is an incoming doc
        if (success) {
```

continues on next page

```
            // call the callback function with the arguments
            this.callBack.apply(this, this.callBackArgs);
        } else {
            // call the server error function
            onServerDisconnect();
        }
    }
    // send the document
    server.execute();
}
```

To quickly summarize, the sendToServer() function takes an object named server and passes it the XML data and the callback function, and then tells server to send the data by calling server.execute(). server is an object of a custom-made class named Serverdata()—its purpose to handle the passing of the data to Java in one neat little package. The following code shows how server is created and its defaults set.

```
global.server = new ServerData();
// set the methods
server.setMethod(server.SEND_AND_LOAD);
// set the language
server.setLanguage(server.JAVA);
// this is the url of server
server.setURL(myurl);
```

Without going into all the detail regarding ServerData(), we'll look at what ServerData.execute() uses to send the XML data to Java: the Flash XML.sendAndLoad() method. The specific line of code inside ServerData() looks like this:

```
docOut.sendAndLoad(url, docIn);
```

where docOut is the XML data being sent to the Java server located at url, and docIn is the variable that contains the result passed back from Java once docOut is sent and processed.

Once a response is returned from Java and Flash receives the data result, Flash automatically runs docIn.onLoad(), which is set up in ServerData() to process the callback function originally set by the handler.

Callbacks: Verifying Data Requests

Let's revisit the code for loginHandler, specifically the declaration of its callback function and the passing of this function to the ServerData() object:

```
loginCallback = function () {
    if (wasSuccessful(this.getDocIn())) {
        // goto email interface
        gotoAndStop("email");
    } else {
        // show error
        message.text = getError(this.getDocIn());
    }
}
// send login request
sendToServer(loginXML, loginCallback);
```

The `loginCallback()` function is sent as the second parameter of sendTo Server, so the ServerData object can call `loginCallback()` automat-ically, upon receiving a response after Java processes the XML. Also notice that `loginCallback`'s action resulting from a successful transaction is to take Joe into the main part of the application (the email screen); it displays an error message for unsuccessful transactions.

Now that we've discussed the create-send-callback method, let's move on to the server and look at how the back-end detects, processes, and responds to the Flash code.

The Back-End: Java

Recall how Flash sends the XML data to Java—it uses the `ServerData()` object and the standard XML.sendAndLoad() method, sending the XML data stored in `docOut` to the server:

```
docOut.sendAndLoad(url, docIn);
```

Also recall that `docIn` is the variable that will contain the result passed back from the server. How does this work? Flash automatically knows that by using the `sendAndLoad()` method, it will wait to receive data into `docIn`. Once the data is in `docIn`, Flash automatically executes the `docIn.onLoad()` method.

Running the `docIn.onLoad()` triggers the execution of the callback function. This is because we preset the `docIn.onLoad()` method to run the callback when `sendToServer()` is executed in the handler code:

```
sendToServer(loginXML, loginCallback);
```

Processing the New User Request

Earlier you saw how Flash created the New User request when Joe clicked the Create button for the registration screen. When the Java server receives and processes the data, it returns to Flash a result indicating whether the process is successful, and as discussed earlier, this result is stored in the Flash variable `docIn`.

Java returns the following code to Flash when Java processes the data unsuccessfully:

```
<Response>
    <Status>
        Error
    </Status>
    <Data>
        <Message>
            Some message on why the new user request failed
        </Message>
    </Data>
</Response>
```

and successfully:

```
<Response>
    <Status>
        Success
    </Status>
    <Data>
        <Message>
            The transaction completed successfully
        </Message>
    </Data>
</Response>
```

Processing the Login Request

Much in the same way that new user requests are handled by Java, the login requests tell Java to generate the following code to send to Flash for an unsuccessful process:

```
<Response>
    <Status>
        Error
    </Status>
```

```
        <Data>
            <Message>
                Some message on why the login failed
            </Message>
        </Data>
    </Response>
```

and for a successful process:

```
    <Response>
        <Status>
            Success
        </Status>
        <Data>
            <Message>
                The transaction completed successfully
            </Message>
        </Data>
    </Response>
```

The Database

On the create new user request, Joe's data updates the Users table of the database, as Java sends the information to the database to be written.

The login request triggers the Java server to allocate a thread for Joe, for handling Joe's connection throughout the life of the time he is logged into the application. The database is unaffected by Joe's login request.

Building Peachmail: Address Book Services

Now that Joe has logged in, he needs to add some friends to his address book. Peachmail's Address Book allows a user to add contacts, remove contacts, and send emails to contacts. Let's look at how Flash MX works with the server to provide Peachmail's address book services.

The Front-End: Flash MX

When Joe clicks Login, he's presented with the main email screen (**Figure 7.11**).

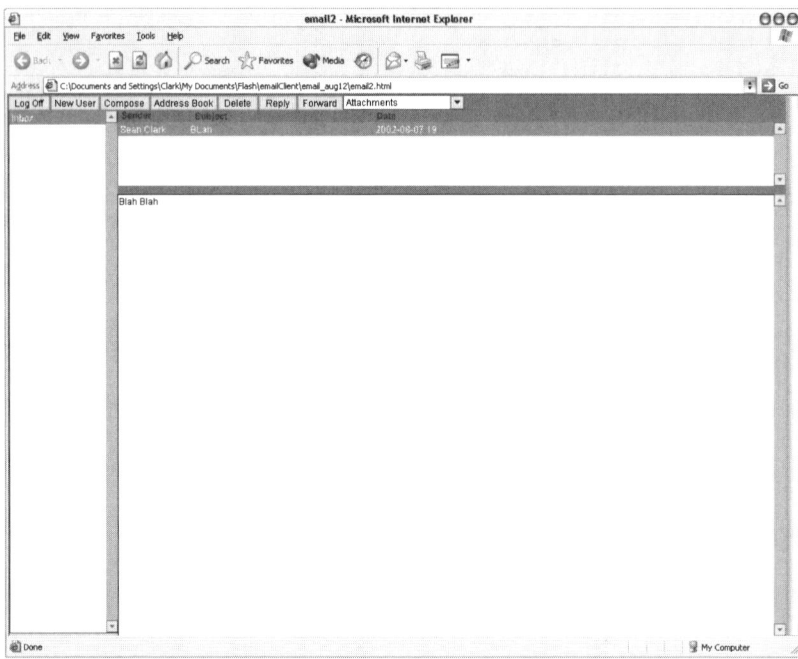

Figure 7.11 *The Peachmail application's main email screen.*

Each button on the screen is handled in much the same way as the buttons in the login and registration section—that is, each button executes a handler when it's clicked. Joe wants to add some friends to his address book, so he clicks the Address Book button. This triggers the `addressBookHandler()`, which simply opens a pop-up browser window to show the Address Book screen.

```
global.openBrowserWindow = function (url, name, width,
→ height) {
    getURL("javascript:void(window.open('" + url + "', '" +
    → name + "', 'resizable=0, toolbar=0, menubar=0,
    → titlebar=0, status=0, width=" + width + ", height=" +
    → height + "'))");
}
addressBookHandler = function () {
```

```
        openBrowserWindow("addressBook.html", "addressBook",
        → 217, 157);
    }
```

The Address Book screen (**Figure 7.12**) contains three buttons that enable Joe to add a new address, delete an address, or send an email to a selected email address.

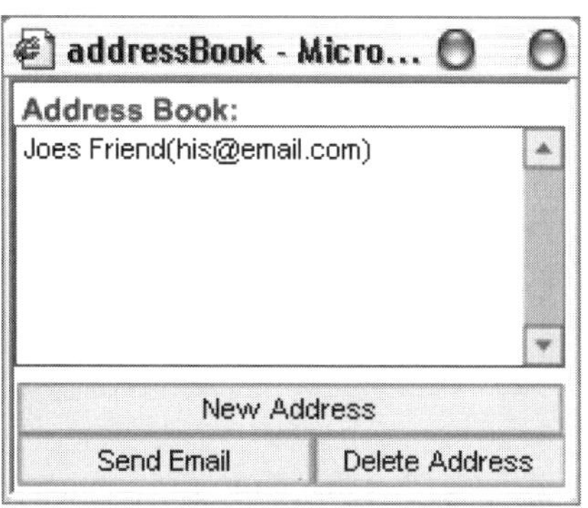

Figure 7.12 *Add a new address, delete an address, or send an email from the Address Book screen.*

Let's take a look at each of these services separately.

Adding a New Address

Clicking the New Address button triggers `newAddressHandler()`, which opens the New Address screen (**Figure 7.13**) for adding a new address:

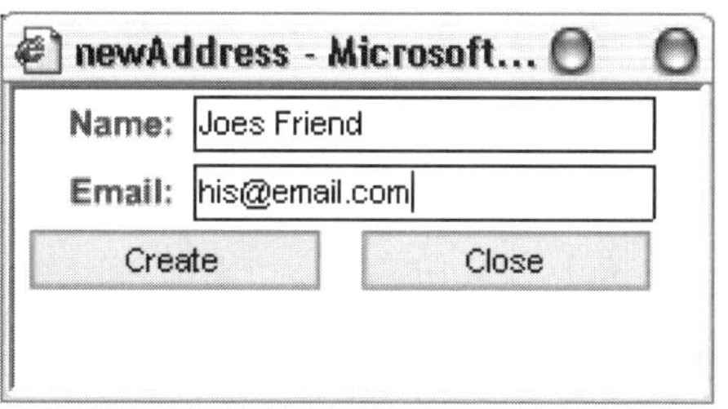

Figure 7.13 *The New Address screen.*

When the New Address screen is loaded, it creates a local connection to the Address Book screen so that it can pass back the newly added address. Local connections allow data to be passed between two external `.swf` files. We'll discuss local connections in more detail at the end of this chapter. For now, let's look at what happens when the Create button is clicked:

```
createHandler = function () {
    // change the address
    newAddressConnection.send("newAddress", name.text,
    → email.text);
    // close this window
    getURL("javascript:void(window.close());");
}
```

The handler takes the text from the name and email textfields and sends them to the local connection's `newAddress()` function – the local connection being the Address Book window – and then it closes itself i.e. the New Address window. The Address Book's `newAddress()` function looks like this:

```
newAddressConnection.newAddress = function (name, email) {
    // create the new address
    addAddress(name, email);
}
```

The `newAddress()` function takes the name and email and sends them to `addAddress()`:

```
addAddress = function (name, email) {
    // make the xml
    addAddressXml = buildAddAddressBookEntryRequest(name,
    → email);
    // make the callback
    addAddressCallback = function (name, email) {
        // check for success
        if (wasSuccessful(this.getDocIn())) {
            // get the dataNode
            var dataNode = findDataNode(this.getDocIn());
            // get the id
            var id = dataNode.firstChild.attributes.ID;
            // add the entry
            addressBook.addAddress(name, email, id);
        }
    }
    // send to server with name and email supplied as arguments
    sendToServer(addAddressXml, addAddressCallback, name,
    → email);
}
```

In this code, the `buildAddAddressBookEntryRequest()` function creates the XML request for the new entry and the `sendToServer()` function passes the request to the server for processing. You'll recall this mirrors the create-send-callback method discussed earlier in the login and registration section. What is interesting here is the callback function: it takes the XML result from the server and parses it, and then it calls `addressBook.addAddress()` to add the new address details to the Address Book's listbox:

```
addressBook.prototype.addAddress = function (name, email, id) {
    // create a temp object to hold values
    var tempObject = {};
    // store the name
    tempObject.name = name;
    // store the email
    tempObject.email = email;
    // store the id
    tempObject.id = id;
    // add the the addresses array
    this.addresses.push(tempObject);
    // add to the listbox
    this.listbox.addItem(tempObject.name + "(" + tempObject.
    → email + ")", this.address.length);
    // store in the ids object
    this.ids[id] = this.listbox.getLength() - 1;
}
```

Note how the code calls the `addItem()` method of Macromedia's listbox component to add the new address to the listbox.

Deleting an Address

Deleting an address involves selecting an address from the listbox and then clicking the Delete Address button. When an item is selected from the listbox, it is marked in the listbox so that it can be retrieved later by the `listbox.getSelectedIndex()` function. When the Delete Address button handler is called it does the following:

```
deleteAddressHandler = function () {
    // get the id from the selected address
    var id = addressBook.getSelectedAddress().id;
    // delete the address
    deleteAddress(id);
}
```

The `addressBook.getSelectedAddress()` function returns a record containing the name, text, and id fields of the selected address, using the `listbox.getSelectedIndex()` function mentioned previously.

```
addressBook.prototype.getSelectedAddress = function () {
    // get the selected item
    var selected = this.listbox.getSelectedIndex();
    // return the object with the item info
    return this.addresses[selected];
}
```

The deleteAddress() function creates an XML request for deleting the address, sends it to the server via sendToServer(), and removes the selected address from the Address Book:

```
deleteAddress = function (id) {
    // make the xml
    deleteAddressXml = buildDeleteAddressBookEntryRequest(id);
    // send the xml
    sendToServer(deleteAddressXml);
    // delete from the address book
    addressBook.deleteAddress(id);
}
```

The final step of the delete address method is addressBook.deleteAddress(), which removes the address from the Address Book's listbox:

```
addressBook.prototype.deleteAddress = function (id) {
    // get the index from the ids object
    var index = this.ids[id];
    // remove from the listbox
    this.listbox.removeItemAt(index);
}
```

Sending Email

To send email, the user must first select an address from the Address Book listbox and then click the Send Email button.

```
sendEmailHandler = function () {
    // get the current email
    var email = addressBook.getSelectedAddress().email;
    // open the compose window
    openCompose(email);
}
```

sendEmailHandler() passes the selected address to openCompose(), which handles the creation of the local connection to the Compose screen and the opening of the Compose screen with the selected email address.

```
openCompose = function (to, subject, message) {
    // create a connection to the compose window
    composeConnection = new popupConnection("compose", false);
    // set the email text fiels contents
    composeConnection.send("setVariable", "to", "text", to);
    // set the subject contents
    composeConnection.send("setVariable", "subject", "text",
    → subject);
    // set the message contents
    composeConnection.send("setVariable", "message", "text",
    → message);
    // close the connection after everything is sent
    composeConnection.onFinishQueue = function () {
        // close the connection
        this.close();
    }
    // open the compose window
    openBrowserWindow("compose.html", "compose", 550, 400);
}
```

The Compose screen (**Figure 7.14**) appears and the user is given the capability to fill in the textfields and click Send (or Cancel, if he changes his mind).

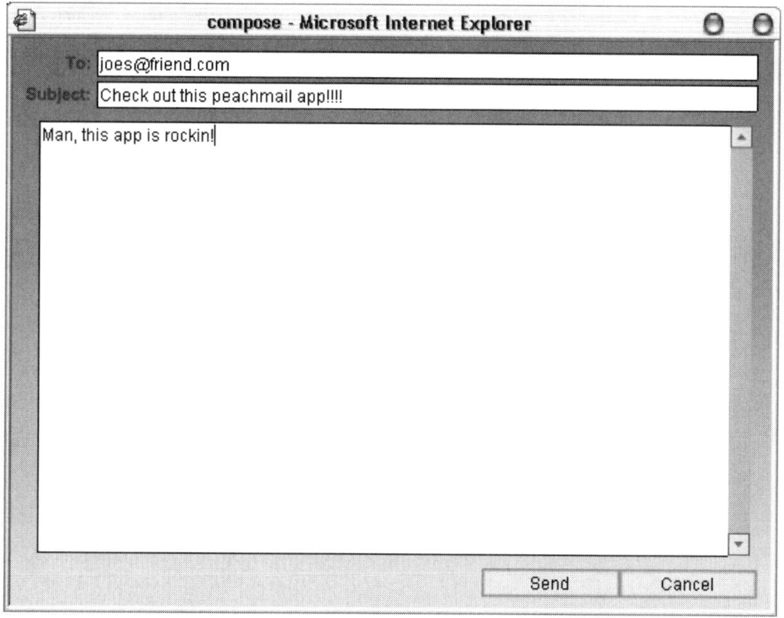

Figure 7.14 *The Peachmail Compose screen.*

The Send button's handler looks like this:

```
sendHandler = function () {
    // make the xml doc
    var sendMsgXml = buildSendMessageRequest(to.text,
    → subject.text, message.text);
    // create the callback
    sendMsgCallback = function () {
        // close the window
        getURL("javascript: void(window.close());");
    }
    // send it to the server
    sendToServer(sendMsgXml, sendMsgCallback);
}
```

You'll notice this handler does nothing more than create and send the XML request to the server, and then its callback closes the window. The server handles the work of sending the message to the specified recipient.

The Back-End: Java

Similar to the server handling in the login and registration, the server handling for the address book services consists of taking an XML document, processing the respective request, and firing back a response indicating whether the processing was successful. In adding an address, the processing includes updating the database with the new address. In deleting an address the processing includes removing an address from the database. Finally, in sending the email, the server is responsible for delivering the message to the recipient.

Processing the Add Address Request

When Joe adds an address to his Address Book, this is an example of what he would send to the server:

```
<Request>
    <TransactionType>AddAddressBookEntry</TransactionType>
    <Data>
        <Entry>
            <Name>Lara</Name>
            <Email>lara@iamlara.com</Email>
        </Entry>
    </Data>
```

```
</Request>
```

This is a typical response returned by the server if the server were added the address to the database successfully:

```
<Response>
    <Status>Success</Status>
    <Data>
        <Entry ID="456" />
    </Data>
</Response>
```

and unsuccessfully:

```
<Response>
    <Status>Error</Status>
    <Data>
        <Message>The address did not add successfully</Message>
    </Data>
</Response>
```

Processing the Delete Address Request

Let's say Joe successfully added a friend to his Address Book, but realizing he made an error in the email address, he decides to delete the address. The XML request would look like this:

```
<Request>
    <TransactionType>DeleteAddressBookEntry</TransactionType>
    <Data>
        <Entry ID="56" />
    </Data>
</Request>
```

On a successful deletion of the address from the database, the server would return this to Flash:

```
<Response>
    <Status>Success</Status>
    <Data>
        <Message>The transaction completed successfully
        → </Message>
    </Data>
</Response>
```

And on an unsuccessful deletion:

```
<Response>
    <Status>Error</Status>
    <Data>
        <Message>The address did not delete successfully
        ➝ </Message>
    </Data>
</Response>
```

Processing the Send Email Request

When Joe decides to send an email, the XML request looks like this:

```
<Request>
    <TransactionType>SendMsg</TransactionType>
    <Data>
        <Addressee>lara@iamlara.com</Addressee>
        <Subject>curious</Subject>
        <Body>Lara, do you miss me?  Curious, Joe</Body>
    </Data>
</Request>
```

The following is an example of the XML response if the server successfully delivers the message to the recipient:

```
<Response>
    <Status>Success</Status>
    <Data>
        <Message>The transaction completed successfully
        ➝ </Message>
    </Data>
</Response>
```

And unsuccessfully:

```
<Response>
    <Status>Error</Status>
    <Data>
        <Message>The email failed to send</Message>
    </Data>
</Response>
```

The Database

On Joe's add address request, the server adds a record to the AddressBookEntries table containing Joe's userID, the new name, and the new email address. The delete address request removes the specified record from the Address-BookEntries table. Finally, the send email request saves the message into the Messages table.

Building Peachmail: Email Services

Joe has completed adding his friends to his Address Book and is now ready to use the email services of Peachmail! The email services include the capability to view, send, receive, and delete email from his account. We've already shown how sending an email works from the Address Book screen. You'll see that sending from the main email screen is not much different.

The Front-End: Flash MX

We covered the New User button and the Address Book button of the main email screen (**Figure 7.15**) in the previous sections. Now we'll look at the remainder buttons: Compose, Delete, Reply, and Forward.

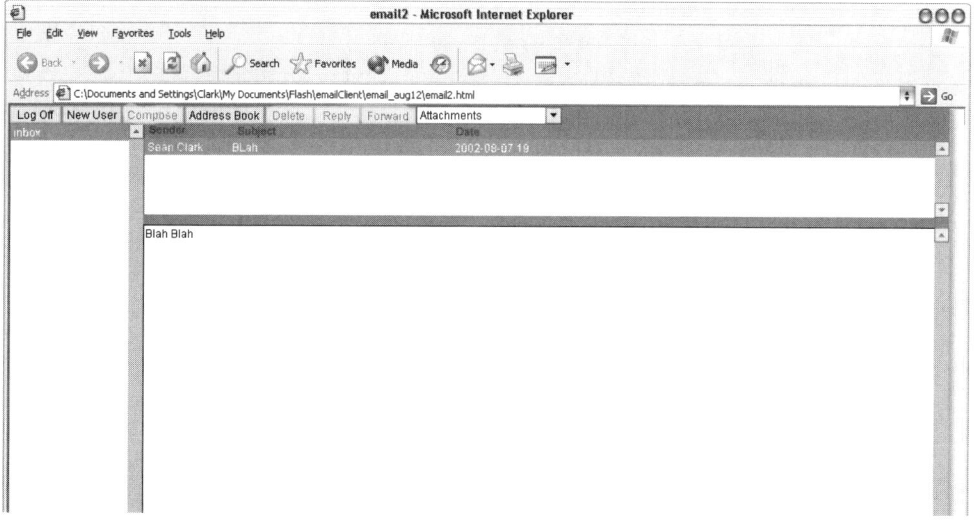

Figure 7.15 *The Peachmail main email screen.*

Sending Email

The Compose, Reply, and Forward buttons involve the process of sending email, with the only difference being how the pop-up Compose screen is set up when the button is clicked. Take a look at the button handlers and notice how they all use the openCompose() method:

```
composeHandler = function () {
    // open the compose window
    openCompose();
}

replyHandler = function () {
    // get the current email
    var email = emailMessages.getSelectedEmail();
    // get the subject, and add "RE: "
    var subject = "RE: " + email.emailObject.subject;
    // get the from address
    var fromAddress = email.email;
    // make the message
    var message = "\n—- Original Message —-\n" +
    → addTicks(emailText.text);
    // open the compose window, and set the variables
    openCompose(fromAddress, subject, message);
}

forwardHandler = function () {
    // get the current email
    var email = emailMessages.getSelectedEmail();
    // get the subject, add "FW: "
    var subject = "FW: " + email.emailObject.subject;
    // get the message
    var message = "\n—- Original Message —-\n" + addTicks
    → (emailText.text);
    // open the compose window with the variable
    openCompose("", subject, message);
}
```

The openCompose() method on this screen is the same as the one in the Address Book screen. Generally, each openCompose() call fills in certain fields in the Compose screen depending on the handler. For instance, clicking Reply fills in the Compose screen's "To:" field, subject, and email body with the sender, subject, and email body of a selected email, respectively.

Clicking Forward fills in the Compose screen's subject and email body with the subject and email body of a selected email, and clicking Compose simply opens the Compose screen with nothing passed to it.

Notice how the Forward and Reply handlers require the selection of an email in order to fill in the Compose screen's fields with the proper content. This is achieved in the handlers by the line:

```
var email = emailMessages.getSelectedEmail();
```

"emailMessages" is an object of the custom emailList class used to manage the processing of the emails. We'll discuss the emailList class in more detail at the end of the chapter. For now, we can show that its getSelectedEmail() method calls the listbox component's getSelectedItem() method and its data variable to retrieve the selected email object:

```
emailList.prototype.getSelectedEmail = function () {
    // return the id
    return this.listBox.getSelectedItem().data;
}
```

The data variable is an object called emailObject, which contains the contents of the email, that is, email.sender, email.email, email.subject, email.ReceiveDate, and so on.

One other thing to point out is the email body that is retrieved by the handlers in the line:

```
addTicks(emailText.text);
```

emailText is a textfield that displays the currently selected email message, and the function addTicks() simply prefixes markers to every line of the message body to indicate it's not part of the new email to be sent.

Once the Compose screen is open, it functions the same way as sending email that we discussed in the address book section.

Receiving Email

Peachmail is built to receive emails into a folder named Inbox. The Inbox folder is in a listbox called folders on the stage, and when it's clicked, Flash sends out a request to select the messages for that folder. To understand the detail of how the messages are retrieved and displayed to the screen, you need to understand how the messages are stored in Flash.

Peachmail contains a custom class called folderList():

```
global.folderList = function (listbox) {
    // store the listbox
    this.listbox = listbox;
    // set the change handler
    this.listbox.setChangeHandler("onChange", this);
    // store an array with the folders
    this.folders = [];
}
```

`folderList()` is used to track all the folders for a specific user. Each folder is displayed on the screen by using Macromedia's `listbox` component. In addition, its details are stored in an array `this.folders`.

When the user logs into Peachmail, the application immediately executes `getFolders()` to retrieve the folders for the current user. As in the handlers discussed in the previous sections, this function performs a create-send-callback action to create the Get Folders XML request, send it to the server, and process the retrieved folder data.

Here is the ActionScript `for getFolders` and its callback:

```
getFolders = function () {
    // create the xml
    var getFoldersXml = buildGetFoldersRequest();
    // create the call back
    getFoldersCallBack = function () {
        // create the folders list
        global.emailFolders = new folderList(folders);
        // if there are already messages, remove them
        folders.removeAll();
        // create the onSelect callback
        emailFolders.onSelect = function (folder) {
            // get the id
            var id = folder.data;
            // get the emails
            getMessages(id);
        }
        // make the folders array
        foldersArray = [];
        // get the data node
        var dataNode = findDataNode(this.getDocIn());
        // get the folders
        var folders = dataNode.firstChild.childNodes;
        // loop through the folders
```

```
        for (var i = 0; i < folders.length; i++) {
            // get the folder
            var folder = folders[i];
            // get the id
            var id = folder.attributes.ID;
            // get the name
            var name = String(folder.firstChild.firstChild);
            // add the folder
            foldersArray.push({id: id, name: name, emails:
            → []});
            // add to the folders list
            emailFolders.addFolder(name, id);
        }
    }
    // send to server
    sendToServer(getFoldersXml, getFoldersCallback);
}
```

You'll notice the `getFoldersCallBack()` callback function is quite heavy compared to the handler callbacks we've seen in the previous sections, so let's step through its process.

The first thing it does is to create a folderList object named `emailFolders` and to set the `emailFolders`.listbox variable to point to the `folders` listbox on the stage:

```
global.emailFolders = new folderList(folders);
```

Next, it clears the folders with the `removeAll()` listbox method, and then creates the `onSelect()` method for `emailFolders`. `onSelect()` is a key method for the retrieval of the email messages, as we'll discuss later. Then, it creates an array `foldersArray`. The callback then parses through the result data. For each folder it finds, it notes the folder name and folder ID, and proceeds to:

1. Store the name and ID into a folder record in `foldersArray`, along with an empty array named `emails`:

   ```
   foldersArray.push({id: id, name: name, emails: []});
   ```

2. Add the name and id into the `emailFolders` object as a new folder:

   ```
   emailFolders.addFolder(name, id);
   ```

The `emailFolders.addFolder()` method updates the `folders` listbox on the screen to display the added folder, in addition to updating the `emailFolders`' `folders` array with a folder record containing the folder name, folder ID, and the listbox index.

Here is the ActionScript for addFolder:

```
folderList.prototype.addFolder = function (name, id) {
    // add item to listbox
    this.listbox.addItem(name, id);
    // store in array
    this.folders.push({name: name, item: this.listbox.
    → getLength(), id: id});
}
```

Now we can see how the handler updates the listbox on the screen. However, it's not so obvious how the code links a handler to the folders listbox for when a folder is clicked. Part of this involves understanding the Macromedia listbox component and how it handles changes.

When a user selects an item from the Macromedia listbox component, the onChange() handler of the listbox is automatically executed. The onChange() handler is not assigned by default, so it executes nothing in its default state. Recall the following line in the constructor for the folderList class:

```
this.listbox.setChangeHandler("onChange", this);
```

When the folderList object emailFolders was created in getFolders Callback(), it executed the preceding line thus assigning the folders listbox's onChange() to the folderList's onChange() method:

```
folderList.prototype.onChange = function () {
    // call callback function, with the selected folder
    this.onSelect(this.listbox.getSelectedItem());
}
```

Notice that the onChange() method executes the onSelect() method. onSelect() was defined in getFoldersCallback() and looks like this:

```
emailFolders.onSelect = function (folder) {
            // get the id
            var id = folder.data;
            // get the emails
            getMessages(id);
        }
```

onSelect() is passed the listbox's selected item, from emailFolders. onChange(). The folder ID is retrieved and then passed to getMessages(). The getMessages() function performs a create-send-callback action to get the messages for a specific folder. Of particular interest here is how much work the callback function getMessagesCallback() does in order to get the received data properly set up for viewing.

Here's the ActionScript for getMessages:

```
getMessages = function (folderId) {
    // create the xml
    var getMessagesXml = buildGetMessagesInFolderRequest
    → (folderId);
    // create the callback
    getMessagesCallback = function () {
        // check for success
        if (wasSuccessful(this.getDocIn())) {
            // create the email list
            emailMessages = new emailList(messages);
            // remove all emails from the listbox
            messages.removeAll();
            // create the handler
            emailMessages.onSelectEmail = function
            → (emailData) {
                // get the details of the message
                getMessageDetails(emailData.id);
                // enable reply and forward buttons
                reply.setEnabled(true);
                forward.setEnabled(true);
                // check to see if there are attachments
                if (emailData.emailobject.hasAttachments ==
                → "True") {
                    // enable the combo box
                    attachmentCombo.setEnabled(true);
                } else {
                    // disable the combo box
                    attachmentCombo.setEnabled(false);
                }
                // keep track of last listbox selected
                global.selectedListBox = "emails";
            }
            // create the delete handler
            emailMessages.onDeleteEmail = function
            → (emailData) {
                // get the id
                var id = emailData.id;
                debug.print(":::" + id);
                // get the xml
```

continues on next page

```
        var deleteEmailXml =
        → buildDeleteMessageRequest(id);
        // send to the server
        sendToServer(deleteEmailXml);
    }
    // get the data node
    var dataNode = findDataNode(this.getDocIn());
    // get the messages
    var messages = dataNode.firstChild.childNodes;
    // loop through the messages
    for (var i = 0; i < messages.length; i++) {
        // get the message
        var message = messages[i];
        // create a temp object
        var messageObject = {};
        // get the id
        messageObject.ID = message.attributes.ID;
        // get the read status
        messageObject.New = message.attributes.New;
        // get the recieve date
        messageObject.ReceiveDate = message.
        → attributes.ReceiveDate;
        // get whether it has attachments
        messageObject.HasAttachments = message.
        → attributes.HasAttachments;
        // parse the sender to get the email and
        → the name
        var sender = message.attributes.Sender.split
        → ("(");
        // get the sender
        messageObject.Sender = sender[1].substring(0,
        → sender[1].length - 1);
        // get the email
        messageObject.email = sender[0];
        // get the subject
        messageObject.Subject = unescape(message.
        → firstChild.firstChild.toString());
        // create the attachments array
        messageObject.attachments = [];
        // add the message to the email list
        emailMessages.addEmail(messageObject);
    }
}
```

```
    }
    // send the xml
    sendtoServer(getMessagesXml, getMessagesCallback);
}
```

The callback function getMessagesCallback() sets up an emailList object named emailMessages using the messages listbox on the stage:

```
emailMessages = new emailList(messages);
```

emailMessages is created to facilitate all aspects of the messaging for a single folder. Next, the callback creates two handlers:

```
emailMessages.onSelectEmail()
emailMessages.onDeleteEmail()
```

which will be called later, when a user selects and/or deletes email from the messages listbox. Finally, the getMessagesCallback() function loops through the received data and adds each message as an object into emailMessages with the following code:

```
emailMessages.addEmail(messageObject);
```

Taking a look at addMail() in detail shows how it updates the messages listbox on the screen using the listbox component's addItem() method:

```
emailList.prototype.addEmail = function (email) {
    // add the email to the email list
    this.listBox.addItem(email.sender, email.subject,
    → email.ReceiveDate, {id: email.id, email: email.email,
    → emailObject: email});
    // get the length of the email list
    var length = this.listBox.getLength();
    // reference the number with the ids object
    this.ids[email.id] = length - 1;
}
```

When an item is selected from the messages listbox, its change handler is automatically invoked. Just like in the emailFolders Class constructor, the emailList Class constructor links the "messages" listbox's change handler to its onChange() method.

Here's the ActionScript for onChange:

```
emailList.prototype.onChange = function () {
    // call callback function, supply the id
    this.onSelectEmail(this.listBox.getSelectedItem().data);
}
```

So when Joe clicks on a message from the messages listbox, emailList.onChange() calls the onSelectEmail() method, defined earlier in our callback, triggering the viewing of the email. At this stage, however, all the emails for the inbox folder are loaded and ready to be viewed. Whew! Joe would be proud.

Viewing Email

We've shown that the user must initiate a request to update the messages listbox by clicking on a folder in the folders listbox, and you've seen that the getMessages() function, executed when the user clicks on a folder, populates the messages listbox with the subject headings of the messages from a given folder ID.

Without going into repetitive detail, getMessages() follows the same pattern as getFolders(): it performs a create-send-callback action to retrieve messages for the specified folder, and within the newly-defined callback, it generates the code necessary to view the message when a message is clicked. Recall that onSelectMail() is invoked when the user clicks on a message, and passes the messageID of the selected email to getMessageDetails():

```
getMessageDetails = function (messageID) {
    // create the xml
    var getMessageDetailsXml = buildGetMessageDetailsRequest
    → (messageID);
    // create the callback
    getMessageDetailsCallback = function (messageID) {
        // check for success
        if (wasSuccessful(this.getDocIn())) {
            // get the data node
            var dataNode = findDataNode(this.getDocIn());
            // get the message
            var message = dataNode.firstChild;
            // get the body
            var body = message.childNodes[2];
            // get the id
            var emailId = message.attributes.ID;
            // get the email
            var email = emailMessages.getEmail(emailId).
            → emailObject;
            // check to see if the email has attachments
            if (email.hasAttachments == "True") {
                // get the attachments
```

```
                    var attachments = message.childNodes[3].
                    → childNodes;
                    // create an array to hold the attachments
                    var attachmentsArray = [];
                    // loop through the attachments
                    for (var i = 0; i < attachments.length; i++) {
                        // get the id
                        var id = attachments[i].attributes.ID;
                        // get the name
                        var name = attachments[i].firstChild.
                        → firstChild.toString();
                        // add it to the array
                        attachmentsArray.push({name: name, id:
                        → id});
                    }
                    // process the attachments
                    processAttachments(attachmentsArray);
                }
                // set the text
                emailText.text = removeTags(body);
            }
        }
        // send the xml to the server
        sendToServer(getMessageDetailsXml,
    getMessageDetailsCallback, messageID);
    }
```

getMessagesDetails() uses the create-send-callback scheme and handles the retrieval of the message from the server, updating the stage's textfield with the text body of the email.

Deleting Email

Deleting email is a two-click process: the user first clicks on a message from the messages listbox, and then clicks the Delete button. Let's start off easy by looking at the Delete button's handler:

```
deleteHandler = function () {
    // delete selected
    emailMessages.deleteSelectedEmail();
}
```

Remembering that emailMessages is an object of the emailList() Class, we see that deleteSelectedEmail() looks like this:

```
emailList.prototype.deleteSelectedEmail = function () {
    // get the selected email
    var email = this.listBox.getSelectedItem().data;
    // get the email number
    var num = this.ids[email.id];
    // remove from the listbox
    this.listBox.removeItemAt(num);
    // call the callback handler
    this.onDeleteEmail(email);
}
```

`deleteSelectedEmail()` facilitates the deletion by removing the message from the listbox, and then calling `onDeleteEmail()`. For convenience, here is the `onDeleteEmail()` method again:

```
emailMessages.onDeleteEmail = function (emailData) {
    // get the id
    var id = emailData.id;
    // get the xml
    var deleteEmailXml = buildDeleteMessageRequest(id);
    // send to the server
    sendToServer(deleteEmailXml);
}
```

Notice how `onDeleteEmail()` only passes one argument to `sendToServer()`, that being the XML request to delete the record from the database. No callback is required because the server simply takes the request to delete and passes the change request to the database.

Let's move on to explore some of the transactional data between Flash and the server to carry out the actions for Email Services.

The Back-End: Java

Email Services are reliant on the server to handle the sending, receiving, viewing, and deleting of the email. Let's look at an overview of the transaction data happening between the Flash front-end and the server.

Processing the Send Request

The XML request and response for sending email are identical to those found in the address book services section.

Processing the Received Request

This request is broken up into two stages: the folders request and the messages request. Here is an example of what Joe would send to the server to request his folder listing:

```
<Request>
    <TransactionType>GetFolders</TransactionType>
    <Data></Data>
</Request>
```

And this is an example of a successful response:

```
<Response>
    <Status>Success</Status>
    <Data>
        <Folders>
            <Folder ID="3">
                <Name>Inbox</Name>
            </Folder>
        </Folders>
    </Data>
</Response>
```

Assuming Joe received a successful response, he clicks on the folder that has now appeared and initiates the messages request:

```
<Request>
    <TransactionType>GetMessagesInFolder</TransactionType>
    <Data>
        <Folder ID="3"/>
    </Data>
</Request>
```

And this is an example of a successful response:

```
<Response>
    <Status>Success</Status>
    <Data>
        <Messages>
            <Message ID="5" New="True" ReceiveDate="2002-
            → 09-18" HasAttachments="False">
                <Subject>Hello there Joe!</Subject>
            </Message>
        </Messages>
    </Data>
</Response>
```

Processing a View Request

When Joe decides to view a message, he clicks on a message in the listbox to fire off the Message request to the server:

```
<Request>
    <TransactionType>GetMessageDetails</TransactionType>
    <Data>
        <Message ID="5"/>
    </Data>
</Request>
```

Assuming the process is successful, the following document is returned:

```
<Response>
    <Status>Success</Status>
    <Data>
        <Message ID="5" ReceiveDate="2002-09-18">
            <Subject>Hello there Joe!</Subject>
            <Body>Joe! You're the best!  Love, Lara</Body>
            <Attachments>
            </Attachments>
        </Message>
    </Data>
</Response>
```

Processing the Deletion Request

Recall how the deletion did not have a callback function. In the case of the deletion request, the document is sent to the server, and the server communicates to the database to remove the specified record. Here is an example of the XML request:

```
<Request>
    <TransactionType>DeleteMessage</TransactionType>
    <Data>
        <Message ID="5" />
    </Data>
</Request>
```

The Database

The three tables that are primarily affected by the Email Services of Peachmail are Folders, Messages, and Attachments.

Prior to the receive email request, the server first retrieves data from the Folders table correlating to a specific user ID and sends it back to Flash. Then when the user clicks on a folder, the server pulls data from the Messages table for the specific folder ID and sends the message listing back to Flash.

When the user clicks on a message to view it, the server requests data from the Messages table correlating with the specific message ID. The Attachments table is queried as needed, if there are any attachments accompanying the message.

Deleting a message involves the removal of the message from the Messages table. The attachments specific to the request are also removed.

Coming Together

So far, we've covered the three fundamental services of Peachmail: login and registration, Address Book, and Email Services. This section discusses some of the more advanced ActionScript concepts used by Peachmail, including custom classes and local connections. In addition, we recap the application's architecture, listing the custom classes that were created specifically for this application and their purpose.

Advanced ActionScript

One of the benefits of Flash MX is the use of components to ease development, with Peachmail making extensive use of Macromedia's listbox component. With this in mind, we'll explore the listbox methods used by Peachmail. We'll also look at how Peachmail uses Local Connection objects to send data between two swf files running externally. Finally, we cover prototyping and how Peachmail creates custom classes, leading right into the discussion of Peachmail's architecture and its custom classes.

Macromedia Components: Using the Listbox Component

Peachmail uses Macromedia's listbox component to display the addresses in the Address Book, the folders in the email folders listing, and the messages in the email messages listing. We'll discuss the most common list box methods used by Peachmail: `addItem()`, `getSelectedItem()`, and `setChangeHandler()`.

addItem() is called when the user adds an address to the address book, or when the user logs in and the folder list is automatically updated, or when the user clicks on a folder and the messages list is updated. For example,

```
this.listbox.addItem(name, id);
```

creates a record in the listbox containing the name and id and displays the name variable on the screen in the listbox—the name variable is the label part of the listbox and the id is the data part. These parts of the listbox can be referred to by the following code:

```
mylabel = this.listbox.getSelectedItem().label;
mydata = this.listbox.getSelectedItem().data;
```

where getSelectedItem() is the currently selected item in the listbox. When Joe selects an item from the listbox, the listbox's onChange() event is automatically invoked. In the case of Peachmail's folder list for example, we showed that by calling the listbox's setChangeHandler() method to reassign its onChange() event, the onChange() event is set to retrieve the messages for the selected folder. The following example shows exactly that, where the "onChange" refers to the onChange() function in the folderList Class:

```
this.listbox.setChangeHandler("onChange", this);
folderList.prototype.onChange = function () {
    // call callback function, with the selected folder
    this.onSelect(this.listbox.getSelectedItem());
}
```

One last thing to point out regarding Peachmail's use of the listbox is how the custom emailList Class uses the addItem() method:

```
this.listBox.addItem(email.sender, email.subject,
→ email.ReceiveDate, {id: email.id, email: email.email,
→ emailObject: email});
```

You'll notice how more than two parameters are being passed to addItem(). This is because the messages listbox is a modified version of the standard Macromedia listbox, and is extended to receive more than one parameter. We'll discuss extending classes a bit later, but for now, this is what the extended addItem() method looks like:

```
FEmailListBoxClass.prototype.addItem = function(name,
→ subject, date, data)
{
    if (!this.enable) return;
    this.dataProvider.addItem({name:name, subject:subject,
    → date:date, data:data});
}
```

SWF to SWF: The Local Connection Class

LocalConnection objects are new in Flash MX and are used by Peachmail in circumstances such as sending data from the `newAddress.swf` in one window to the `AddressBook.swf` in another window. A local connection requires a sender `.swf` and a receiver `.swf` (**Figure 7.16**).

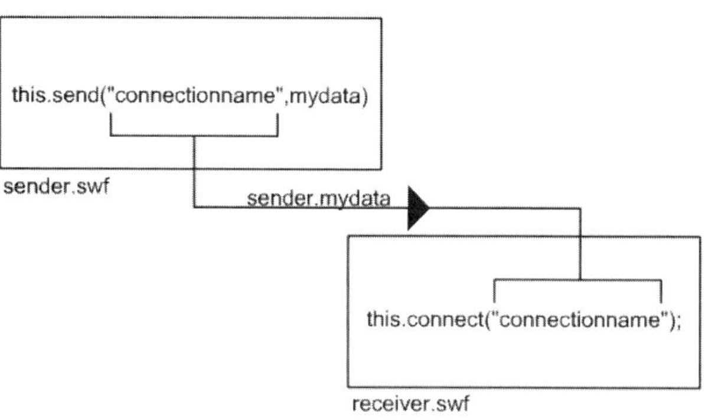

Figure 7.16
Connecting two external `.swf` *files.*

The receiver `.swf` contains the following code:

```
RecvLC = new LocalConnection();
RecvLC.myfunc = function(msg) {
    trace("The sender has just sent me a message:");
    trace(msg);
}
RecvLC.connect("TheLC");
```

To communicate with the receiver, the sender `.swf` has the following code:

```
SendrLC = new LocalConnection();
SendrLC.send("TheLC", "myfunc", "Your fly is open.");
```

When the example runs, the receiver readies itself for a connection from an external source to `"TheLC"`. When the sender sends the message to `"TheLC"`, it calls the receiver's `"myfunc"` function passing a string, which the receiver traces to the Flash MX Output window.

In Peachmail, the local connection for the Address Book screen looks like this:

```
newAddressConnection = new popupConnection ("newAddress",
→ false);
newAddressConnection.newAddress = function (name, email) {
    // create the new address
    addAddress(name, email);
}
```

Notice how newAddressConnection is a popupConnection object rather than the LocalConnection object. popupConnection is a custom class that handles the creation of a LocalConnection object and calls the connect() method to set this swf up as a receiver. Let's take a look at popupConnection's constructor:

```
global.popupConnection = function(connectionName, popup) {
    // store the connection name
    this.connectionName = connectionName;
    // store whether this is a popup
    this.popup = popup;
    // start a queue
    this.queue = [];
    // start up the popup connection
    this.start();
};
// inherit from local connection
popupConnection.prototype = new LocalConnection();
```

When a popupConnection is constructed, it inherits from LocalConnection(), meaning it attains the same properties and methods of LocalConnection() with the potential to extend the class. *Extending* the class means to define a new method for this class while still having access to the methods of the parent class—you'll see an example of this later. The last line of the constructor for popupConnection() triggers the class' start() method:

```
popupConnection.prototype.start = function() {
    // check whether this is a popup
    if (this.popup) {
        // connect
        this.connect(this.connectionName+"Popup");
    } else {
        // connect
        this.connect(this.connectionName);
    }
    // call the onConnect function in the other window
    this.send("onConnect");
};
```

Because this.popup is false in this scenario—defined false when newAddressConnection was created previously—the start() method goes on to run the connect() method of the popupConnection class, which by inheritance is the connect() method of the LocalConnection class:

```
this.connect("newAddress");
```

So now the Address Book is ready to receive data from any external `.swf` sending to `newAddress.swf`.

Before we get on to the sender code in the newAddress window, you may be curious about why the last line of the `start()` method calls the `send()` method of the `popupConnection` class. The `send()` method is actually extended from the parent class' `send()` method. This means all the functionality of the original `LocalConnection` class' `send()` is intact, but calling `send()` from a `popupConnection` object executes a different `send()` method. `popupConnection.send()` looks like this:

```
popupConnection.prototype.send = function() {
    // check whether this is a popup
    if (this.popup) {
        // add the connection name to the arguments
        arguments.unshift(this.connectionName);
    } else {
        // add the connection name to the arguemnts
        arguments.unshift(this.connectionName+"Popup");
    }
    // if this is connected or this is a popup
    if (this.connected or this.popup) {
        // call function in the other window
        super.send.apply(this, arguments);
    } else {
        // put in queue
        this.queue.push(arguments);
    }
};
```

To access the `LocalConnection.send()` from within `popupConnection`, the `popupConnection` class uses `super.send()` and the `Function.apply()` method:

```
super.send.apply(this, arguments);
```

This results in calling the `send` method of the parent class with "`arguments`" as its list of arguments, and "`this`" is used to make the parent's `send` method relative to the `popupConnection` class.

When `popupConnection.send()` is called in the `AddressBook.swf`, it adds `"newAddressPopup"` to the beginning of its arguments in the line:

```
arguments.unshift(this.connectionName+"Popup");
```

and then adds the arguments to the queue:

```
this.queue.push(arguments);
```

so that at this stage, newAddressConnection.queue would contain:

```
[ ["newAddressPopup", "onConnect"] ]
```

Moving on to the Local Connection object for the sender, the NewAddress.swf contains the following code:

```
newAddressConnection = new popupConnection("newAddress",
→ true);
```

Tracing through the construction of newAddress.swf's newAddressConnection, we can see that one of the first actions is to set itself up as a data receiver in "newAddressPopup" with the line:

```
this.connect(this.connectionName+"Popup");
```

The next step calls the send() method:

```
this.send("onConnect");
```

which adds the string "newAddress" to the beginning of the arguments:

```
arguments.unshift(this.connectionName);
```

and then calls the Local Connection send() method:

```
super.send.apply(this, arguments);
```

so that the final call looks like this in the newAddress.swf:

```
newAddress.super.send("newAddress", "onConnect");
```

This sets up newAddress.swf to connect to a local connection named "newAddress" and execute newAddress' onConnect() method. Because we set up AddressBook to be the newAddress receiver, the onConnect() method of the AddressBook's local connection object is executed:

```
// called when connected with the popup
popupConnection.prototype.onConnect = function() {
    // change the connected flag
    this.connected = true;
    // loop through queue
    for (i = 0; i < this.queue.length; i++) {
        // send function
        super.send.apply(this, this.queue[i]);
    }
    // call the onFinishQueue handler
    this.onFinishQueue();
};
```

As you can see, the AddressBook's connected flag is set to true and it communicates back to newAddress.swf that it is connected by looping through its queue and applying the queue element to super.send() to get:

```
newAddressConnection.super.send("newAddressPopup",
→ "onConnect");
```

On the newAddress.swf side, its onConnect() method is triggered and thus its connected flag is also set to true. As it doesn't contain any elements in its queue, the connection process ends there. So finally, after all this, we have two-way communication between AddressBook.swf and newAddress.swf.

Keeping in mind everything we've discussed so far is just to set up the communication between the two .swfs, the actual code to send the new address data from newAddress.swf to AddressBook.swf is executed when the Create button in newAddress.swf is clicked and its handler is triggered:

```
createHandler = function () {
    // change the address
    newAddressConnection.send("newAddress", name.text,
    → email.text);
    // close this window
    getURL("javascript:void(window.close());");
}
```

This finally calls the Address Book's newAddressConnection.newAddress() method, defined at the beginning of the Address Book discussion in this section, to process the name.text and email.text data from newAddress.swf.

Prototyping: Creating Custom Classes

By definition, a class is a group of properties, methods and events used to create objects in Flash. The MovieClip() class for example, contains properties such as _x, _width, _name, _visible, and so on; methods such as gotoAndStop(), attachMovie(), getDepth(), hitTest(), and so forth; and events like onEnterFrame and onLoad.

Peachmail contains several custom classes, such as ServerData(), buildBaseRequest(), folderList(), emailList(), and AddressBook(). We'll use ServerData() as an example to see how a custom class is created.

In Peachmail, server is made an object of the ServerData() class using the new operator:

```
global.server = new ServerData();
```

This gives server the properties, methods, and events of the ServerData() class. For example, the following are now valid:

```
server.setMethod(server.SEND_AND_LOAD);
server.setLanguage(server.JAVA);
```

where setMethod and setLanguage are methods of the ServerData() class.

Creating a class first involves creating the constructor function. This function is called when an object is created from a class, such as when the new operator is used, as in the previous example. A constructor's purpose is to initialize the newly created object with any startup parameters. If no initialization is required, an empty function is still valid, such as:

```
function myClass() {
}
```

Here is the constructor for the ServerData() class:

```
function ServerData() {
    // Create all language constants
    this.NOT_SPECIFIED = 0;
    this.COLD_FUSION = 1;
    this.ASP = 2;
    this.ASPNET = 3;
    this.PHP = 4;
    this.JAVA = 5;
    // Create all method constants
    this.SEND = 1;
    this.LOAD = 2;
    this.SEND_AND_LOAD = 3;
    // Default the language
    this.setLanguage(this.NOT_SPECIFIED);
    // Default the method
    this.setMethod(this.SEND_AND_LOAD);
    // Default ignore white to true
    this.setIgnoreWhite(true);
}
```

An important distinction to point out is the reference of this—it is used to qualify the respective property and/or method, insuring that it belongs to the current class. After the creation of the constructor, the next step is creating the class methods.

Class methods are defined by using the prototype property. For example:

```
myClass.prototype.mymethod = function() {
// mymethod's code goes here
}
```

Here are some examples of ServerData's methods, namely setLanguage() and execute():

```
ServerData.prototype.setLanguage = function(language) {
this.language = language;
}
ServerData.prototype.execute = function() {
    // Blank out the status
    this.setStatus("");
    // Chose which method to execute
    switch(this.getMethod()) {
        // handle send
        case this.SEND:
            // execute the send method
            results = this.executeSend();
            break;
        // handle load
        case this.LOAD:
            // execute the load method
            results = this.executeLoad();
            break;
        // handle send and load
        case this.SEND_AND_LOAD:
            // execute the send and load method
            results = this.executeSendAndLoad();
            break;
        // handle anything that doesn't match
        default:
            // No method specified, throw an error
            this.setStatus("Error: Invalid method defined!");
            return false
    } // end switch
    // if the results are positive, no errors were encountered
    if(results) {
        this.setStatus("Command executed properly");
    }
    // return whatever the specified method returned
    return results;
}
```

Completing the discussion on classes is the concept of inheritance. Classes can be made a subclass of a parent class, thereby inheriting all the properties, methods, and events of the parent class. This is the case with the popupConnection class we showed earlier in the section on Local Connections. popupConnection() is made a subclass of the LocalConnection class using the new operator:

```
popupConnection.prototype = new LocalConnection();
```

Therefore, popupConnection() is a subclass of LocalConnection() and has access to all of LocalConnection's methods. Lastly, when popupConnection.send() was defined, it overrode LocalConnection.send() without eliminating the capability to access the parent class' send() method. This is part of the idea of extending a class: to create a subclass of a parent class and adding your own methods to the subclass.

Peachmail Architecture

This section revisits some of the concepts of the Peachmail architecture: specifically, the create-send-callback action, standardized transactions, and listbox handling. For each area, a custom class was defined to handle the details of the work involved. This discussion briefly comments on each concept and shows details of its respective class.

Create-Send-Callback (The ServerData Class)

The create-send-callback action was used extensively throughout the Peachmail application. ServerData() is created to assist in putting together an object to handle the complexity of creating an XML transaction request, sending it to the server, and processing a callback function based on the result of the processed request.

The constants for ServerData()'s language getter/setter are:

- NOT_SPECIFIED (default)
- COLD_FUSION
- ASP
- ASPNET
- PHP
- JAVA

The constants for ServerData()'s method getter/setter are:

- SEND
- LOAD
- SEND_AND_LOAD (default)

Table 7.2 lists the methods for ServerData().

Table 7.2 ServerData() Methods

METHOD	DESCRIPTION
execute()	Performs the method specified by getMethod() onto the XML specified by getDocOut() and/or getDocIn().
executeSend()	Called by execute() to perform an XML Send with data from getDocOut(); the data is formatted to the getLanguage() specs before sending.
executeLoad()	Called by execute() to perform an XML Load with data from getDocIn().
executeSendAndLoad()	Called by execute() to perform an XML Send and Load with data from getDocOut() and getDocIn() respectively; the data is formatted to the getLanguage() specs before sending.
loaded(success)	Called internally when an XML Load operation has completed, its purpose is to ensure the code can extend and add more functionality later; this also executes ServerData's onLoad() method.
onLoad(success)	Stubbed method for onLoad. Override this method to capture the data when the data is done loading.
getMethod()	Default is SEND_AND_LOAD.
setMethod(method)	To be used with method constants.
getDocIn()	Getter function for Serverdata.docIn, which contains the xml object to populate with the servers response.
setDocIn(xmldoc)	Setter function for Serverdata.docIn.
getDocOut()	Getter function for Serverdata.docOut, which contains the XML document to send to the server.
setDocOut(xmldoc)	Setter function for Serverdata.docOut.
getURL()	Getter function for the URL property of the xml object.
setURL(url)	Setter function for the URL property of the xml object.
getLanguage()	Default is NOT_SPECIFIED.
setLanguage(language)	To be used with language constants.
getIgnoreWhite()	Default is True.
setIgnoreWhite(value)	Set the ignoreWhite property for the XML.
getStatus()	Getter function for ServerData.status; status is a verbose message indicating the state of an XML transaction.
setStatus(status)	Setter function for ServerData.status.
toString()	Returns the string "ServerData".

Standardized Transactions (The buildBaseRequest Class)

The XML transactions have a specific layout that is used throughout Peachmail. Standardizing the XML Transaction requests and responses provides great benefits to developers and programmer analysts, as a strict syntax makes it easy to grasp the data layout for faster development and future modifications and enhancements. Looking back at the XML requests discussed earlier in this chapter, we can see that all the XML requests have the following pattern:

```
<Request>
    <TransactionType>
        [ some transaction type ]
    </TransactionType>
    <Data>
        < [data var 1] >
            [some data]
        </[data var 1]>
            .
            .
            .
        < [data var n] >
            [some data]
        </[data var n]>
    </Data>
</Request>
```

The purpose of buildBaseRequest is to centralize where the request is generated so that any future changes can be made with ease. The majority of the XML request setup takes place in the constructor, so it has been listed here for your reference.

Here's the `buildBaseRequest()` constructor:

```
function buildBaseRequest(transactionType) {
    // Create the XML Object
    this.doc = new XML();
    // Create the request node
    var requestNode = this.doc.createElement("Request");
    // Create the transaction node
    var transactionNode = this.doc.createElement
    → ("TransactionType");
    // Create the transaction value
```

```
    var transactionNodeValue = this.doc.createTextNode
    → (transactionType);
    // Populate the value of the transaction node
    transactionNode.appendChild(transactionNodeValue);
    // Create the data node
    var dataNode = this.doc.createElement("Data");
    // Append the transaction node to the request node
    requestNode.appendChild(transactionNode);
    // Append the data node to the request node
    requestNode.appendChild(dataNode);
    // Append the request node to the parent doc
    this.doc.appendChild(requestNode);
    // Return the completed document
    return this.doc;

} // end buildBaseRequest function
```

Table 7.3 lists the methods of buildBaseRequest.

Table 7.3 *buildBaseRequest Methods*

METHOD	DESCRIPTION
addData (newData, value, attributes)	**Adds data to the XML document.**
getDoc()	**Returns the XML document.**

Listbox Handlers (the AddressBook, folderList, and emailList Classes)

Three classes—AddressBook(), folderList(), and emailList()—were created to handle each of the listboxes of the Peachmail application. We've covered the details on how they are used throughout the chapter. For your reference, the following are the constructor and a table listing the methods for each of these classes (see **Tables 7.4–7.6**).

The AddressBook() constructor:

```
_global.addressBook = function (listbox) {
    // store the listbox reference
    this.listbox = listbox;
    // create an array to hold addresses
    this.addresses = [];
    // create an object to hold ids, for easy access
    this.ids = {};
}
```

Table 7.4 AddressBook() Methods

METHOD	DESCRIPTION
addAddress (name, email, id)	Adds an address to the AddressBook list.
deleteAddress (id)	Deletes an address from the list given its id.
deleteSelectedAddress()	Deletes the currently selected address from the list.
getSelectedAddress ()	Returns the currently selected address in the list.
getSelectedIndex ()	Returns the index of the currently selected address in the list.

The folderList() constructor:

```
global.folderList = function (listbox) {
    // store the listbox
    this.listbox = listbox;
    // set the change handler
    this.listbox.setChangeHandler("onChange", this);
    // store an array with the folders
    this.folders = [];
}
```

Table 7.5 folderList() Methods

METHOD	DESCRIPTION
addFolder (name, id)	Adds a folder to the Folders list.
deleteFolder(name)	Deletes the folder from the list given its name.
deleteSelectedFolder ()	Deletes the selected folder from the list.
onChange()	Calls the callback function.

The emailList() constructor:

```
emailList = function (listbox) {
    // store listbox reference
    this.listBox = listbox;
    // create a new array to hold the emails
    this.emails = [];
    // create an object for easy referencing with ids
    this.ids = {};
    // change the change handler
    this.listBox.setChangeHandler("onChange", this);
}
```

Table 7.6 *emailList() Methods*

METHOD	DESCRIPTION
`setFolder (folder)`	Sets a folder to be the current folder.
`addEmail(email, folder)`	Adds a message to the Messages list.
`addAttachment (emailId, name, id)`	Adds an attachment to the Attachments combobox.
`deleteSelectedEmail ()`	Deletes the selected email from the list.
`getEmail(id)`	Returns the email given the id from the list.
`setAttachments(emailed, attachments)`	Links an email to a set of attachments.
`onChange()`	Calls the callback function.
`getSelectedEmail()`	Returns the selected email from the list.

Summary

This chapter walks through the process of building an Email Client application, from looking at customer requirements to building a functionality blueprint, from creating the data definition to finally developing and coding our processes. It shows how an application consists of the front-end (Flash), the server back-end (Java), and the database (Microsoft Access). Peachmail demonstrates the use of Flash MX to develop our concept.

Peachmail follows a create-send-callback routine to process data requests and responses. It uses XML as its data format and creates a class to adhere to strict data request definitions. It shows the use of prototyping to create custom classes for specific data requirements, like data request handling and listbox handling. It enables you to see how local connections serve to interface external `.swfs` so that data transactions can occur between them.

Best of all, Joe, our resident Peachmail user, is now enjoying his vacation, thanks to Peachmail. What a jolly good fellow!

8: Multiple-Communication Application

By William B. Sanders

New technology like the Flash Communication Server MX (FlashCom) can be an end in itself, but it really should not be. FlashCom can be a lot of fun, and it also serves a purpose and is intended to get a job done, as you will soon see. The application discussed in this chapter is designed to be a practical communication device that two people could use to communicate via video, voice, and text chat and to present data from a database. The multiple communication features enable users with different Internet and computer capacities to pass information back and forth in real time. In testing the application, users with phone modems, DSL lines, cable modems, and T1/T3 lines served as real-world test benches. Modifications after testing include controls for the user's Internet connection to reflect actual communication conditions over the Internet.

The metaphor first offered for a two-way audio/visual/text chat application was that of a "Customer Service" center. As such, it developed along the lines of what a customer service representative would want to communicate and what a customer would need to know. Each side of the customer service equation is developed as a separate module, but most of the features, and certainly most of the script, are the same for both parts. The two modules share a common server-side script and reside in the same application folder.

With areas for two video screens and a text chat area, no room remained for the database. After considering opening a separate window or jumping to another frame, I settled on overlaying the database on top of the chat area, and set up controls so that one or both users could activate the database. By loading the database module into a separate level, it could be placed directly on top of the text chat area. The overlay strategy makes it unnecessary to go through the camera-permission segment whenever a video is introduced in a page.

To best understand the application, we'll first look at the hardware and software required for the video portion of the application. Several tests were made between Connecticut and London with fellow beta tester and owner of www.d-street.com, aYo Binitie. In testing the application with another fellow beta-tester, Sudhir Kumar in India, I found that even without a camera and a phone, we were able to maintain voice and text chat communication.

The chat application is as simple as I could make it. It's developed along minimalist lines to get the job done in a single chat room. Originally devised for two people, it's expanded to any number. In a customer service environment, others may want to be consulted, and while two-way audio and video needed to be limited for bandwidth considerations, this was not the case with text chat. Finally, the data module is discussed as a generic front end for any number of different modules that could be appended to this one.

Setting Up the Embedded Video

Starting off the project is quite simple. All you need for a two-person audio-visual application is two video windows. Setting them up and providing them with instance names is the first task to complete. Here are the steps:

1. Open the Library panel. In Flash MX, the Embedded Video object is tucked away in a pop-up menu in the Library panel.
2. To access the Library panel's Options menu, click the pop-up menu arrow in the upper-right hand corner of the Library panel. It's a very small arrow, so if you are not familiar with it, you might miss it.

3. Select New Video from the Options menu. As soon as you make the selection, you see Embedded Video 1 in the bottom pane of the Library panel.

4. Drag one instance of Embedded Video 1 to the top of the left side of the stage and another instance below the first one. Position the top video object at X=12.5, Y=21.8, and the bottom one at X=12.5, Y=182.9 (the large Xs in **Figure 8.1**). On a layer beneath each of the video windows I included background rectangles to help frame the videos. When selected, video objects have blue outlines, and the big X is the layer color. Be careful not to put them beneath an opaque object: They'll disappear just like any other object on the stage.

5. Select the top Embedded Video, and in the Properties panel, give it an instance name of `rep`.

6. Select the bottom Embedded Video, and in the Properties panel, give it an instance name of `cus`.

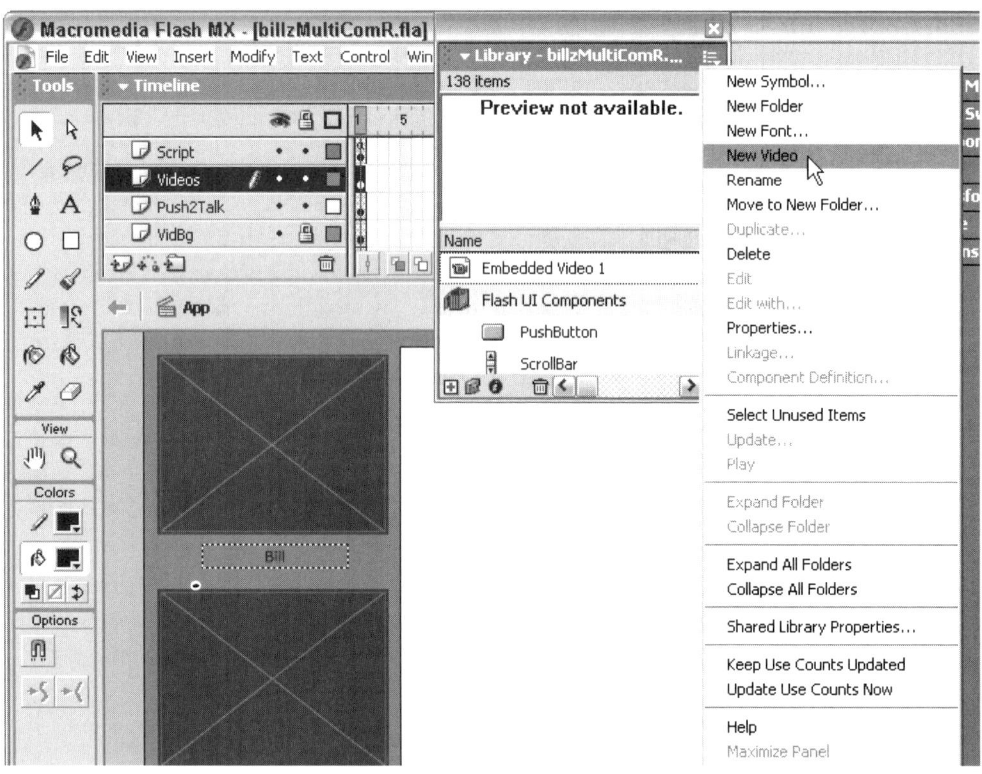

Figure 8.1 *Place two instances of the Embedded Video object on the stage.*

The first phase is complete. Both objects are placed on the stage and supplied with instance names just as you would do with any other object in Flash MX. Given the movie clip quality of having an instance name, Embedded Video objects can be dynamically changed, including being dragged. (When you have an application with several users coming and going, draggable video objects can be helpful in positioning partially-viewed members into spots abandoned by members who've left the video chat.)

Videos and Video Settings

In dealing with the video aspect of this application, two matters must be considered: the hardware and the software. The hardware is the camera and the ports for connecting the camera (for example, USB, IEEE 1394 port) you use with the application. The software refers to the settings that you can control with Client-Side Communication ActionScript. You can also control aspects of the video using Server-Side Communication ActionScript, but this application only uses the client-side version.

Video Cameras

The hardware configuration for Flash Communication Server MX proved to be both simple and complex. The cameras themselves were the simple part. I tested three Webcams and two digital video cameras (DVs), and they all worked well with the application. The DVs used were a Canon Ultura and a newer Canon Optura100, primarily on a Windows XP platform using a Dazzle IEEE 1394 card. On a Macintosh 400mhz/640mg RAM I used one of the available Firewire (IEEE 1394) ports with an iBOT camera. Also I tested a D-Link USB WebCam on both the XP and iMac. Initially, I tried using a PYRO IEEE 1394 with little success on either the Mac or PC. I learned that the problem using the PYRO was not the camera. Neither the iBOT nor PYRO could be configured to the Dazzle IEEE 1394. It has some type of DV configuration that worked with DVs but not with Webcams, or at least the ones I tested. Using a generic IEEE 1394 card on an XP Pro platform with the PYRO IEEE 1394 camera, I found it to be an excellent Webcam for use with Flash Communication Server MX. **Table 8.1** shows the video cameras and drivers Macromedia tested and certified for use with Flash Player 6. Three of the cameras I tested (the PYRO IEEE 1394, Canon Ultura, and Canon Optura 100) are not on the list but worked fine once configured correctly.

Table 8.1 *Camera, Drivers, Platforms and Flash 6 Players Requirements*

MANUFACTURER/ MODEL	DRIVER VERSION	PLATFORMS	MEETS REQUIREMENTS
3com Home Connect	6.6.4	Win2000, WinMe, Win98	Yes
Creative WebCam Go Plus	1.0	WinMe, WinXP, Win98	Yes
D-Link USB WebCam (DSB-C100)	0921	Win2000, WinMe, Win98, WinXP, Mac 9.1, Mac 9.2	Yes
IBM Ultraport Camera 2	Most Current	Win2000	Yes
Intel Deluxe PC Camera	1.0	Win2000, WinXP	Yes
Intel Easy PC Camera	1.0	Win2000, Win98, WinXP, WinMe	Yes
Irez Kritter USB	1.02b4	Mac 9.1, Win2000, WinMe, Win98	Yes
Irez StealthFire	1.2	Mac 9.0.4, Mac 9.1, Mac 9.2	Yes
Logitech QuickCam Traveler	6.0.1	Win2000	Yes
Logitech QuickCam Web	6.0.1	Win2000	Yes
Logitech QuickCam Express	6.0.1	Win2000	Yes
Logitech QuickCam Pro 3000	6.0.1	Win2000, Mac 9.1, WinMe, Mac 9.2, WinXP	Yes
Logitech QuickCam VC	Windows - 4.1.5 Macintosh - 2.1.2	Win2000, Mac 9.0, Mac 9.1, Mac 9.2, Mac OSX	Yes
Orange Micro iBOT Pro Firewire	4.10.22 Mac 9.2	Win2000, Mac OS X,	Yes
Veo Stingray	5.0.0.0	Win98, WinXP, Win2000, WinMe	Yes

- QuickCam Express driver version 5 causes crash in IE 5.5 on Win 2000 when using certain mode settings. To avoid this issue, upgrade your driver to version 6.
- Kritter USB 2.1 camera (clear-bodied) is known to cause occasional crashes on Mac OS 9 and Windows in Flash Player 6.
- If you have multiple cameras on your Windows operation system: the D-Link USB WebCam (DSB-C100) driver may cause other camera drivers to not work right. To remedy this issue, reinstall drivers for all cameras except the D-Lin USB WebCam.
- On Mac OS 9.2: D-Link USB WebCam (DSB-C100) shows very gradual fade-in every time the camera is used in Flash Player 6.
- The ATI Multimedia Video Driver is known to have problems in Flash Player 6. Crashes may occur if you use this driver.
- DV cameras have exhibited some problems: possible slow performance and possible problems with audio.
- Two or more 3Com Home Connect cameras are known to use more memory than expected.

One further issue involving cameras and using Flash Communication Server MX is the Macintosh running OS X. At the time of this writing the primary Webcam driver for OS X was relatively unstable. The driver problem is being addressed, and by the time you read this, that issue may be solved. However, I found that running this application under pure OS 9.2 did not pose the problems encountered with OS X. So while the OS X drivers are being updated, Mac users can run Flash Communication Server MX with a Webcam under OS 9.2 without any problems at all.

For some reason, when my DV was attached to the Macintosh running under OS X, it took a telephoto shot when testing the Customer Service application, necessitating placing it far away from the focal point. That is another mystery left to OS X driver developers.

The Camera Object and Its Settings

Client Side Communication ActionScript's primary software tool for setting your video is the Camera object. Creating a Camera object is unlike other objects in Flash and ActionScript because you address an actual piece of hardware rather than a construct. However, once the Camera object is created and placed in your script, it has the same characteristics as other objects created in Flash MX ActionScript. The Embedded Video instance pulled out of the Library panel provides a convenient target for the Camera object. Once the Camera object is defined, it can then be associated with an Embedded Video instance or simply with an outgoing video stream.

To create a Camera object in a computer with a single video camera attached to it use the get() method with no parameters to define a Camera object. For example,

```
myCamera = Camera.get();
```

creates the object, myCamera, that is addressed much like any other user object created in Flash MX ActionScript.

Once the Camera object is created the next step is to define its qualities. For this application, the following Client-Side Communication ActionScript is employed:

```
//Camera setup
cam = Camera.get();
cam.setMode(160,120,9);
cam.setQuality(0,90);
cam.setKeyFrameInterval(5);
//Connetion Type
_root.conType.text="Default";
```

These settings represent the faster end of Internet connections, somewhere between a DSL line and cable modem or LAN. Each of the setting methods needs to be addressed separately. (On the Customer module, the user can choose from three bandwidth settings, and it's necessary to include some kind of message indicating that the current settings are the default. A line of script is sent to a dynamic text field stating this, and the same text field receives information about any other of the options the user has selected.)

Camera.setMode(width, height, fps, [favorSize])

Using the `Camera.setMode()` method is generally unproblematic. If you use the Embedded Video object's default size, you can use identical dimensions for the *width* (160) and *height* (120) parameters. Larger or smaller frames can be set, depending of the size of video image required for an application. After experimenting with different sizes, and given the bandwidth limitations inherent in the Internet, it's not a bad tradeoff between quality of picture streamed and detail size.

The default fps (frames per second) setting is 15. However, on slower connections, especially phone modems, the rate is unrealistic. The setting used in the application is 9. That frame rate represents a fairly fast rate for a DSL, but a good one for cable modems yet slower than optimally achieved on a LAN. (I list recommended settings for different types of connections in the "Typical Camera Object Settings for Different Bandwidths" section later in the chapter.)

To handle the tradeoff between the frame size and frame rate, the optional `favorSize` parameter can be set to a Boolean value. The default is `true`, which favors size over frame rate. That means that your animation will appear slow or jerky if a size/speed conflict arises but your picture dimensions are better maintained. By setting the `favorSize` parameter to false, fps is maintained, providing better video animation (as measured by frame rate) at the expense of picture dimensions.

Camera.setQuality(bandwidth, frameQuality);

The `bandwidth` argument represents the maximum amount of bandwidth, measured in bytes per second, sustainable by the outgoing video feed. The default value is 16384, but by setting `bandwidth` to 0, you can specify that Flash MX video can use what is needed to sustain the `frameQuality`.

The `frameQuality` parameter ranges from 0 to 100, with 100 being the highest quality. Higher quality demands more bandwidth; to make sure that you have the bandwidth to sustain the quality, set `bandwidth` to 0. The settings used in the application, `setQuality(0,90)` represent high quality, ensuring a minimum quality of 90 regardless of the amount of bandwidth required. Flash MX generates video transmission at a given bandwidth with a set quality. **Table 8.2** shows Macromedia's suggested settings for different bandwidth speeds.

Table 8.2 *Camera.setQuality() Parameter Settings with Different Bandwidth Speeds*

BANDWIDTH	EFFECT	CODE
Modem	Lower image quality, higher motion quality	`cam.setQuality(4000,0)`
	Higher image quality, lower motion quality	`cam.setQuality(0,65)`
DSL	Lower image quality, higher motion quality	`cam.setQuality(12000,0)`
	Higher image quality, lower motion quality	`cam.setQuality(0,90)`
LAN	Lower image quality, higher motion quality	`cam.setQuality(400000,0)`
	Higher image quality, lower motion quality	`cam.setQuality(0,100)`

Camera.setKeyFrameInterval(keyframeInterval)

The concept of video keyframes is similar to the tweening action in a Flash MX movie. The value set for `keyframeInternval` determines the number of video frames in a stream that will be treated as keyframes. The default value is 15, which means that every 15th frame will be treated as a keyframe. The other frames are interpolated by the Flash MX video compression algorithm.

However, the parallel between tweening and the video compression algorithm is only an analogy. The Flash MX video compression algorithm attempts to transmit only what has changed since the previous video frame has been transmitted. For relatively still actions—like those encountered by a video surveillance camera set to watch a hallway of a closed office—the number of keyframes set can be fairly high. However, to pick up more animation, forcing more frames to be treated as keyframes provides better quality pictures and animation.

Determining the best `keyframeInterval` value is very much a matter for self-testing. A higher value (fewer keyframes) reduces bandwidth use because fewer demands are placed on sending an entire frame. Fewer keyframes, though, can mean more time to place the playhead at a given point in the video. A greater number of prior video frames may need interpolation before the video starts up again. Given the relatively low number of fps used (9), a lower `keyframeInterval` will mean that close to two frames per second will be keyframes. Because the application is face-to-face communication, enough gestures can be clearly generated to convey an expression, and the talking movement is relatively sedentary. (Those who are generous with their gestures may appear a little jerky but not comically so.)

Typical Camera Object Settings for Different Bandwidths

In creating this application, it was easy to add buttons to the customer's side of the application. Assuming that the representative would have a standard Internet connection, I added option buttons only to the customer side so that users with different bandwidths could click the button that most closely represented their system. The following are `Camera` object configurations for a 56k phone modem, a DSL connection, and a LAN connection:

```
//56k Modem
cam.setMode(160,120,2);
cam.setQuality(0,75);
cam.setKeyFrameInterval(5);

//DSL
cam.setMode(160,120,5);
cam.setQuality(0,85);
cam.setKeyFrameInterval(5);

//LAN
cam.setMode(160,120,15);
cam.setQuality(0,90);
cam.setKeyFrameInterval(10);
```

All of these settings can be dynamically changed, using the buttons for the viewer to make changes based on his Internet connection. Alternatively, if you plan on implementing this application and you have a good idea with whom you will be communicating, you can tailor the settings for their connections.

Camera Selection

One final matter is the choice of the camera. One of my computers has drivers for both a DV camera and camcorder. Having installed and used the DV first, its driver was the default one and blocked the iBOT WebCam I later installed. However, once you have the application up and running, the Flash 6 player provides a handy context menu. These steps take you to the right set of options:

1. Right-click (Control+click on the Macintosh) on the video portion of the page while connected through the application.
2. Select Settings from the pop-up menu.

3. In the Macromedia Flash Player Settings window, select the Webcam icon.
4. In the pop-up menu select the camera and driver you want. In **Figure 8.2**, the Microsoft DV Camera and VCR driver is selected.

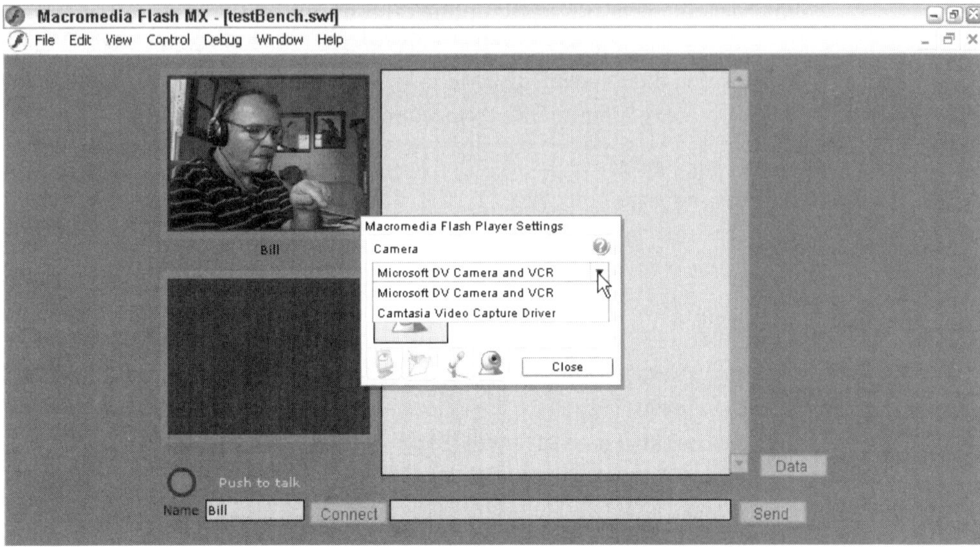

Figure 8.2 *Check to see that the correct camera and driver are selected.*

If you still have problems getting your camera to perform check Table 8.1 to see if the camera and driver you are using is compatible with the Flash 6 Player.

Microphones and Audio Settings

The audio portion of Flash Communication Server MX is relatively simple both in terms of choices of equipment and settings. Many computers, including laptops and all iMacs, come with built-in microphones. Others have microphone jacks for external microphones, and USB ports can be used as jacks with USB microphones. Likewise, a wide selection of headset-microphone combinations is available for computers as well.

Microphone Devices

The audio portion of the application is very easy to set up. The application was tested with two different types of USB microphones on a Windows XP platform and with the built-in microphone and a USB microphone on a

Macintosh OS X. All worked, but all seemed to require different volume levels with a common set of microphone settings. A Telex USB microphone was tested on two different XP platforms and an iMac running OS X, and it worked the best of all. The second USB microphone was a Telex H-551 combination headset and microphone. A combined headset and microphone placed the sending and receiving audio components right where they belonged and worked well. The built-in microphone on the iMac was set to a medium volume but required shouting into the microphone hole. However, in tests using either USB microphone, speaking in a natural voice was sufficient. Sudhir Kumar, with whom I tested the application in India, used an Intex backphone, and while we had problems with the sound stream stopping, the quality of the audio received was very high.

The Microphone Object and Its Settings

Client Side Communication ActionScript's primary software tool for setting audio is the `Microphone` object. Making a `Microphone` object is almost identical to creating a `Camera` object, but Flash MX does not have a microphone symbol in the library analogous to the Embedded Video.

To create a `Microphone` object you use the `get()` method with no parameters in a similar fashion as you did with `Camera` object. For example,

```
myMicrophone = Microphone.get();
```

creates the object `myMicrophone`. All of the properties and methods associated with the new object name can be applied to it.

The script for setting up the microphone is similar to the camera's script, with the important difference that this application begins with the microphone turned off by setting the gain to zero. The following script is the one used in the application:

```
//Microphone set up
mic = Microphone.get();
mic.setGain(0);
mic.setRate(22);
```

The application uses a push-to-talk button, so the gain was set to the off position, and no sounds will be emitted from the microphone until the button script executes.

Microphone.setGain(gain)

The `setGain()` method allows you to specify the amount the microphone should boost the signal. By setting the gain to zero, as was done in this application, it is possible to keep sounds muted until the user wants to talk. This approach was taken initially to see if we could improve on the sound transmission, and while it may have worked to some extent, the main advantage was found to lie in both avoiding cross-talk and feedback squeal.

The range for `setGain()` is 0 to 100, and in this application 75 is set when a button is pressed. Setting the gain to 75 allows the speaker to be heard. When the button is released, the gain is reset to 0 and the user cannot be heard:

```
//Push to talk
talk.onPress = function() {
    mic.setGain(75);
};
talk.onRelease = function() {
    mic.setGain(0);
};
```

The button object was assigned the instance name `talk` so that the script for the button could be placed with the main script all in one place. Otherwise, the script would have to be placed in direct association with the button object. As much as possible, all script is kept together, adhering to Macromedia's recommended scripting practices for ActionScript.

A suggested alternative to using the `Microphone.gain()` method was to use the Microphone object's `muted` property. The `muted` property of the Microphone object is controlled by the user and is a read-only property. Unfortunately, the user control aspect occurs at the beginning of the camera connection sequence where the Flash 6 player detects a camera object and microphone object and accepts or rejects the connection to her camera and microphone. As a result, there is no way to use `Microphone.muted` to turn the microphone on and off other than to have the user connect and disconnect from the application.

Microphone.setRate(kHz)

The microphone rate setting specifies the rate (measured in kilohertz) at which the microphone is to capture sound. However, rather than having a full range, only five settings are acceptable: 5, 8 (the default), 11, 22, and 44. The application sets the rate to 22, but in the customer module, other rates can be set by selecting different bandwidth variation buttons. The action

```
mic.setRate(22);
```

at the beginning of the script establishes 22kHz as the microphone capture rate.

Typical Microphone Object Settings for Different Bandwidths

Like the different settings for the Camera object, the Microphone object can be re-set by the customer for optimizing audio. The same functions used to change the camera settings also change the Microphone.setRate() value. The following are Microphone object configurations for a 56k phone modem, a DSL connection, and a LAN connection:

```
//56k phone modem
mic.setRate(5);

//DSL
mic.setRate(11);

//LAN
mic.setRate(22);
```

These values are subject to the type of microphone and what it can handle. You might want to experiment with different models to see what setting is optimum for the Internet connection and type of microphone you have.

Establishing Connections

Once you have your Camera and Microphone objects defined, the next step is to make different connections and links. You link the Embedded Video object to the camera, and then you make links to streaming video going out and coming in. The first step involves the Video object and getting hardware and streams attached to the Embedded Video object.

Video.attachVideo(source|null)

The instance name of the Embedded Video is the Video object. In this application, the names rep and cus are used for the customer representative and customer portions of the application. The null argument means that the video will no longer be shown in the Video object. The Flash Communication Server MX is not required for the video to appear in the Video object. The attachVideo() method is the only Video object method employed in the application, and none of its properties is used.

First, you must attach the camera source to the `Video` object (the Embedded Video is the `Video` object.) The following code attaches the camera to the `rep` and `cus` instances of the Video object:

```
//Customer Rep movie only
rep.attachVideo(cam);

//Customer movie only
cus.attachVideo(cam);
```

All these statements do is to vector video input from your camera to the Embedded Video object. Once the Flash Communication Server MX is activated, you can attach the video images to streams going out, and connect your Embedded Video object to video streams coming in.

Post-Connection Attachments

The application requires a stream of audio and video going out and coming in. The customer side only sends out a stream showing what the customer's camera sees and the microphone hears. The customer representative side streams in what the customer's camera shows and microphone hears, while streaming out the data from its own camera and microphone. As a point of reference, the following script segment does the bulk of the work for sending a stream and receiving a stream. However, the connection must be made first (connecting to Flash Communication Server) before you can attach outgoing or incoming steams.

```
//Make the connection
function connect() {
    config.data.user = user;
    config.flush();
    //Make the connecton
    hookup = new NetConnection();
    hookup.connect("rtmp:/billzMultiCom", user);
    //
    //Customer app configuration only
    //Out to customer rep
    outStream = new NetStream(hookup);
    outStream.publish("cusStream", "live");
    outStream.attachVideo(cam);
    outStream.attachAudio(mic);
    //
```

```
//Customer app configuration only
//Stream in from customer rep
inStream = new NetStream(hookup);
inStream.play("repStream");
rep.attachVideo(inStream);
```

First, the `connect()` function (a user function) begins with two lines that set up the text chat portion of the module. Those will be ignored for the time being since they have nothing to do with the audio/video streams.

The NetConnection Object

Next, you make the actual connection *to an application* on the Flash Communication Server, not to FCS. You create an object by assigning an identifier a new `NetConnection()` value like any other object. In this application, `hookup` is the object name used because it is unambiguous and is easily differentiated from other terms. Once the client-side `NetConnection` object has been defined, use the `connect()` method to identify the application on the Flash Communication Server. The application is not a file reference, but rather a folder where the Flash MX SWF files and various supporting files can be found. Using Real-Time Messaging Protocol (RTMP), the script identifies the Uniform Resource Identifier (URI) to the target folder. In looking at the statement

```
hookup.connect("rtmp:/billzMultiCom", user);
```

you can see that only a single slash (/) is employed. When both the application (SWF file) and server are running on the same machine, which is a typical authoring environment, you can use a single slash. If the server is on a different computer, then use a double slash but the same RTMP protocol. If the server you place the application on also runs a Flash Communication Server, you can use the single slash. Were the application move to another server, the line would change to:

```
hookup.connect("rtmp://someServer.someDomain.com/
→ billzMultiCom", user);
```

In addition to specifying the URI when invoking the `connect()` method, you can optionally specify a parameter of any type to be passed to the target URI. In this case, `user` is part of the text chat module and can be ignored as far as setting up two-way audio/visual communication. (However, for the overall application, it is important, as you'll see later in this chapter.)

Essentially this process allows the Flash client to open a TCP socket on FCS for streaming RTMP data. These data are steams of video and audio. Text can be streamed as well, and so all three types of data are passed through the open socket.

Streaming Out with NetStream(object)

The NetConnection object named hookup now must be sent out to a recipient. In this application, the recipient is either the Customer or Representative module. Also, the object must capture data coming in over the open socket. To accomplish this goal, you need to create two NetStream objects—one to escort data out and one to escort it in.

To send audio/video data out from the Flash client, you need three NetStream methods:

```
NetStream.publish(whatToPublish | false [, howToPublish])
NetStream.attachVideo(source | null [,
snapShotMilliseconds]))
NetStream.attachAudio(source)
```

First, define a NetStream object. To help identify the outbound stream, the NetStream object identifier is outStream:

```
outStream = new NetStream(hookup);
```

Second, you provide a string that will identify what is being sent out or published. The string "cusStream" is used to indicate that it is the customer's string. This same name will be used by subscribers to this stream to view the video and hear the audio. The second parameter is one of three publishing values—record, append, and live. The default is "live" and although it isn't required, it is included here to emphasize the streaming nature of the data:

```
outStream.publish("cusStream", "live");
```

What is being published in the NetStream object can be defined in terms of sources, and in this case the sources are the video camera and microphone. So again, attachVideo() method is used, but instead of attaching it to an Embedded Video, it is attached to an outgoing stream. Likewise, you use attachAudio() to attach the audio to the same NetStream object:

```
outStream.attachVideo(cam);
outStream.attachAudio(mic);
```

In some ways it's like throwing twigs in a running stream. Whatever you throw in can be caught downstream.

Streaming In with NetStream(object)

In the same way that media can be streamed out, it can be streamed in. The Customer module of the application sends out "cusStream" and streams in "repStream". The script invokes the NetStream object, but instead of publishing the stream, the code plays it using the `play()` method. The string `"inSteam"` identifies it in the script as the stream of data coming into the computer:

```
inStream = new NetStream(hookup);
inStream.play("repStream");
```

Finally, the data streaming into the computer needs a place be displayed, and so the `attachVideo()` method is needed again:

```
rep.attachVideo(inStream);
```

Incoming audio is vectored to the speakers or headphones. This aspect does not require an attachment to any hardware.

Text Chat

The text chat is added to accommodate those without audio contact. Sometimes the audio portion of the application cannot send sound, either because one user lacks a microphone or because of connection problems. In this section of the chapter, the text chat portion of the script functions has been extracted and collapsed into a segment and all of the material from the `Camera` and `Microphone` objects along with their steams have been omitted to better clarify the text chat structure. The client-side listing is discussed first, followed by the server-side.

Setting Up the Client-Side Text Chat

The `connect()` function begins by using the `SharedObject` named `config`. The `SharedObject.data` property is a read-only one; to assign a value, add an attribute and assign a value to the object that you want to share. In this case the attribute `user` is assigned the value `user`. Next the `flush()` method writes a locally persistent shared object to a local file.

The connection uses the same `NetConnection` object, hookup, with the `onStatus` event handler to check the connection status. Then the `hookup` object assigns the `chatBox` instance (the large dynamic text field) a function literal that establishes the field as the source for placing the `msg` variable. The `msg` variable is the message sent from any user.

The next step defines users as a `SharedObject` so that all participants will have their `msg` (what they type in the message box) sent from their message box to the chatBox. Then they are connected using the common NetConnection object, hookup, as an argument when the users' SharedObject invokes the connect method. The msg is cumulatively defined as the text in the chatBox object. The TextFiled.scroll property is defined at 1000, which should be plenty unless you run into an impossibly talkative user.

Next, the sent() function simply defines the movement of the text typed into the message text field. It does this using the NetConnection.call method to invoke a method or command in the server-side script. (See the "Server-Side Text Chat ActionScript" section later in this chapter.)

The Text Chat Client-Side Script

The rest of the text chat script toggles the UI buttons, creates the config SharedObject, and automatically connects the user to the chat. This sets up a remote shared object. Remote shared objects are created on the client, but they are available to the server as well. Local shared objects can store information on users' computers, but they are not available to the server. The following listing shows the text chat portion of the script in its entirety:

```
function connect() {
    config.data.user = user;
    config.flush();
//The NetConnection is here using object name, "hookup"
//...............
//The Camera and Microphone and streams go here
hookup.onStatus = function(info) {
        trace(info.code+newline);
        if (info.code == "NetConnection.Connect.Closed") {
            _root.chatBox.text = "";
        }
    };
    //NetConnection with the main text field
    hookup.chatBox = function(msg) {
        _root.chatBox.text = msg;
    };
    msg = "";
    //Establishes shared object with all users
    users = SharedObject.getRemote("users", hookup.uri, false);
    users.onSync = function(list) {
    };
```

```
    users.connect(hookup);
    users.message = function(msg) {
        _root.chatBox.text += msg;
        _root.chatBox.scroll = 1000;
    };
    _root.sendButton.setEnabled(true);
}
//Send the text in the message box to the shared chat area
→ function send() {
    if (length(message.text)>0) {
        hookup.call("message", null, message.text);
    }
    message.text = "";
}
sendButton.setEnabled(false);
// Create the config SharedObject
config = SharedObject.getLocal("config");
// Auto-connection
user = config.data.user;
connect();
```

A Scroll Pump

One of the many challenges encountered while developing this application was the coordination of actions coming over the Internet and a script. Whenever the text reaches the bottom of the text window, I want it to automatically scroll to the bottom without the user having the do so manually. The timing between when an action is issued and when it occurs is often problematic. One unique Flash feature that can overcome timing issues is to place the action outside of the main timeline and handle it with a movie clip. This idea, originally suggested by Sudhir Kumar, works very well. The clip is placed beneath an embedded video on the bottom layer. The movie clip consists of two frames with the following script in the first frame:

```
var lastPlace = _root.chatScroll.maxPos;
var pump = _root.chatScroll.getScrollPosition();
if (pump != lastPlace) {
    _root.chatScroll.setScrollPosition(lastPlace);
} else {
    stop();
}
```

The maximum scroll (maxPos) position is compared with the current position (pump). If the two values are not the same, the setScrollPosition() method is invoked until they are equal. Then the movie clip stops until the next time a play() action is issued by the send() function. Be sure to include the instance name pumper for the movie clip so that it can be addressed by the main script.

An Enter Button

Because sending a message is accomplished easier by pressing the Enter (Return) key than by clicking the Send button, an event handler for the Enter key was required. The send() function moves the text from the message box to the main chat area. A button with the instance name sender was created and then associated with the following script:

```
on (keyPress "<Enter>") {
    _root.send();
}
```

The button is hidden with the movie clip on the bottom layer.

Server-Side Text Chat ActionScript

The server-side script is divided into three parts. The first part sets up the shared objects for the users who will connect to the application. The second part, the heart of the script, connects the users to the chat, and the third part takes care of the disconnect. Like all server-side scripts using Flash Communication Server MX applications and Server-Side Communication ActionScript, this file is saved as main.asc. Each application folder can have no more than a single main.asc file.

In Server-Side Communication ActionScript, the most ubiquitous object is application. It is the link between your application instance and the server-side script and contains information about the application instance. The application instance can handle more than a single instance of an application at the same time.

The first part of the script involves the initial detection of an application using the text chat. This is done with the application.onAppStart event handler. The shared object is accessed using the SharedObject.get method. The method returns a reference to a shared object specified in the first argument ("users"). It then initializes the text chat instance (chatBox) and defines an ID property.

The second part is a function that gathers in all who would visit. This allows more than two visitors to the chat room. While only two people can use the video, no limit is set on the number of those who can chat. During testing, it was found that steaming video on a single application had exponential weight that slowed down considerably when additional video streams were added. However, this did not seem to be the case with text, and so more than two users can use the text function at the same time. In a real-world application, for example, more than a single customer representative might want to help answer a customer's question.

The final part of the script simply removes the user from the ID list and voids the ID and name. The following script is the main.asc in its entirety. It was constructed in a text editor apart from Flash MX.

```
//All Flash Communication Server MX ActionScript
//Server-side scripts are saved as main.asc
//Part I–Event handlers traces application starting
//Event handler detects the application has started.
application.onAppStart = function()
{
trace("begin chat");
application.users = SharedObject.get("users", false);
application.chatBox = "";
application.nextId = 0;
}
//Part II–Event handler detects connection
application.onConnect = function(newClient, name)
{
newClient.name = name;
newClient.id = "u" + application.nextId++;
trace("connect: " + name + newClient.id);
application.users.setProperty(newClient.id, name);
application.acceptConnection(newClient);
// send the initial chatBox
newClient.call("chatBox", null, application.chatBox);
// accept a chat message and send it back out
newClient.message = function(msg) {
//The user's name is concatenated with the message variable
→ and sent
```

continues on next page

```
//with a newline. It is sent to all users.
msg = this.name + ": " + msg + "\n";
application.chatBox += msg;
application.users.send("message", msg);
}
}
//Part III—Disconnect event handler.
application.onDisconnect = function(client)
{
trace("disconnect: " + client.id);
 application.users.setProperty(client.id, null);
}
```

Remember to save this script in the `main.asc` text file and place it in the same folder as the application. Only one server-side script named `main.asc` can be in the folder.

The Customer Representative Module

The Customer Representative module (**Figure 8.3**) is designed for a stable platform and connection. Therefore, it was unnecessary to add buttons for different Internet connection speeds. Also, you can place a name in the text field beneath the top video since it would be expected that each representative would have her own application.

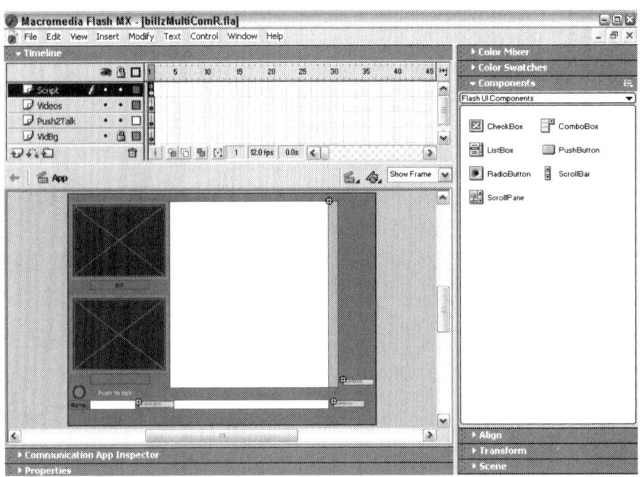

Figure 8.3 *The basic layout and layers of the customer representative module.*

Organizing the Representative Module Objects

The parts that make up the bulk of the objects on the stage are standard Macromedia Flash MX elements. Four standard UI components, five text fields, two buttons, and a movie clip need to be named and placed on the stage. All references to names for the text fields, buttons, and movie clip are Instance names. Here's a complete list of what you need:

UI Components

NAME	CLICK HANDLER
Connect	connect
Send	send
Data	dataCall
NAME	**TARGET**
chatScroll	chatBox

Text Fields

INSTANCE NAME	TYPE
repName	Dynamic
cusName	Dynamic
cusName	Dynamic
message	Input

Text Fields

VAR NAME	TYPE
user	Input

Buttons

INSTANCE NAME	SYMBOL TYPE
talk	Button
sender	Button

Movie Clip

INSTANCE NAME	SYMBOL TYPE
pumper	Movie Clip

Client-Side Script

Here's the Customer Representative module script:

```
stop();
//Camera and Mic setup
cam = Camera.get();
cam.setMode(160, 120, 5);
cam.setQuality(0, 90);
mic = Microphone.get();
mic.setRate(22);
mic.setGain(0);
```

continues on next page

```
rep.attachVideo(cam);
//Make the connection
function connect() {
    config.data.user = user;
    config.flush();
    hookup = new NetConnection();
    hookup.connect("rtmp:/billzMultiCom", user);
    //Stream out to customer
    outStream = new NetStream(hookup);
    outStream.publish("repStream", "live");
    outStream.attachVideo(cam);
    outStream.attachAudio(mic);
    //Stream in from customer
    inStream = new NetStream(hookup);
    inStream.play("cusStream");
    cus.attachVideo(inStream);
    hookup.onStatus = function(info) {
        trace(info.code+newline);
        if (info.code == "NetConnection.Connect.Closed") {
            _root.chatBox.text = "";
        }
    };
    hookup.chatBox = function(msg) {
        _root.chatBox.text = msg;
    };
    msg = "";
    users = SharedObject.getRemote("users", hookup.uri, false);
    users.onSync = function(list) {
    };
    users.connect(hookup);
    users.message = function(msg) {
        _root.chatBox.text += msg;
        _root.chatBox.scroll = 1000;
    };
    root.sendButton.setEnabled(true);
}
function send() {
    if (length(message.text)>0) {
        hookup.call("message", null, message.text);
    }
```

```
        message.text = "";
        root.pumper.play();
    }
    sendButton.setEnabled(false);
    // disable until we connect
    config = SharedObject.getLocal("config");
    // auto connect
    user = config.data.user;
    connect();
    talk.onPress = function() {
        mic.setGain(75);
    };
    talk.onRelease = function() {
        mic.setGain(0);
    };
    //Bring up data
    function dataCall() {
        if (fetchData.getLabel() == "Data") {
            loadMovieNum("data.swf", 2);
            fetchData.setLabel("Close");
        } else if (fetchData.getLabel() == "Close") {
            unloadMovieNum(2);
            fetchData.setLabel("Data");
        }
    }
```

Customer Module

The Customer module began life as nothing more than the representative module with the streams going in opposite directions. However, over time, it developed in two different and important ways. First, I added three more UI component buttons to it for selecting bandwidth and an additional text field to inform the user which bandwidth was currently selected (**Figure 8.4**). This was important because of the different bandwidths of those with whom I tested it. Second, and belatedly, I began a login module (**Figure 8.5**). This module is simply an entry point where the customer-user can log in. At this point, it is somewhat redundant because login is automatic, but it is useful for the user entering her name and seeing it appear beneath her video.

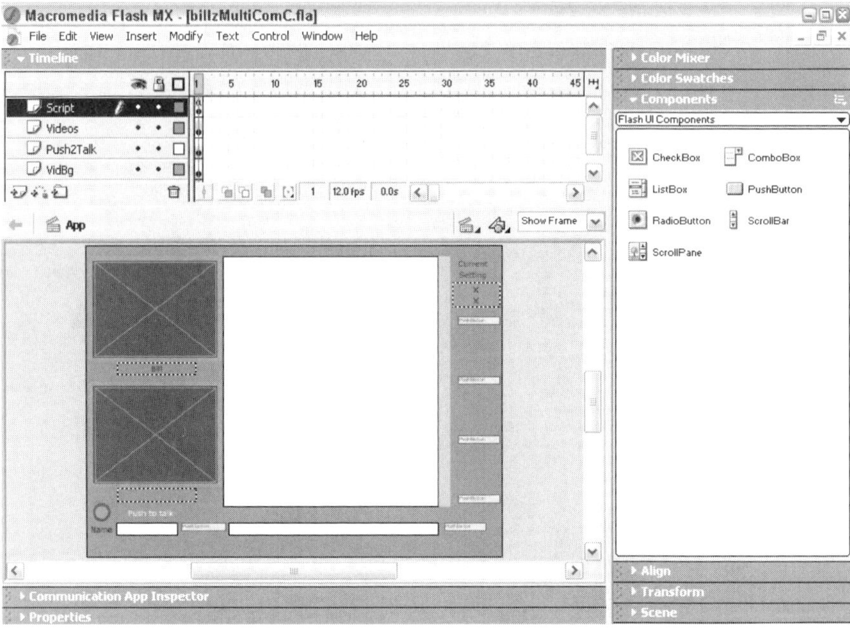

Figure 8.4 *The customer module has three added buttons on the right side to adjust for different connection speeds.*

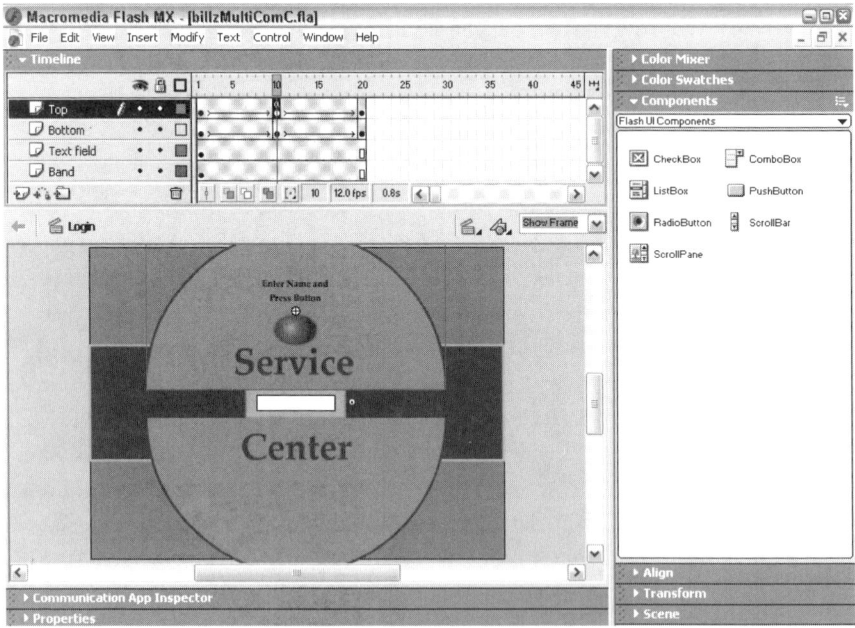

Figure 8.5 *The entry module (Login scene) provides a place where the users can enter names to appear beneath their pictures.*

Organizing the Customer Module Objects

The parts that make up the bulk of the objects on the stage for the Customer module are the same as for the Representative module; however, three additional UI components are added to give the customer an opportunity to adjust the connection parameters on the right side of the stage. Here's a list of what you need:

UI Components

NAME	CLICK HANDLER
Connect	connect
Send	send
Data	dataCall
LAN	lan
DSL	dsl
Modem	modem
NAME	**TARGET**
chatScroll	chatBox

Text Fields

INSTANCE NAME	TYPE
repName	Dynamic
cusName	Dynamic
cusName	Dynamic
message	Input

Text Fields

VAR NAME	TYPE
user	Input

Buttons

INSTANCE NAME	SYMBOL TYPE
checkIn	Button (In movie clip, instance name: top)
talk	Button
sender	Button

Client-Side Script

Here's the Customer module script:

```
Scene: Login
//Script for button checkIn
on(release) {
    _global.CusUser=_root.uname.text;
    _root.play();
}

Scene: App
```

Frame 1:

```
stop();
cusName.text = CusUser;
//Camera and Mic setup
cam = Camera.get();
cam.setMode(160, 120, 5);
cam.setQuality(0, 90);
mic = Microphone.get();
mic.setRate(22);
mic.setGain(0);
cus.attachVideo(cam);
//Connetion Type
_root.conType.text = "Default";
//Make the connection
function connect() {
    config.data.user = user;
    config.flush();
    hookup = new NetConnection();
    hookup.connect("rtmp:/billzMultiCom", user);
    //Out to customer rep
    outStream = new NetStream(hookup);
    outStream.publish("cusStream", "live");
    outStream.attachVideo(cam);
    outStream.attachAudio(mic);
    //Stream in from customer rep
    inStream = new NetStream(hookup);
    inStream.play("repStream");
    rep.attachVideo(inStream);
```

```
    hookup.onStatus = function(info) {
        trace(info.code+newline);
        if (info.code == "NetConnection.Connect.Closed") {
            _root.chatBox.text = "";
        }
    };
    hookup.chatBox = function(msg) {
        root.chatBox.text = msg;
    };
    msg = "";
    users = SharedObject.getRemote("users", hookup.uri, false);
    users.onSync = function(list) {
    };
    users.connect(hookup);
    users.message = function(msg) {
        root.chatBox.text += msg;
        root.chatBox.scroll = 1000;
    };
    root.sendButton.setEnabled(true);
}
function send() {
    if (length(message.text)>0) {
        hookup.call("message", null, message.text);
    }
    message.text = "";
    root.pumper.play();
}
sendButton.setEnabled(false);
// disable until we connect
config = SharedObject.getLocal("config");
// auto connect
user = config.data.user;
connect();
//Push to talk
talk.onPress = function() {
    mic.setGain(75);
};
talk.onRelease = function() {
    mic.setGain(0);
};
```

continues on next page

```
//Bring up data module
function dataCall() {
    if (fetchData.getLabel() == "Data") {
        loadMovieNum("data.swf", 2);
        fetchData.setLabel("Close");
    } else if (fetchData.getLabel() == "Close") {
        unloadMovieNum(2);
        fetchData.setLabel("Data");
    }
}
//Setting Options
//Phone Modem
function modem() {
    root.conType.text = "Phone Modem";
    cam.setMode(160, 120, 2);
    cam.setQuality(0, 75);
    cam.keyFrameInterval(3);
    mic.setRate(5);
}
//DSL
function dsl() {
    root.conType.text = "DSL";
    cam.setMode(160, 120, 5);
    cam.setQuality(0, 85);
    cam.keyFrameInterval(5);
    mic.setRate(11);
}
//LAN—T1, T3, Cable Modem
function lan() {
    root.conType.text = "LAN";
    cam.setMode(160, 120, 15);
    cam.setQuality(0, 90);
    cam.keyFrameInterval(10);
    mic.setRate(22);
}
```

Data Module: ActionScript, PHP and MySQL

This module is strictly for demonstration and proof-of-concept. Example data were put into a MySQL database and the PHP script accesses the data. It illustrates other ways to communicate with the application (**Figure 8.6**). Several more such applications could be superimposed on top of the text chat portion of the application. Any database or backend middleware would provide the same functionality.

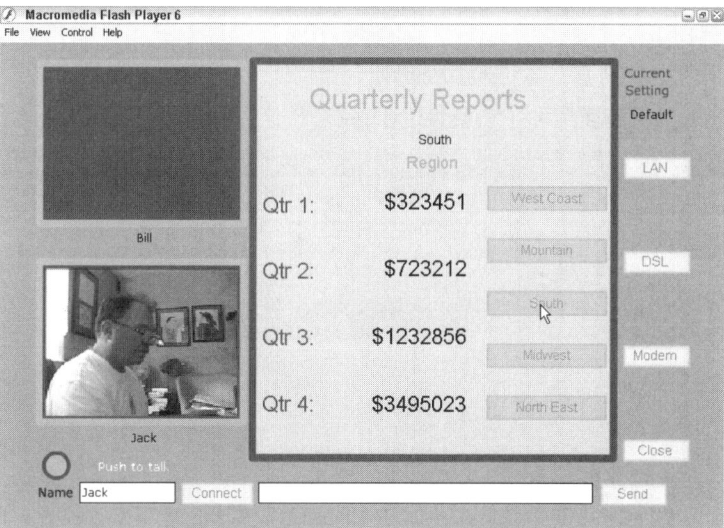

Figure 8.6 *The data module allows one additional mode of communication: data from a database.*

Passing Data Between Flash and PHP

Five functions make up the client-side ActionScript. The new `LoadVars()` object in Flash MX seems to be a much more effective and efficient way of passing variables and data between Flash and a backend than the older `loadVariables()` and `loadVariablesNum()` functions. The `sendAndLoad()` method enables you to send data in one `LoadVars()` object and receive it in another. For each function, I made a "Load" and "Hold" `LoadVars()` object. The "Load" object would load the variable that was to be passed to the PHP script and the "Hold" object would store the MySQL data sent through PHP. Then, using the `LoadVars.onLoad` method, with the "Hold" object, the data were passed to the text fields and a "$" added to the front. The variable passed to the PHP script is `regNum`, and so it was attached to the "Load" object for definition. The variables passed from PHP were `qt1wc`, `qt2wc`, `qt3wc`, and `qt4wc`, each representing a different quarterly profit.

Organizing the Data Module Objects

Standard Flash MX UI components and text fields makes up the objects on the Data module stage. The example is meant to be a generic one, and a further enhancement would be to make them all shared objects so that when one user opened the module, it would open it for all connected users. Here's a list of what you need:

UI Components

NAME	CLICK HANDLER
West Coast	west
Mountain	mountain
South	south
NAME	**TARGET**
North East	northeast

Text Fields

INSTANCE NAME	TYPE
q1	Dynamic
q2	Dynamic
q3	Dynamic
q4	Dynamic

ActionScript

```
function west() {
    root.region.text = "West Coast";
    westLoad = new LoadVars();
    westLoad.regNum = 0;
    westHold = new LoadVars();
    westHold.onLoad = function() {
        root.q1.text = "$"+this.qt1wc;
        root.q2.text = "$"+this.qt2wc;
        root.q3.text = "$"+this.qt3wc;
        root.q4.text = "$"+this.qt4wc;
    };
    westLoad.sendAndLoad("http://www.sandlight.com/
    → getReport.php", westHold);
}
```

```
function mountain() {
    root.region.text = "Mountain";
    mtLoad = new LoadVars();
    mtLoad.regNum = 1;
    mtHold = new LoadVars();
    mtHold.onLoad = function() {
        root.q1.text = "$"+this.qt1wc;
        root.q2.text = "$"+this.qt2wc;
        root.q3.text = "$"+this.qt3wc;
        root.q4.text = "$"+this.qt4wc;
    };
    mtLoad.sendAndLoad("http://www.sandlight.com/
    → getReport.php", mtHold);
}
function south() {
    root.region.text = "South";
    southLoad = new LoadVars();
    southLoad.regNum = 2;
    southHold = new LoadVars();
    southHold.onLoad = function() {
        root.q1.text = "$"+this.qt1wc;
        root.q2.text = "$"+this.qt2wc;
        root.q3.text = "$"+this.qt3wc;
        root.q4.text = "$"+this.qt4wc;
    };
    southLoad.sendAndLoad("http://www.sandlight.com/
    → getReport.php", southHold);
}
function midwest() {
    root.region.text = "Midwest";
    mwestLoad = new LoadVars();
    mwestLoad.regNum = 3;
    mwestHold = new LoadVars();
    mwestHold.onLoad = function() {
        root.q1.text = "$"+this.qt1wc;
        root.q2.text = "$"+this.qt2wc;
        root.q3.text = "$"+this.qt3wc;
        root.q4.text = "$"+this.qt4wc;
    };
    mwestLoad.sendAndLoad("http://www.sandlight.com/
    → getReport.php", mwestHold);
}
```

continues on next page

```
function northeast() {
    root.region.text = "Northeast";
    northLoad = new LoadVars();
    northLoad.regNum = 4;
    northHold = new LoadVars();
    northHold.onLoad = function() {
        root.q1.text = "$"+this.qt1wc;
        root.q2.text = "$"+this.qt2wc;
        root.q3.text = "$"+this.qt3wc;
        root.q4.text = "$"+this.qt4wc;
    };
    northLoad.sendAndLoad("http://www.sandlight.com/
    → getReport.php", northHold);
}
```

Server-Side PHP

The PHP script is simple as befits a demo. Four values are passed from a row in the MySQL table with the row value passed from Flash MX. The PHP variable, `$regNum`, receives values from 0 to 4 which it uses to select from MySQL fields, qt1, qt2, qt3, or qt4. (For those of you unfamiliar with PHP, a variable passed to PHP is placed into a variable of the same name with a dollar-sign [$] in front of it.) Each field in each row contains a value representing fictitious quarterly profits from a small corporation.

Once all of the data are placed into the PHP variables, they are re-formatted for Flash MX. The format

```
varName1=val1&varName2=val2....
```

is used to place all of the data into a single PHP variable, `$qtData`. Using the PHP echo statement, the results are sent back to the Data module:

```
<?php
//Setup and connect
$server="localhost";
//Server name
$user="sandligh_streame";
//User name
$pass="tincan";
//Password
```

```
$flashbase ="sandligh_flash1";
//database name
$billz_table="reports";
//table name

//Make the connection
$hookup = mysql_connect($server, $user, $pass);

//Select database
mysql_select_db($flashbase,$hookup);

//Query specific table in database
$result = mysql_query("SELECT * FROM $billz_table",$hookup);
$q1wc=(mysql_result($result,$regNum,"qt1"));
$q2wc=(mysql_result($result,$regNum,"qt2"));
$q3wc=(mysql_result($result,$regNum,"qt3"));
$q4wc=(mysql_result($result,$regNum,"qt4"));

//Format for Flash
$qtData="qt1wc=$q1wc&qt2wc=$q2wc&qt3wc=$q3wc&qt4wc=$q4wc";
echo "$qtData";
?>
```

Next Steps

Some applications are done when shipped and others are an ongoing project. For me, this multiple-communication application is an ongoing project. Each time I thought it was complete, I found ways to improve it, and friends have found many more ways to make improvements. At the time of this writing, the Flash Communication Server MX was just about ready to be shipped, and so it is safe for me to say that what I have done is only the beginning.

As a tool, I believe that the Macromedia Flash Communication Server MX offers unforeseen opportunities for developing communication software. With email, billions of Web pages, and mobile phones everywhere, one might wonder what yet another communication format has to offer. Plus, for years, anyone with a Webcam and Internet connection has been able to see and talk with anyone similarly equipped. For me, and the many others with whom I shared the early development process of FCS, the idea that we could design and configure our own communication application easily opened new doors. In my case, I wanted something for only two people with the ability to communicate in many different ways. It is a tool to solve any kind of communication challenge or opportunity that may present itself. As such, not only does it empower a wide range of people with different communication needs, it provides the ability to experiment with a wider range of communication modes. As the saying goes, "You ain't seen (or heard) nothing yet!"

On the CD-ROM

In the Chapter 8 folder on this book's CD-ROM, you'll find 10 files in a folder named billzMultiCom. Usually a folder name doesn't mean much, but with Flash Communication Server MX, it does. The folder is the app or application. The name of the folder must be consistent with the NetConnection.connect() line in the Representative and Customer modules:

```
hookup.connect("rtmp:/billzMultiCom", user);
```

You can change the application's name to JoezMultiCom or SuezMultiCom or any other name you want. However, when you do so, be sure to change the NetConnection.connect() method so that the reference is consistent with the folder name.

Of the 10 files, the three FLA files are the only ones you do not need in the folder to successfully run the application. (If you're not using a browser, you don't need the HTML files, either.) However, unless you are placing the files on a remote hosting service, leave the FLA files in the same folder. That way, if you want to customize the files to suit your needs, it is easy to save and publish them where you need them.

If you are running the developer's or trial version of FlashCom, you need to place the folder inside the applications folder that is inside the flashcom folder. Depending on where your Web server is located, you will want the flashcom folder at the root level of the Web server. For example, a typical path on Windows XP Pro would be:

```
C:\Inetpub\wwwroot\flashcom\applications\billzMultiCom
```

When you launch your application, one user selects billzMultiComR.html (or .swf) and the other user selects billzMultiComC.html (or swf). If used with a browser, on your own computer, you would use an address something like the following:

```
http://localhost/flashcom/applications/billzMultiCom/billzMultiComR.html
```

The person with whom you want to chat would enter:

```
http://IPaddress/flashcom/applications/billzMultiCom/billzMultiComC.html
```

where IPaddress would be the actual IP address (such as 12.201.34.701). If you want to place the materials on your hosting service, be sure to check that it has a FlashCom server running and how it wants you to configure your application.

A: Multiuser Servers

by Michael Grundvig

When we work with multiplayer games, such as the one in Chapter 5, we use a socket server called ElectroServer, along with an ActionScript object called ElectroServerAS. In this appendix, we discuss what a socket server is, how one works, and how you can use one for your own games. More specifically, we talk about ElectroServer. We also discuss how to install ElectroServer on almost any computer, from a desktop model to a multiprocessor Sun server.

What Is a Socket Server?

Before we can get into the details of installing and using a socket server, it's important to understand what a socket server is. Put simply, a socket server—also called a *multiuser server*—is a server that listens for inbound client connections on a port and allows those clients to communicate with each other over a common protocol (which in the case of ElectroServer is XML). That's quite a mouthful! Let's break this concept down into more digestible parts. We'll start with a review of the Internet basics on which a socket server depends.

Internet Basics

While I'm sure everyone reading this uses the Internet just about all the time, it's surprising to learn how little most developers know about how it actually works. I've always felt that the more knowledge you have about something, the more effective you can be in using it. In the case of socket servers, this knowledge can help you avoid the sticky deployment and security issues that so many people run into.

IP Address

While the Internet Protocol (IP) address isn't even close to being the lowest level of networking on the Internet, it's the lowest layer we need to worry about. An IP address means just what it says: It's essentially the address of a computer on the Internet. While there are exceptions, it's easiest to assume that each computer on the Internet has a unique IP address (**Figure A.1**). An IP address, coupled with some other Internet technologies, is enough to let any machine find and communicate with any other machine over the Internet.

An IP address typically takes the form `XX.XX.XX.XX`, where each segment can be a one, two, or three-digit number. For example, one of the Web servers for Macromedia.com is `65.57.83.12`.

These numbers are called *dotted quads* or just *IPs*. A single segment in the IP is called an *octet* because its maximum size is 2^8, defined as a range of 0–255. At first glance, it may seem as if the number of IP addresses available is huge and we will never run out; but in reality we are already getting uncomfortably close to the limit. The current IPv4 specification allows for about 4.3 billion addresses, but with the explosive growth of users on the Internet, more and more IPs are needed every day.

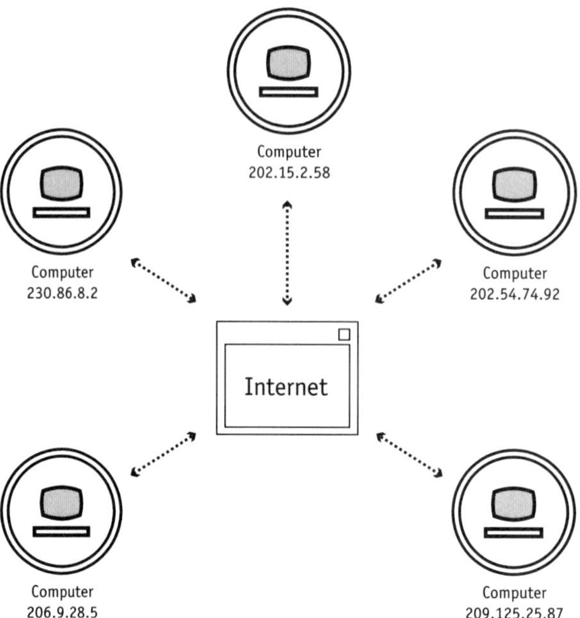

Figure A.1 *Generally, each computer on the Internet has a unique IP address.*

To this end, a new version of the IP specification called IPv6 is in the works. This specification adds improved multimedia streaming and better performance. But most important, it increases the IP address size from 32-bit to 128-bit.

How do you get an IP? In the case of home users, you are assigned an IP address when your machine connects to your ISP. If you are on dial-up, this means that every time you connect to the Internet, you typically get a new IP address. For the most part, cable and DSL modems work the same way, but as you are always connected, your IP usually won't change unless you reboot your machine. There are some exceptions to this, however. Many DSL providers are using a technology named PPPoE (Point-to-Point Protocol over Ethernet), which allows you to disconnect and reconnect with your machine still running. When this happens, you could be assigned a new IP address. Also, it is possible to "release" your current IP address and get another one, but the method for doing so depends on your operating system and there is no guarantee that it will be a new IP address.

Figure A.2 shows the typical home computer setup with a DSL or cable modem. You can also have something called a *static IP address*. This means that your IP doesn't change from one day to the next but stays the same even after your connection goes down or you have to reboot. Servers on the Internet almost always have static IP addresses, and there are few cases where you wouldn't want one.

So do you have to be online to get an IP address? Not at all! Any machine that supports TCP/IP (the protocol the Internet uses) always has an IP available to it. This is a reserved IP called the *loopback IP*, and you can connect to it using the IP 127.0.0.1 or the host name `localhost`. This IP is used for diagnostics and testing but can also be used by us Flash developers to run socket servers locally without anyone else's being able to access them. We'll talk more about this later.

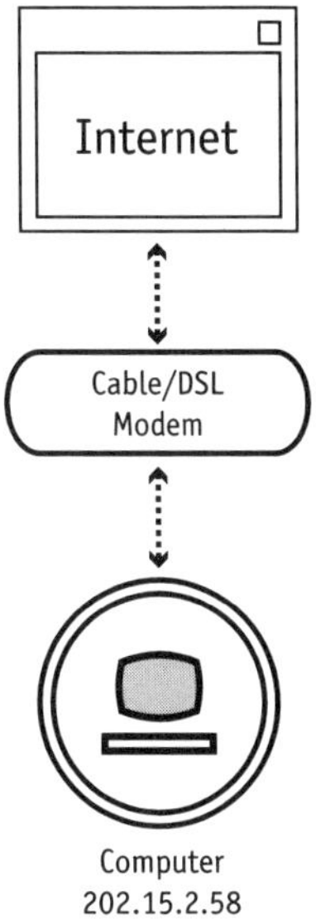

Internet

Cable/DSL
Modem

Computer
202.15.2.58

Figure A.2 *A DSL or cable modem connects a home computer with the Internet.*

I said previously that each computer on the Internet has a unique IP address, and also that this is not strictly true. You've probably heard of firewalls and routers. These devices can be used to hide IP addresses from the Internet in various ways. Now before any of you groan and skip ahead, know that I bring this up because it directly relates to running a socket server on your home machine and getting people to see it on the Internet. Kind of important!

Here's a real-life example to illustrate the situation. If a small corporation wanted to provide its 20 employees with Internet access from their workstations through the company's dedicated ISDN line, how would it do this? One possible way would be to contact the company's ISP and have 20 IP addresses made available to its network. This constitutes a maintenance headache and a lot of administrative overhead. A simpler way would be to use a technology called Network Address Translation (NAT). NAT enables one computer to act as a gateway to the Internet for other computers. This computer would have one connection to the Internet with an externally available IP address, and another connection to the internal network with an internal address (**Figure A.3**). This is usually accomplished by having two network cards. By "internal address," I mean an IP that only the internal network will understand. Often these start with *10* in the first octet. Each computer on the internal network would also have its own unique internal IP and would understand that to connect to the Internet, it needs to go through the gateway.

I bring this up because many people with cable modems or DSL access use small router/firewall appliances made by companies such as Linksys, 3Com, or Intel. When you use one of these appliances, you cannot run a socket server on the internally designated IP address and expect people on the external Internet to see it without some configuration changes. Specifically, you can start the server without any problems, but when you give out your IP and port, people will not be able to connect to it. If this happens, you may need to use the DMZ, port, or IP forwarding feature of your appliance to allow external clients to connect to your server. A DMZ allows your computer to be in an unsecure location on your network, and thus the firewall allows anyone in. Port and IP forwarding are ways to tell your firewall to send all IP requests on a given port to your server rather than blocking them. One other solution to this problem is to open up that port on your firewall so that it is not restricted. Implementing any of these solutions is beyond the scope of this appendix. Look in your router/firewall appliance's documentation to see which will work best for you.

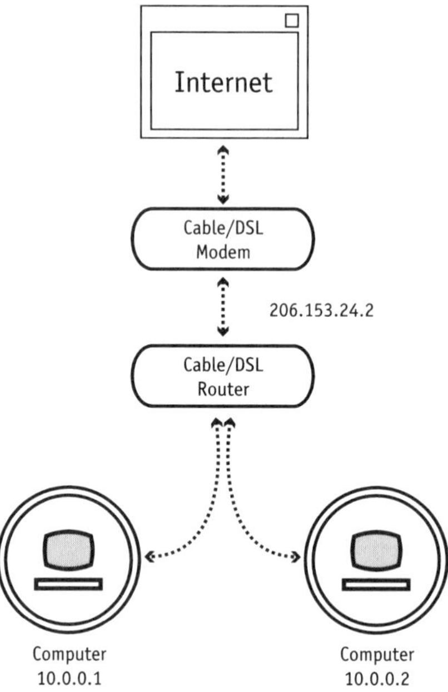

Figure A.3 *Computers on the internal network have IP addresses that only their network understands.*

Ports

Thus far, we have talked about a computer's address on the Internet. This is a valid analogy on the surface, but it still needs some refinement. The typical computer on the Internet has one IP address but is often running many different Internet-related applications at the same time. As you know, Web browsers, instant messengers, email clients, multiplayer games, and other applications can all run simultaneously.

With only one address, how does your computer know which application needs the data you are receiving? This is where ports come into play. There are 65,536 ports associated with every IP address on a computer. If you think of each IP address as the real-world address of an apartment building, a port would be an apartment number.

This means that, theoretically, your desktop computer could be talking to 65,000+ remote computers at the same time without getting confused. (Realistically, a desktop machine couldn't handle that, but some servers are more than able to.) So when talking to a remote computer, you use not just the IP address but also a specific port to uniquely identify both the computer *and* the service/application with which you wish to communicate.

You would think that with 65,536 ports available, there would be enough for every service imaginable. And for the most part, there are—but still, you have to be careful. Many ports are reserved for a specific functionality, such as HTTP, FTP, POP, SMTP, and many others. The general rule of thumb is that you should never use any port below 1024 for your own applications. In the case of Flash with XMLSocket, this is a hard rule—Flash is unable to use a port below 1024. Table A.1 lists common ports used by various services.

Table A.1 *Commonly Used Ports*

INTERNET SERVICE	TCP PORT	INTERNET SERVICE	TCP PORT
HTTP	80	FTP	21
HTTPS	443	Telnet	23
SMTP	25	NMTP	119
POP3	110		

Sockets

A socket is simply one endpoint of a two-way connection over a network. Any socket is defined by an IP and a port. When a server application is running, it "listens" on a socket for inbound connections from a client. A client, such as a Web browser, knows the IP or host name and port number of the server, and attempts to connect. If all goes properly, the server accepts the connection and then moves the client's connection to a different socket, which it picks internally. This is so that the server can continue listening for clients on the original socket, in order to accommodate more than one client at a time. Once they are connected through the internally picked socket, both the client and the server are able to communicate with each other directly.

Let's follow through with our example of a Web browser. You open your favorite Internet browser and type in `http://www.macromedia.com`. Through the wonder of DNS (that's a Domain Name Server, which maps an IP address to a domain name), that domain name is translated to `65.57.83.12`. The browser knows you are using HTTP, so it knows the port is 80. This is enough information to attempt to establish a socket connection to `65.57.83.12:80`. Internally, the Web browser does exactly that. The Macromedia Web server accepts the connection and shuffles your browser to a different socket on its side. At this point, your browser is able to request a Web page. Once you have finished getting the page you want, your browser automatically closes the connection to the server and is able to move on. This is a very simple description of what happens, but it gives you the basic idea.

Where Does Flash Fit In?

We have now talked about the basic underlying technologies used to establish TCP connections between computers on the Internet, and how a common application handles this transaction. Now, how does Flash accomplish this? Easy—exactly the same way!

Flash does not handle sockets any differently than your Web browser does. The only difference is the protocol that's used. In a Web browser it's HTTP. When you receive email, it's POP3 or IMAP. For sending email, it's SMTP. In Flash, it's XML, which you define yourself to best customize it to your task. (And Flash hasn't chosen a specific port number, so you can pick whatever port you want, as long as it's above 1024.)

Now that you have all that background material under your belt, let's talk specifically about socket servers and how they work with Flash.

Socket Servers

A socket server is just a server that listens on a socket for a connection from a Flash client, and accepts those connections when it hears them. That seems straightforward enough, but now you are probably wondering: What makes a socket server different from a Web server? Well, two things specifically: A socket server uses a different protocol, and its connections are state-full.

A *state-full* connection is one that remembers the user between interactions. This critical difference dramatically extends Flash's abilities over an application based on the HTTP protocol. The HTTP protocol is not state-full. There are many clever methods to make it *appear* to remember a client between requests, but in reality a Web page doesn't know if you visited it five minutes or five days ago. It is always up to the non-state-full application (any Web application using HTTP) to determine who you are, as well as to store any data it needs to remember about you. Conversely, the connections to a socket server are held open until you explicitly close them with code, or until you close the Flash application. This means that many transactions can occur over one connection, and that the server can remember you between transactions with little difficulty. This is necessary for chat functionality such as game history, accurate counts of people in a room, and so on.

The protocol for a Web server is HTTP. The high-level protocol for a socket server, as we've said, is XML. This is where the power and flexibility of a socket server come into play. By using XML as the high-level protocol, you can define your own specific (that is, user-defined) protocol for the application at hand.

Introducing ElectroServer

As you can see, a socket server is a simple yet powerful communication tool. The specific implementations of a socket server may vary, but the basic idea is the same. There are several major socket servers available for Flash and quite a few minor ones. Here we'll introduce you to the one we know best, and which, of course, is best suited for the online gaming environment: ElectroServer. ElectroServer is a high-performance socket server designed by your friends at Electrotank (`www.electrotank.com`) with multiplayer Flash games in mind. Throughout this book, the multiplayer games have all used ElectroServer and its various features. Over the next few pages, we will discuss those features and how you can install, use, and administer ElectroServer for your own use.

If you're planning to run the server, make sure to read "Properties File" in the "Configuring ElectroServer" section of this appendix.

On the CD-ROM we've included a full version of ElectroServer and a demo license key. The demo license key is limited to five concurrent connections and works on any IP address. This means that up to five people can be connected to the server at once. ElectroServer running in demo mode must be able to connect to the Internet every time it is started, or it shuts itself down. For the most recent information on ElectroServer, or if you are interested in a copy that accepts more than five concurrent connections, visit `www.electrotank.com/ElectroServer`.

Features

ElectroServer has several unique abilities that other socket servers don't support, and that allow for some sophisticated game functionality. Let's start with the basic features and work toward the more advanced ones.

Many features are configurable via a properties file (which we'll discuss in "Configuring ElectroServer" a little later in this appendix).

Rooms. ElectroServer supports a room model for all chatting and games. This means that when you connect to the server, you are not automatically in a room, and you must join one to do anything.

Rooms can be either visible or hidden (in which case they don't show up on the room list). The `ElectroServerAS` object used in this book (and discussed in further detail in Appendix B) takes care of this for you. Making a game room invisible keeps people from attempting to join it.

When the number of users in a room changes, all rooms set to receive updates are notified of the new room size. This is useful for getting a count of users in any given room. But rooms can also be configured to ignore these updates for performance reasons, and many people prefer that configuration.

Room list. All clients (users) receive an accurate list of all visible rooms on the server. This list contains the number of users in all rooms as well. It does not contain rooms that have been marked invisible.

User list. Within each room is a list of users for that room. This list is updated every time someone enters or leaves the room, so it is always up-to-date.

Private messages. ElectroServer supports the capability for users to send private messages to any specific player on the server.

Administrators. ElectroServer supports the concept of administrators. Administrators are users who have access to kick and ban functionalities (discussed next). To create or remove an administrator account, you use the built-in administrator console application (explained later).

Kick user. If a user is acting up (and believe me, this happens a *lot*), then you can kick the user from the server. This does not work in the same way as a kick in IRC (which only removes you from a room). In ElectroServer, the kick command disconnects a user totally from the server and gives him a message about why he was booted. This command is available only to users who have administrator-level status.

Ban user. If a user is being particularly bad, you can ban her from the server. Ban is based on the user's IP address, so it is not foolproof. But it is permanent—if you ban her and restart the server, she is still banned from the system.

An administration tool is provided to remove users from the ban list. The ability to ban is available only to users who have administrator-level status.

Logging. ElectroServer provides extensive logging functionality to ensure smooth operation. When the server starts, it initializes all necessary components and logs that information to the screen. Once the components are started and the server is listening for users, it starts logging instead to whatever location is specified in the properties file. If requested, the server will roll log files—rename the old file and start a new one with the original name—at startup. The server supports configurable levels of logging, allowing you to determine how much or how little information you want to capture. All error, kick, and ban messages are logged no matter what.

Language filtering. ElectroServer supports the capability to determine if a player is using words that are prohibited on the site. The prohibited words are listed in a text file specified in the properties file. This feature can be enabled or disabled and has many configurable options, including the capability to kick offenders from the server.

System messages. A system message is one transmitted to all users in all rooms, regardless of their status. It can be used to inform users of events about to occur, such as a server restart or a celebrity chat. Only administrator-level users can send out system messages.

Room variables. A room variable is defined at the room level by a user. These variables have various configurable behaviors. For instance, a room variable can be configured to remove itself when the user who created it leaves the room. A room variable can be locked to protect it from being overwritten, or it can be persistent and maintained even when the user who created it leaves the room. Room variables are automatically sent to all users when they are created, modified, or deleted. A user gets all the room variables in a room when he joins the room. Room variables are one of the features that make ElectroServer especially well suited for games.

Object serialization. This powerful ElectroServer feature actually stems from its client-side object. The `ElectroServerAS` object supports the capability to take most ActionScript objects not bound to physical resources (such as movie clips and sound clips) and send them to the room the user is in, or even use them as room variables. This makes it quick and easy to send complicated data structures to anyone.

Detect updates. ElectroServer supports the capability to automatically check for updates to its code over the Internet. When the server first starts, it makes an HTTP connection to `www.electrotank.com` and checks the available versions. It determines if the version online is newer than your current version and notifies you.

Administration. ElectroServer supports several console-based administration applications to ease administering the server. You can manage the administrator accounts, as well as the banned-user lists, from simple console applications.

Installing ElectroServer

While this is a production-quality server, you can very easily run it on your local workstation. In fact, that is the recommended way to develop multi-user applications.

There are several ways to install ElectroServer. Because ElectroServer is written completely in Java, it runs on any platform that supports the 1.3.1 Java Virtual Machine. Sun Microsystems currently has downloads for Windows, Solaris, and Linux; and many other platforms support Java as well, such as Mac OS X and HPUX.

The first thing you need to do, regardless of platform, is install the Java Virtual Machine. For Windows, Solaris, or Linux you can find it at Java.Sun.com (`http://java.sun.com`). For Mac OS X, you can find it at Mac OS X Java Runtime Environment (`http://developer.apple.com/java`).

Follow the directions listed with the download and install the Java environment. When you are completely finished, you should be able to type `java` from a command prompt and get a response that looks something like this:

```
C:\WINDOWS\Desktop>java
Usage: java [-options] class [args...]
        (to execute a class)
    or  java -jar [-options] jarfile [args...]
        (to execute a jar file)
```

This is how it looks for the 1.4 JVM, so yours might look a little different. At this point, your computer should be able to run Java applications, and you can proceed with the actual installation of ElectroServer, which should be very simple.

Windows Installation

Run the Windows installer (`setup.exe`) for ElectroServer from the CD-ROM included with this book. You'll find it in the Demos\ElectroServer\Windows folder. Run this application as you would any other, and follow the onscreen prompts to finish installing ElectroServer. This installation creates a Start-menu group as well as a script you can use to start and stop the server as needed. The setup application also creates an uninstaller.

Unix Installation

Locate the Demos\ElectroServer\Unix folder on the CD-ROM. Copy the files in that directory to the location from which you want the server to run. Usually it's something like /usr/local/ElectroServer, but that is completely at your discretion. Then execute the `Setup.sh` script. It extracts the contents of the .tar file into your current directory. The server should now be installed correctly.

Other Platform Installation

Locate the Demos\ElectroServer\Generic folder on the CD-ROM. Take the .zip file in that folder and manually extract it to wherever you want the server to execute.

The difference between this installation and the other installation methods is that this one won't create easy-to-use start and stop scripts for you.

Configuring ElectroServer

Now that you have the server and Java installed, you need to configure it to reflect your desired environment, startup options, and features. Configuring ElectroServer is quite simple; everything you need to manage or change can be done through either an easy-to-use console application or the text-based properties file.

Properties File

Most of the ElectroServer configuration occurs through the ElectroServer.properties file that is created in the installation directory. You can open this file in any text editor, such as Notepad or VI. The various configuration options for the ElectroServer.properties file are documented right in the file, so we won't cover that information here. Any changes to the properties file require you to restart the server.

There are two configurations that are crucial to starting the server. The first is:

```
General.LicenseFileLocation
```

This option points to the ElectroServer license file in the installation directory, without which the server cannot start. By default, it points to the demo license file, which lets you run the ElectroServer on any IP address and port, but with a maximum of five connections at once. This license also requires the server to be able to connect to the Internet, or it won't start. If you have any settings in the properties file that don't match your license file, the server informs you of that, and shuts down.

The second crucial configuration is:

```
ChatServer.IP
```

This setting is used for the chat server's IP address. By default, it is set to 127.0.0.1. This is the loopback IP for your machine, as we discussed previously. You will have to change this if you want other people on the Internet to connect to the server.

Administrator Accounts

If you want to have administrators for your chat server, you have to set the `ChatServer.AdministrationEnabled` setting in the properties file to `true`. Once this is done, you need to run the ElectroServer administration tool to add administrators. Here's how you can run the tool in various platforms:

Windows—Either choose the Start Administrator option from the Start menu or go to ElectroServer's installation folder and run the file `StartAdministrator.bat`.

Unix—From ElectroServer's installation folder, run `StartAdministrator.sh`.

Other platforms—From ElectroServer's installation folder, run:

```
java -cp ElectroServerV2.jar com.electrotank.electroserver.
➥admin.ElectroAdmin
```

Please note that no matter how this looks onscreen, it's one command line.

Once in the tool, choose the Manage Administrator Accounts option and follow the onscreen prompts.

Language Filter

The Language filter manages a customizable list of any words you want blocked on your chat server. You simply specify the location of the bad-word list in the ElectroServer.properties file. This list is a plain-text file in this format:

```
Badword1
Badword2
...
Badword10
```

You can change this file at any time, but you need to restart the server in order to see those changes.

Banned IPs

If some IP addresses have been banned on the server and you want to remove them from the restricted list, you need to run the ElectroServer administration tool. You can run the tool in the same way you did for administering admin accounts. Once in the tool, choose the Manage Banned IP Addresses option, and then follow the onscreen prompts.

Running ElectroServer

Running ElectroServer is similar to running the Administrator—very simple. As you can imagine, the server must be started before you can jump into testing, playing, or chatting.

Starting the Server

Windows Choose the Start ElectroServer option from the Start menu, or go to the ElectroServer installation folder and run `StartElectroServer.bat.`

Unix Run `StartElectroServer.sh` from the ElectroServer installation folder.

Other platforms Run

```
java -cp ElectroServerV2.jar
com.electrotank.electroserver.ElectroServer
ElectroServer.properties
```

from the ElectroServer installation folder.

Stopping the Server

Windows Choose the Stop ElectroServer option from the Start menu, or go to the ElectroServer installation folder and run `StopElectroServer.bat`.

Unix Run `StopElectroServer.sh` from the ElectroServer installation folder.

Other platforms Run

```
java -cp ElectroServerV2.jar
com.electrotank.electroserver.StopES
ElectroServer.properties
```

from the ElectroServer installation folder.

ElectroServer has been around from almost the beginning of Flash 5 and has seen a lot of use for many different applications. It's been used by numerous companies on many platforms with great success. With a little effort, you should have no trouble adapting it for your needs.

B: The ElectroServerAS Object

by Jobe Makar

The ElectroServerAS object allows you to easily create chats, multiplayer games, and any other types of multiuser entertainment applications you are interested in developing. It is an ActionScript object that has tons of properties and methods to make your job as a Macromedia Flash developer much easier. With this object, you do not need to write a single line of XML to talk to the ElectroServer socket server; it does that for you!

For instance, if you want to send a chat message, all you need to do is execute a line of ActionScript like this:

```
ElectroServerAS.sendMessage(info, "room")
```

The `info` variable contains the message you wish to send. The second parameter, "`room`", specifies whether you want to send the message to the room at large or as a private message to another user. When this line of ActionScript is executed, the `ElectroServerAS` object takes the information passed in, determines which XML tags are necessary, formats the data, and sends it to the server.

But the `ElectroServerAS object` can do more than just send and receive messages. It can create variables at the room level on the server itself. Also, to make multiplayer games easier to program, we have enabled the `ElectroServerAS` object (with the help of the `WDDX_ms.as` script, created by Branden Hall of Fig Leaf Software) to send objects to other users. This is a big advantage over other multiuser server systems (server and Flash client working together), because it means that when a player makes a move in a game, instead of having to format an awkward string or XML packet with a zillion attributes, she can just send the object itself. Also, if you find it useful, which I'm sure you will, you can create variables in a room on the server. Whenever these variables are created, updated, or deleted, everyone in the room is informed. This makes creation of a card-based game like poker or hearts (which involves shuffling the deck and informing the players of the card arrangement) more elegant. Without this feature, you'd need a round-robin type of procedure—which I find very annoying—in which everyone messages everyone else privately. Room variables get around this and enable some really cool possibilities in games.

You can certainly develop chats and multiplayer games without the use of the* `ElectroServerAS` *object, but it would require a lot of work—writing and parsing XML documents—as well as numerous hours of debugging.

Earlier, I mentioned that ElectroServer's ability to send ActionScript objects to other users gives it a great advantage over other multiuser servers. I want to also make it clear that there is nothing keeping other multiuser servers from doing this, since it is actually a feature of the `ElectroServerAS` object and not the socket server. If you use a socket server other than ElectroServer, you can add this ability yourself, but it will take quite a bit of time to write.

In order to use much of the `ElectroServerAS` object's functionality, you must understand event handlers. An *event handler* is a function that is called when an event occurs. There are many multiuser events that can occur, such as receiving a chat message, receiving a move in a game, receiving an update of the room list, and receiving a game challenge from another user. While you probably won't ever need to use all of the methods and properties `ElectroServerAS` offers, you will want to know they are there—and how to use them. In this appendix we list and describe every method and property of the `ElectroServerAS` object.

Evolution Is Ongoing!

Just as with every innovation that makes our lives easier, we are always finding new ways to increase the usefulness of the `ElectroServerAS` object. To download the most recent version of this object (and any—gulp—bug fixes or documentation fixes), please visit Electrotank's ElectroServer page (`www.electrotank.com/ElectroServer`).

In the AppendixB folder on the CD-ROM, you'll find two functional chats that were created using the `ElectroServerAS` object. Chat_fullfeatured.fla has all the features of a good chat. Chat_barebones.fla has the absolute minimum features needed to create a working chat.

Click-and-Drag Actions

We've mentioned that there are a lot of methods and properties in the `ElectroServerAS` object, and many of them are really useful for game development. But don't think you have to remember the syntax for even the ones you use all the time. You can install these actions directly into the Actions toolbox in the Actions panel in Flash (that's a lot of Action!), and drag and drop them into the script pane whenever you want to use them. This installation will also enable color-coding for all `ElectroServerAS` actions.

1. Open Flash.
2. Locate the install.swf file in the AppendixB directory, and open it inside the Flash environment (as a SWF—don't import it!).
3. Click the Install ElectroServerAS Object Actions button.

   The actions are now installed. Close the SWF and look in the Actions panel. You'll see that the `ElectroServerAS` object is now an option in the Actions panel. Currently there is no documentation (reference help) installed with these actions; this appendix will serve as the documentation.

However, by the time this book is published, there will probably be an updated installer for these actions (see www.electrotank.com/ElectroServer) that should contain the reference help.

4. For the color-coded version, close Flash and then reopen it.

In order for all of these actions to work, you must include the file ElectroServerAS.as within the Flash file that is to make use of the ElectroServerAS object. ElectroServerAS.as is a text file that contains all of the ActionScript used to define the methods and properties of the ElectroServerAS object. You don't ever need to open or edit this file (unless you want to extend the object's capabilities).

To include ElectroServerAS.as with your movie (which you must do to make use of its actions) follow this simple procedure:

1. Copy the ElectroServerAS.as file into the directory where your Flash movie is saved.
2. Copy WDDX_mx.as into that same directory.

   This file enables the ElectroServerAS object to send ActionScript objects.
3. Add this line of ActionScript to the main timeline anywhere before you need to start using the ElectroServerAS object:

   ```
   #include "ElectroServerAS.as"
   ```

That's it. Now when you create a SWF movie, all of the information in the ElectroServerAS.as file will be pulled into it. You do not need to insert an include action for WDDX_mx.as, because ElectroServerAS.as does that for you automatically.

Methods and Properties of ElectroServerAS

And now, without further ado, here is the list of all events and functions that the ElectroServerAS object can perform.

Please note that all of the methods included here are intended to be used with Flash Player 6; the version that supports and correctly interprets them is Flash Player 6.

ElectroServer works with Flash 5 and with Flash MX. However, the `ElectroServerAS` ***object works only with Flash MX, because of the function scoping changes that are new to Flash MX.***

ElectroServerAS.addToHistory

Usage: `ElectroServerAS.addToHistory(message)`

Parameter: `message`—This parameter is the string to add to the chat history.

Returns: Nothing.

Description: Method; appends a string to the `history` property, `ElectroServerAS.history`.

Example: The following line adds a chat message to the `history` property:

```
ElectroServerAS.addToHistory("Anyone for a game of golf?")
```

ElectroServerAS.ban

Usage: `ElectroServerAS.ban(who, why)`

Parameters:

`who`—This is the user name of the person whom you wish to ban.

`why`—This parameter shows the reason why you wish to ban this user.

Returns: Nothing.

Description: Method; disconnects a user from the ElectroServer socket server and bans him or her from connecting from that IP address again. This method is only available to users with administrator-level access. See also `ElectroServerAS.login`.

Example: The following line bans a user:

```
ElectroServerAS.ban("meanie", "Offensive language")
```

ElectroServerAS.cancelChallenge

Usage: `ElectroServerAS.cancelChallenge()`

Parameters: None.

Returns: Nothing.

Description: Method; cancels the challenge request you sent out. The `ElectroServerAS.challengeCancelled` event is fired on the challengee's side.

ElectroServerAS.challenge

Usage: `ElectroServerAS.challenge(who, game)`

Parameters:

`who`—This is the user name of the person whom you wish to challenge.

`game`—This parameter is a string that is the name of the game to which you are challenging a user.

Returns: Nothing.

Description: Method; challenges a user to a game. The `ElectroServerAS.challengeReceived` event is triggered on the challengee's computer. The property `ElectroServerAS.challenging` is set to `true`.

Example: The following line is an example of how to challenge a user:

```
ElectroServerAS.challenge("jobem","Mini Golf")
```

ElectroServerAS.challengeAnswered

Usage: `ElectroServerAS.challengeAnswered(which)`

Parameter: `which`—This is a string value indicating the response from the person challenged (`"accepted"`, `"declined"`, or `"autodeclined"`).

Returns: Nothing.

Description: Method; a callback function invoked by the `ElectroServerAS` object when a person you have challenged responds to that challenge. If the user accepts your challenge, `which` is `"accepted"`. If the user declines your challenge, `which` is `"declined"`. If for any number of reasons the user's Flash client declines your challenge automatically, `which` is `"autodeclined"`.

Example: The following lines create a function to be called when a challenge request is answered:

```
function challengeAnswered(which) {
    if (which == "accepted") {
        root.gotoAndStop("game");
    } else if (which == "declined") {
        trace("declined");
    } else if (which == "autodeclined") {
        trace("auto declined");
    }
}
ElectroServerAS.challengeAnswered = this.challengeAnswered;
```

ElectroServerAS.challengeCancelled

Usage: `ElectroServerAS.challengeCancelled`

Parameters: None.

Returns: Nothing.

Description: Method; a callback function invoked by the `ElectroServerAS` object when a challenge request that has been sent to you is cancelled.

ElectroServerAS.challengeReceived

Usage: `ElectroServerAS.challengeReceived(who, game)`

Parameters:

`who`—This is the user name of the person who challenged you.

`game`—This is the game you were challenged to.

Returns: Nothing.

Description: Method; a callback function invoked by the `ElectroServerAS` object when a challenge is received. You can be challenged to a game by other users. The `who` parameter contains the user name of the person who challenged you, and the `game` parameter contains the name of the game.

ElectroServerAS.challenging

Usage: `ElectroServerAS.challenging`

Description: Property; this is a Boolean value. If `true`, then a challenge has been sent and no response has yet been received. If, while this is `true`, you are challenged, then an automated decline message is sent back to the challenger. If `challenging` is not `true`, then you can receive challenges. This property is used internally by the `ElectroServerAS` object.

ElectroServerAS.chatReceiver

Usage: `ElectroServerAS.chatReceiver(info)`

Parameter: `info`—An object containing the properties `from`, `type`, and `body`.

Returns: Nothing.

Description: Method; a callback function invoked by the `ElectroServerAS` object when a chat message is received. When this method is called, an object is passed in. The properties of this object are `from`, `type`, and `body`.

The from property is the user name of the person who sent the message. The type property is the type of message that arrived. If type is "public", then it is a message to the room; if type is "private", then it is a private message to you. The body property is a string value that contains the chat message.

Example: The following lines create a function that is to be called when a message is received:

```
function messageArrived(info) {
    var from = info.from;
    var type = info.type;
    var body = info.body;
    if (type == "public") {
        var msg = from+": "+body+newline;
    } else if (type == "private") {
        var msg = from+"(private): "+body+newline;
    }
    chat.window.text = ES.addToHistory(msg);
    chat.bar.setScrollPosition(chat.window.maxscroll);
}
ElectroServerAS.chatReceiver = this.messageArrived;
```

ElectroServerAS.connectToServer

Usage: ElectroServerAS.connectToServer()

Parameters: None.

Returns: Nothing.

Description: Method; this method uses the ElectroServerAS.port and ElectroServerAS.IP properties, and initializes a socket connection with the ElectroServer socket server. See ElectroServerAS.port and ElectroServerAS.IP for more information.

Example: The following line makes a connection with the ElectroServer socket server:

```
ElectroServerAS.connectToServer()
```

ElectroServerAS.createVariable

Usage: `ElectroServerAS.createVariable(name, value, deleteOnExit, lock)`

Parameters:

`name` —The name of the server variable you wish to create in your current room.

`value` —The string value of the variable.

`deleteOnExit` —Either `true` (or `"True"`) or `false` (or `"False"`). If `true`, then the variable is deleted when you exit the room. If `false`, then the variable is not deleted when you exit the room.

`lock` —Either `true` (or `"True"`) or `false` (or `"False"`). If `true`, then the variable cannot be updated. If `false`, then the variable can be updated. The variable can be deleted using `ElectroServerAS.deleteVariable()` no matter what value `lock` has.

Returns: Nothing.

Description: Method; creates or updates a variable in your current room on the socket server. Whenever a variable is created, updated, or deleted, all users in that room are informed via the `ElectroServerAS.roomVariablesChanged` event. All room variables are stored in an object on the `ElectroServerAS` object called `roomVars`.

Example: The following line creates a room variable:

```
ElectroServerAS.createVariable("secret_door","door3",true,
false)
```

ElectroServerAS.deleteVariable

Usage: `ElectroServerAS.deleteVariable(name)`

Parameter: `name` —The name of the room variable you wish to delete.

Returns: Nothing.

Description: Method; deletes a room variable of the name you specify. The variable is deleted even if it is locked (see `ElectroServerAS.createVariable()`). Once it's deleted, all users in that room are informed.

Example: The following line deletes a room variable:

```
ElectroServerAS.deleteVariable("secret_door")
```

ElectroServerAS.disconnectFromServer

Usage: `ElectroServerAS.disconnectFromServer()`

Parameters: None.

Returns: Nothing.

Description: Method; closes the connection between Flash and the ElectroServer socket server.

Example: The following line disconnects the Flash client from the ElectroServer socket server:

```
ElectroServerAS.disconnectFromServer()
```

ElectroServerAS.getHistory

Usage: `ElectroServerAS.getHistory()`

Parameters: None.

Returns: The string `ElectroServerAS.history`.

Description: Method; returns the chat history. The chat history is stored as a string in `ElectroServerAS.history` and gets added to using the `ElectroServerAS.addToHistory()` function.

Example: The following line sets a variable from the chat history:

```
myHistory = ElectroServerAS.getHistory()
```

ElectroServerAS.getRoomList

Usage: `ElectroServerAS.getRoomList()`

Parameters: None.

Returns: An array of objects.

Description: Method; returns an array. Each element of the array is an object that describes a room and has two properties: `name` and `total`. The property `name` is the name of the room; the property `total` is the number of people in that room.

continues on next page

Example: The following ActionScript loops through the room list and shows the names and number of people in each room in the output window:

```
var theRooms = ElectroServerAS.getRoomList();
for (i in theRooms) {
    trace(theRooms[i].name);
    trace(theRooms[i].total);
}
```

ElectroServerAS.getUserList

Usage: `ElectroServerAS.getUserList()`

Parameters: None.

Returns: An array of objects.

Description: Method; returns an array. Each element of the array is an object that describes a user and has only one property: `name`. The property `name` is the user name of one person in your room.

Example: The following ActionScript loops through the room list and shows the names and number of people in each room in the output window:

```
var theUsers = ElectroServerAS.getUserList();
for (i in theUsers) {
    trace(theUsers[i].name);
}
```

ElectroServerAS.history

Usage: `ElectroServerAS.history`

Description: Property; this is a string value that stores the chat history. Currently this method just returns the `history` property. However, in future revisions of the `ElectroServerAS` object, the history may be stored in a different manner, in which case the `getHistory()` method will be more useful. So it would be a good idea to get into the practice of using the `ElectroServerAS.getHistory()` method.

Example: The following line is an example usage of this property:

```
myHistory = ElectroServerAS.history
```

ElectroServerAS.inGame

Usage: `ElectroServerAS.inGame`

Description: Property; this is a Boolean value (`true` or `false`). If it's `true`, then you are currently in a game. If it's `false`, then you are not currently in a game. If you receive a challenge and `ElectroServerAS.inGame` has a value of `true`, then a decline message is sent automatically. This property is used internally by the `ElectroServerAS` object.

ElectroServerAS.ip

Usage: `ElectroServerAS.ip`

Description: Property; stores the IP address of the server you wish to connect to. It (as well as `ElectroServerAS.port`) must be set before the `ElectroServerAS.connectToServer()` method will perform properly. This can be the numeric IP address of a server or the domain name (such as `"23.244.81.5"` or `"macromedia.com"`).

Example:

```
ElectroServer = new ElectroServerAS();
ElectroServerAS.ip = "localhost";
ElectroServerAS.port = 8080;
ElectroServerAS.connectToServer();
```

ElectroServerAS.isResponding

Usage: `ElectroServerAS.isResponding`

Description: Property; this is a Boolean value (`true` or `false`) used internally by the `ElectroServerAS` object. If you receive a challenge, this property is set to `true`. If while it's `true` you receive another challenge, a decline message is automatically sent. Once you respond to this challenge by either accepting it or declining it, `isResponding` is set to `false`.

ElectroServerAS.joinRoom

Usage: `ElectroServerAS.joinRoom(name)`

Parameter: `name`—The name of the room you want to join.

Returns: Nothing.

continues on next page

Description: Method; changes the room you are in to the room specified in the `name` parameter. If the room does not yet exist, then it is created. The name of the room you have chosen to join is stored in the property `ElectroServerAS.myRoom`.

Example: The following line changes the room you are in to "`Lobby`":

```
ElectroServerAS.joinRoom("Lobby")
```

ElectroServerAS.kick

Usage: `ElectroServerAS.kick(who, why)`

Parameters:

`who`—The user name of the person you wish to kick.

`why`—The reason why you are kicking this person.

Returns: Nothing.

Description: Method; disconnects a user from the ElectroServer socket server. You must have administrator-level access to the server in order to initiate this method.

Example: The following line kicks a user from the server:

```
ElectroServerAS.kick("meanie")
```

ElectroServerAS.leaveAlone

Usage: `ElectroServerAS.leaveAlone`

Description: Method; this is a Boolean value (`true` or `false`); the default is `false`. If `true`, then all incoming challenge requests are automatically declined.

ElectroServerAS.login

Usage: `ElectroServerAS.challenge(name, password)`

Parameters:

`name`—This is the user name you wish to have.

`password`—This is an optional parameter containing a password.

Returns: Nothing.

Description: Method; logs in a user to the server. If a password is used, the log-in information is compared with the user name and passwords listed for administrator-level users. If no password is used, the user is just logged in. An administrator is created using tools provided with the ElectroServer socket server.

Example: The following line logs in the user:

```
ElectroServerAS.login("jobem")
```

The following line logs in the user as an administrator:

```
ElectroServerAS.login("important_person","his_password")
```

ElectroServerAS.loginResponse

Usage: `ElectroServerAS.loginResponse(success, reason)`

Parameters:

`success`—This is a Boolean value (`true` or `false`). If `true`, then the login was successful; if `false`, then it was not.

`reason`—This is a string value saying why the login was not accepted.

Returns: Nothing.

Description: Method; a callback function invoked by the `ElectroServerAS` object when a response has been received from the server after a log-in has been attempted. The first parameter, `success`, is `true` if the log-in was a success and `false` if it was not. If the log-in failed (`success false`) then the `reason` parameter (a string value that contains the reason why the log-in attempt failed) is passed in.

Example: The following lines create a function that is to be called when a response to the log-in attempt is received:

```
function loginResponse(success, reason) {
    if (success) {
        ElectroServerAS.joinRoom("Lobby");
        chat.gotoAndStop("chat");
    } else {
        trace("reason="+reason);
    }
}
ElectroServerAS.loginResponse = this.loginResponse;
```

ElectroServerAS.moveReceived

Usage: `ElectroServerAS.moveReceived(object)`

Parameter: `object`—A custom object that an opponent created.

Returns: Nothing.

Description: Method; a callback function invoked by the `ElectroServerAS` object when an opponent sends you a move in a game. This custom object can contain any data type, including arrays, XML objects, and variables.

Example: The following lines create a function and set that function to be called when a move is received. The function simply traces the names and values of all properties of the custom object passed in.

```
function moveReceived(ob) {
    for (i in ob) {
        trace(i+"="+ob[i]);
    }
}
ElectroServerAS.moveReceived = this.moveReceived;
```

ElectroServerAS.myRoom

Usage: `ElectroServerAS.myRoom`

Description: Property; stores as a string the name of the room you are currently in.

ElectroServerAS.onConnection

Usage: `ElectroServerAS.onConnection(success)`

Parameter: `success`—This is a Boolean (`true` or `false`). If `true`, then the connection was successfully established; if `false`, then it was not.

Returns: Nothing.

Description: Method; a callback function invoked by the `ElectroServerAS` object when a connection to the ElectroServer socket server has been established and verified. A value of `true` is passed into the callback function if the connection was a success; a value of `false` is passed in if it was not. The server must successfully send a message verifying that the connection is valid before this event is fired. In other words, making the connection to the server is not enough to fire this event—you need confirmation of the connection.

Example: The following lines create a function that is to be called when a connection to ElectroServer is established and verified:

```
function connectionResponse(success) {
    if (success) {
        chat.gotoAndStop("login");
    } else {
        trace("connection failed");
    }
}
ElectroServerAS.onConnection = this.connectionResponse;
```

ElectroServerAS.onPlayersInRoomChange

Usage: `ElectroServerAS.onPlayersInRoomChange(num)`

Parameter: `num`—A number representing the total number of people in your room.

Returns: Nothing.

Description: Method; a callback function invoked by the `ElectroServerAS` object when the number of people in your room changes. This happens whenever a person joins or leaves your room.

Example: The following lines create a function and set it to be called when the number of people in your room changes. The function checks to see if there are two people in your room. If there are, then it is time to initialize the game (assuming it is a two-player game).

```
function numPlayers(num) {
    if (num == 2) {
        startGame();
    }
}
ElectroServerAS.onPlayersInRoomChange = this.numPlayers;
```

ElectroServerAS.onRoomVarChange

Usage: `ElectroServerAS.onRoomVarChange(roomVars, type, name)`

Parameters:

`roomVars`—An object containing variables.

`type`—A string specifying the type of room-variable change that has occurred (`"list"`, `"update"`, or `"delete"`)

`name`—The string name of the changed variable.

Returns: Nothing.

Description: Method; a callback function invoked by the `ElectroServerAS` object when the list of variables associated with your current room (stored on the socket server) changes or when you first enter a room. When you first enter a room, this event occurs and you are sent a list of all of the variables in that room. The `type` parameter is `"list"` when this happens. When a variable in your room is created or modified, then the `type` parameter is `"update"` and the `name` parameter contains a string name of the variable that changed (or was created). When a variable in your room is deleted, then the `type` parameter is `"delete"`, and the `name` parameter contains a string name of the variable that has been deleted.

ElectroServerAS.opponent

Usage: `ElectroServerAS.opponent`

Description: Property; stores the name of your opponent. This property is created when you and another person have agreed to play a game.

ElectroServerAS.player

Usage: `ElectroServerAS.player`

Description: Property; stores your "player number" within a game. If you are in a game with only two players, then this property has a value of 1 for one person and a value of 2 for the other.

Example: The following is an example of a snippet of code you might find at the beginning of a chess game:

```
if (ElectroServerAS.player == 1) {
    myChessPieceColor = "white";
} else if (ElectroServerAS.player == 2) {
    myChessPieceColor = "black";
}
```

ElectroServerAS.port

Usage: `ElectroServerAS.port`

Description: Property; stores the IP address of the server you wish to connect to. It must be set (as well as `ElectroServerAS.ip`) before the `ElectroServerAS.connect()` method will perform properly. This can be the numeric IP address of a server or the domain name (for example, `"23.244.81.5"` or `"macromedia.com"`).

Example:

```
ElectroServer = new ElectroServerAS();
ElectroServerAS.ip="localhost";
ElectroServerAS.port=8080;
ElectroServerAS.connect();
```

ElectroServerAS.roomListChanged

Usage: `ElectroServerAS.roomListChanged(rooms)`

Parameter:

`rooms`—This is an array of objects.

Returns: Nothing.

Description: Method; a callback function invoked by the `ElectroServerAS` object when the list of visible rooms changes. When it's called, an array is passed in. Each element in the array is an object representing a room with the properties `name` and `total`. The `name` property is the name of the room, and `total` is the number of people in that room.

Example: The following lines create a function and set it to be called when the room list changes. The function populates a text field with room names that take the format `Lobby(32)`.

```
function roomListChanged(roomList) {
    roomList.text = "";
    for (var i = 0; i<roomList.length; ++i) {
        chat.roomList.text +=
roomList[i].name+"("+roomList[i].total+")"+newline;
    }
}
ElectroServerAS.roomListChanged = this.roomListChanged;
```

ElectroServerAS.rooms

Usage: `ElectroServerAS.rooms`

Description: Property; an array that stores information about each room. Every element in the array is an object with the properties of name and total. The name property contains the name of the room; total is the number of people in that room. It is recommended to use the `ElectroServerAS.getRoomList()` method; currently `ElectroServerAS.getRoomList()` just returns the rooms property, but in future revisions of the `ElectroServerAS` object, the room list may be stored in a different way.

ElectroServerAS.roomVars

Usage: `ElectroServerAS.roomVars`

Description: Property; an object that stores the room variables. Every time a variable is created, updated, or deleted from the server, it is also reflected in this object. If you define an event handler using `ElectroServerAS.onRoomVarChange`, you will be informed when this happens.

Example: The following example shows the names of all the server variables in the output window, along with their values:

```
ob = ElectroServerAS.roomVars;
for (i in ob) {
    trace(i+"="+ob[i]);
}
```

ElectroServerAS.sendData

Usage: `ElectroServerAS.sendData(msg)`

Parameter:

`msg`—The data you would like to send to the server.

Returns: Nothing.

Description: Method; sends the information found in the `msg` parameter to the server. This method is used internally by the `ElectroServerAS` object, and it is unlikely to be needed for anything other than extending the `ElectroServerAS` object.

ElectroServerAS.sendMessage

Usage: `ElectroServerAS.sendMessage(msg, who)`

Parameters:

`msg`—The chat message you would like to send.

`who`—A string value stating to whom you would like this message to go. If the string is `"All"`, then the message will be sent to everyone in your current room. If the string specifies a user name (in any room), then the message will be sent to that user as a private message.

Returns: Nothing.

Description: Method; sends a chat message to the room or to a user. This is the method used for regular chatting and private messaging.

Example: The following line sends a message to the room:

```
ElectroServerAS.sendMessage("Good morning Raleigh!","All")
```

The following line sends a message to `"jobem"`:

```
ElectroServerAS.sendMessage("Hey man, where've you been?",
"jobem")
```

ElectroServerAS.sendMove

Usage: `ElectroServerAS.sendMove(who, what)`

Parameters:

`who`—The player to whom you want to send the move.

`what`—The object you would like to send.

Returns: Nothing.

Description: Method; sends an object to the specified user. The object is of type `object` and can contain any other data objects, such as arrays, date objects, or XML objects. This method is how moves are made in a game.

Example: The following sends a move to `"jobem"`:

```
myObject=new Object();
myObject.ball_x=32;
myObject.ball_y=413;
ElectroServerAS.sendMove("jobem",myObject);
```

ElectroServerAS.sendSystemMessage

Usage: `ElectroServerAS.sendSystemMessage(msg)`

Parameter: `msg`—A string value of the message you want to send.

Returns: Nothing.

Description: Method; sends a message to every user in every room on the server. This is only available to users with administrator-level access to the server.

Example: The following line of ActionScript sends a message to everyone connected to the server:

```
ElectroServerAS.sendSystemMessage("The server is about to be
rebooted. Please refresh in 1 minute.")
```

ElectroServerAS.userListChanged

Usage: `ElectroServerAS.userListChanged(users)`

Parameter: `users`—An array of objects.

Returns: Nothing.

Description: Method; a callback function invoked by the `ElectroServerAS` object when the list of users in your room changes. When you first enter a room, this event occurs, and you are sent a list of all the users in the room. The `users` parameter is an array of objects. Each object represents one user and has one property, `name`, which stores the user name of the user whom it represents.

Example: These lines of ActionScript create a function and set it to be called whenever the list of users in the room changes. The function uses the Flash ListBox component to display the list of users.

```
function userListChanged(userList) {
    var path = chat.userList;
    path.removeAll();
    for (var i = 0; i<userList.length; ++i) {
        path.addItem(userList[i].name);
    }
}
ElectroServerAS.userListChanged = this.userListChanged;
```

ElectroServerAS.username

Usage: `ElectroServerAS.username`

Description: Property; the name with which you are logged in.

ElectroServerAS.users

Usage: `ElectroServerAS.users`

Description: Property; an array of objects. Each object represents a user in your room with one property, `name`, that stores the user name of that person. It is recommended that you use `ElectroServerAS.getUserList()` to retrieve the user list. In future revisions of this object, the user list may be stored differently.

ElectroServerAS.usersInMyRoom

Usage: `ElectroServerAS.usersInMyRoom`

Description: Property; an integer that specifies the total number of people in your room.

new ElectroServerAS()

Usage: `new ElectroServerAS()`

Parameters: None.

Returns: Nothing.

Description: Constructor; creates a new `ElectroServerAS` object. You must use the constructor method to create an instance of the `ElectroServerAS` object before calling any of the `ElectroServerAS` object methods.

Example: The following line creates an instance of the `ElectroServerAS` object with a reference of `ES`:

```
ES = new ElectroServerAS();
```

Index

A

B

C

D

E

F

G

H

I

J

K

L

M

N

O

P

R

S

T

Macromedia Press...helping you learn what the Web can be

Reality

Macromedia Press proudly introduces the Reality series–this is your invitation to join a crack team of experts as they confront real-world development problems and work out practical solutions. As a virtual member of these development teams, you'll create a series of complete, configurable, high-quality applications that are defined, discussed, used, and then analyzed. Not only do you get an insider's view of real world case studies, but you also learn best practices and create complete applications that you can use or adapt for your own work.

Reality Macromedia ColdFusion MX: Intranets and Content Management
By Ben Forta, et al
ISBN 0-321-12414-6 • 528 • $39.99

Reality Macromedia ColdFusion MX: J2EE Integration
By Ben Forta, et al
ISBN 0-321-12948-2 • 576 pages • $39.99

Reality Macromedia ColdFusion MX: Flash MX Integration
By Ben Forta, et al
ISBN 0-321-12515-0 • 432 pages • $39.99

Reality J2EE: Architecting for Macromedia Flash MX
By Steven Webster
ISBN 0-321-15884-9 • 504 pages • $39.99

Other Macromedia Press Titles

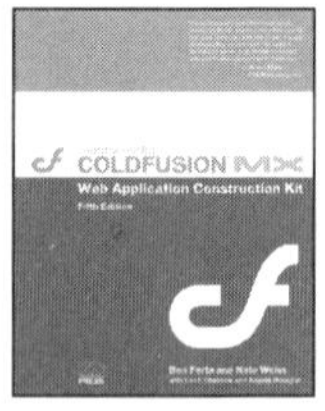

ColdFusion MX Web Application Construction Kit
By Ben Forta, et al
ISBN 0-321-12516-9 • 1536 pages • $54.99

Advanced ColdFusion MX Application Development
By Ben Forta
ISBN 0-321-12710-2 • 1200 pages • $49.99

Macromedia Flash MX Creative Web Animation and Interactivity
By Derek Franklin
ISBN 0-321-11785-9 • 952 pages • $44.99

Certified Macromedia Flash MX Designer Study Guide
By Christopher Hayes
ISBN 0-321-12695-5 • 408 pages • $35.00

Macromedia Flash MX: Creating Dynamic Applications
By Michael Grundvig, et al
ISBN 0-321-11548-1 • 504 pages • $44.99

Macromedia Showcase: Flash Interface Design
By Darci DiNucci
ISBN 0-321-12399-9 • 304 pages • $34.99

Macromedia Flash MX Accelerated Learning Workbook
By MD Dundon
ISBN 0-321-12398-0 • 448 pages • $44.99

Certified Macromedia Flash MX Developer Study Guide
By John Elstad, et al
ISBN 0-321-15730-3 • 304 pages • $35.00

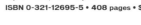

www.peachpit.com